Tough Ain't Enough

Contents

Tough Ain't Enough

1

The Teller and the Tale

• •

An Introduction to the
Films of Clint Eastwood

LESTER D. FRIEDMAN AND
DAVID DESSER

> Never trust the teller, trust the tale.
> —D. H. Lawrence

Why Clint Eastwood?

At age eighty-five, Clint Eastwood became the oldest person ever to direct a film nominated for a Best Picture Oscar, surpassing legendary figures like John Huston, Robert Altman, and David Lean. A decade earlier, he had become the oldest person ever to win an Oscar in the directing category. Nominated four times for Best Director and five times for Best Picture, he also received the Irving G. Thalberg Memorial Award in 2013, given to "creative producers whose bodies of work reflect a consistently high quality of motion picture production." At the moment, Eastwood and Warren Beatty remain the only two filmmakers nominated twice for Best Director and Best Actor in the same movie. Six of Eastwood's films have been selected for competition at the Cannes Film Festival, whose organizers presented him with a lifetime achievement Palme d'Or in 2009, joining Ingmar Bergman (who won in 1997) as one of only two directors in this exclusive club. Nominated five times as Best Director by the

Director's Guild of America and winning three times, Eastwood was also given a Life Achievement Award by the American Film Institute in 1996—almost twenty years and seventeen films ago. More recently, *American Sniper* garnered a higher domestic gross than all the previous Iraq War films combined, and its box-office take topped that of the other eight films nominated for Best Picture at the 2014 Oscars put together. Prior to *American Sniper* and *Sully* (2016), films starring Eastwood always tallied greater box-office grosses than those he directed but in which he did not appear. But the domestic earnings generated by *American Sniper* ($350,126,372) and *Sully* ($125,070,033) demonstrate that, at the respective ages of eighty-four and eighty-six, Eastwood no longer needs to perform on-screen for his movies to turn a very handsome profit. As these honors, awards, and financial accomplishments convincingly demonstrate, Clint Eastwood has become the most productive and profitable actor/producer/director in film history.

FIGURE 1.1   Clint Eastwood holding his Oscars for Best Picture and Best Director for *Unforgiven* at the 1993 Academy Awards ceremony in Los Angeles. Frame enlargement.

Were Eastwood "only" an actor, his career would be of interest in the same way, say, that Paul Newman or Steve McQueen command attention—as enduring, bankable stars who distilled some crucial element of their era's zeitgeist and embodied it within their screen performances. But the critical and popular success of his directing efforts—some thirty-five films over the course of forty-four years—has allowed Eastwood to transcend the image of star and enter the ranks of genuine auteurs. From the biopic to the military movie, from the musical to the police thriller, from the Western to the melodrama, Eastwood has produced a sprawling range of genre movies interlaced with a series of subjects that, like leitmotifs within a symphony, have engaged him for decades. In doing so, he has skillfully manipulated genre conventions to tackle some of the most pressing, and complex, concerns of our time. In creating these films, Eastwood has maintained a long-standing reputation for keeping his pictures within their budgets, completing them on time, successfully working with a range of actors, shooting few takes, rarely storyboarding or blocking out scenes, working almost exclusively with a single camera, usually turning a profit, and contributing haunting musical scores to his movies. Whether in front of or behind the camera, therefore, Clint Eastwood has emerged as one of America's most popular, influential, and respected moviemakers, a truly remarkable evolution that few would have thought possible in the early days of his career.

Because of his stature as an enduring iconic figure, Eastwood has hardly been ignored by both popular critics and academic writers. As early as 1974, Stuart Kaminsky published a slim book on Eastwood, followed by Christopher Frayling's (1992) brief look at his life and career, Richard Schickel's (1997) far more comprehensive tome, and Patrick McGilligan's (2002) controversial look at Eastwood's offscreen personality, followed by Marc Eliot's (2009) and Sara Anson Vaux's (2014) biographies. On the more academic side of things, Paul Smith (1993), Dennis Bingham (1994), and Laurence Knapp (1996) wrote early analyses of his cultural significance, film work, and macho persona; Leonard Engel edited two collections of essays (2007, 2012); Drucilla Cornell (2009) examined issues of masculinity in the director's work; Sara Anson Vaux investigated Eastwood's moral agenda; David Sterritt (2014) and Sam B. Girgus (2014) produced studies of the director's entire career; James L. Neibaur (2016) focused on his Western movies; and Robert E. Kapsis and Kathie Coblentz (2013) updated a collection of his interviews. Much preproduction and some behind-the-scenes materials also exists, the most informative being Michael Goldman's (2012).[1]

Another, equally potent, reason scholars and cultural commentators have engaged with Eastwood's films are the controversies many of them have engendered. The debates that swirl around the ideological signification of his movies are often filtered through Eastwood's public persona as an old-fashioned, some would characterize as retrograde, rugged individualist, a spokesman for Republican policies, and the most famous conservative within generally liberal Hollywood. Critics, for example, often decried the violent, cynical, and unscrupulous nature of his enigmatic "Man with No Name" character, the self-interested antihero in the spaghetti Westerns he made with director Sergio Leone—a dark alternative to his popular portrayal of Rowdy Yates on *Rawhide* from 1959 to 1965.

A more vehement crescendo of attacks, led by the *New Yorker*'s Pauline Kael, accosted his portrayal of San Francisco police inspector Harry Callahan—the Magnum-toting, antiauthoritarian loner in director Don Siegel's *Dirty Harry* (1971)—as "fascist medievalism" and a "right wing fantasy."[2] Her famous remarks in a career filled with them became a pithy stamp that other critics adopted and that dogged much of Eastwood's subsequent acting and filmmaking career. Even a reasonably sympathetic critic, Dennis Bingham, in his review of our manuscript, remarked on "how dreadful and even morally reprehensible some of Eastwood's films were in the peak star period of the 1970s and 1980s." Protesters at the 1971 Oscar ceremony agreed, holding up signs such as "Dirty Harry is a rotten pig."[3] The release of *Unforgiven* (1992) lead to a stream of conflicting readings regarding its attitudes toward violence: Did this film condemn the glorification of violence so closely associated with Eastwood's earlier Westerns or ultimately revel in its display, despite some

FIGURE 1.2 Eastwood as Rowdy Yates in the television Western *Rawhide* (1959–1965) might not have presaged his phenomenal career in the years to follow. Frame enlargement.

sentiments about its corrosive effects on the human psyche? *Million Dollar Baby* (2004), whose main character becomes a quadriplegic, inspired equally heated disagreements between those who favored a person's right to choose euthanasia and disability rights activists who saw Eastwood as resorting to damaging, outmoded stereotypes. Bile from the left and adulation from the right greeted the release of *American Sniper* (2014): Was it a pro- or antiwar statement, and was Chris Kyle a murderer or a hero?

The Teller and the Tale

Given his rambling performance with an empty chair at the 2012 Republican National Convention and his recent praise, but not endorsement, of Donald Trump ("He's onto something, because secretly everybody's getting tired of political correctness, kissing up. That's the kiss-ass generation we're in right now. We're really in a pussy generation."[4]), Clint Eastwood has explicitly stepped into John Wayne's boots as the most outspoken, and famous, conservative in Hollywood. As such, and particularly for scholars who consider themselves liberals, writing about a man whose stated political positions you find repugnant but whose films you admire raises some thorny issues; in particular, it poses a knotty question that critics have struggled with for a very long time: in an examination of artistic work can/should one ever separate the dancer from the dance, the maker from the product? A far more dramatic

FIGURE 1.3 Eastwood addressing an empty chair holding an invisible Barack Obama at the GOP national convention in 2012. Frame enlargement.

example of this question has always haunted those who admire the artistry of Leni Riefenstahl's movies, particularly her panegyric *Triumph of the Will* (1935), while vehemently rejecting her admiration of Hitler and Nazi sympathies. More recently, films and books have detailed the reportedly sadistic behavior of Alfred Hitchcock, a revered and influential figure in film circles, toward his leading ladies, particularly Tippi Hedren's sordid revelations that the director sexually harassed her while filming *The Birds* (1963) and *Marnie* (1964), revealed in Donald Spoto's biography.[5]

Neither Riefenstahl nor Hitchcock is alive to defend themselves, but Eastwood's forays into politics are well documented. He was elected as mayor of his hometown (Carmel-by-the-Sea, California), served as vice-chairman of the California State Park and Recreation Commission panel (2004), and supported Republican candidates as far back as Dwight Eisenhower and as recently as Ronald Reagan, John McCain, and Mitt Romney. At times, however, he has championed Democrats in California as well, such Gray Davis, Sam Farr, and Fred Keeley, and he strongly opposed the wars in both Iraq and Afghanistan. If a self-described political label is necessary, Eastwood habitually characterizes himself as a libertarian, but he never declared support for the 2016 Libertarian candidates for president and vice-president, Gary Johnson and William Weld. Richard Schickel claims that "Clint is a fiscal conservative and subject to grumble fits about intrusive government, but on social issues ranging from gun control to abortion rights he is liberal—or maybe I should say libertarian of the non-intrusive kind."[6] He did, for example, sign an amicus brief supporting same-sex marriage in the Supreme Court's *Hollingsworth v. Perry* case (2013) that ultimately lead to legalization of these unions. In a 2012 discussion with Ellen DeGeneres on her show, an appearance that occurred after his widely ridiculed soliloquy at the Republican National Convention, Eastwood said the following about his creed of pragmatic libertarianism: "Libertarian means you're social liberal—leave everybody alone—but you believe in fiscal responsibility, and you believe in government staying out of your life."[7]

Despite these self-proclamations and socially progressive actions, some critics consistently label Eastwood a reactionary. A conspicuous example of this characterization of Eastwood's political ideology permeates Patrick McGilligan's unauthorized biography, *Clint: The Life and Legend*, an unflattering demythologizing of Eastwood's public image that the author himself describes as "in many ways the antithesis of the legend and certainly the antithesis of his authorized biography."[8] In an interview with Allen Barra in *Salon*, McGilligan asserted that

> Clint's career has been a pro-gun career. He pioneered the huge body count and death toll in cop vigilante films, and his war movies do the same exponentially.

The not-deep idea is that Americans—Men with No Name or Chris Kyle's name—have to use their guns and military hardware to save the town or the world, because other people aren't up to the task, and yes, innocent people die in the crossfire, but that's the price to pay for being America. . . . The film's success is a sad commentary on how little has been learned from Iraq.[9]

Later, in an interview with Roger Ebert, McGilligan claimed,

Eastwood is a right-wing subject. Some have argued he's iconoclastic, or he is a libertarian, but for me, you can't approach him factually unless you concede that about him politically. He supported Reagan, Nixon, and all of the Bushes, and for people to argue he's not right-wing, I just wonder, what planet are you on. I write auteurist books, about directors and actors, and examine their personalities and values and see how it transfers into the films. . . . Clint's a towering figure in our culture . . . but he is also very emblematic of what's wrong with Hollywood.[10]

The common, and quite debatable, contention that media, in this case Hollywood, is primarily responsible for America's love affair with gun violence remains a controversial position that belongs more properly in another book. But we do need to question McGilligan's conception of auteurist criticism.

In the interest of full disclosure, we both often practice auteur criticism, particularly in the previous book we wrote together, *American Jewish Filmmakers*, and other studies of Kurosawa, Spielberg, Ozu, Huston, and Penn. Although sufficient space is not available to plunge into an extensive discussion of film criticism and theory, McGilligan's contention that an auteurist approach necessarily entails delving deeply into how a filmmaker's personality and values gets reflected into their movies cries out for some correction. The French New Wave critics (before they became directors), such as Francois Truffaut and Jean-Luc Godard, who first formulated this approach to film analysis barely incorporated any biographical information about the directors they admired, such as Hawks, Hitchcock, and Ford. They focused on the product, not the artist's personal history or personality. To take an obvious example, Godard's radical politics were totally antithetical to those of the far more conservative John Ford and the right-wing John Wayne, yet Godard considered *The Searchers* (1956) a masterpiece and compared sections of it to *The Odyssey*. In a famous passage, Godard reveals that he realized "the mystery and fascination of this American cinema" when he viewed the climactic scene in *The Searchers* when Ethan Edwards (Wayne), finally ending his obsessive quest to find his kidnapped niece, picks up Debbie (Natalie Wood) to take her home. "How can I hate John Wayne upholding Goldwater and yet love him tenderly when abruptly he takes Natalie Wood into his arms in the last reel of *The Searchers*?"

Godard wonders, adding that he broke into uncontrollable tears at this point in the movie.[11] Godard detests John Wayne's politics, but he connects with the character on the screen, not the offscreen actor who embodies him or the man who directed him. As this example among countless others demonstrates, one can love a movie while not particularly liking, having anything in common, or sharing similar political views with the people who created it.

Let us extend McGilligan's contention even further: one can do a perfectly valid auteurist reading of a movie without knowing very much, if anything at all, about the biography of its filmmakers. In fact, a good argument could be made for knowing very little about the people who produce works of art, for biographical knowledge often generates as much smoke as light; it can corrupt one's reading of a work of art as surely as it can enlighten, and it cannot help but influence one's reception. Can anyone see Woody Allen's *Manhattan* (1979) in the same way after Mia Farrow's charges of his pedophilia, although vehemently denied by the director, as before those allegations were publicized? We bet not. Allen's text is exactly the same in 2017 as it was in 1979, yet biographical information compels us to view Isaac's (Allen) relationship with Tracy (Mariel Hemingway) as far more problematic than when it first appeared and has tainted the reputation of what is, otherwise, one of Allen's finest movies. We could go on almost indefinitely citing similar cases of how biographical information necessarily affects a viewer's readings of works by actors and directors, such as Mel Gibson's anti-Semitic diatribes, Rock Hudson's homosexuality, Roman Polanski's rape of an underaged girl, Lindsay Lohan's drunken antics, Bill Cosby's assault on women, or most anything reported daily on TMZ. But the question remains: Should offscreen activities be taken into consideration when analyzing a work of art, or is it prejudicial, and ultimately wrong, to consider the actions of its producer as part of that process?

The fundamental notion at the base of auteurist criticism, as the essays in this volume demonstrate, is that a series of visual texts by the same person (usually a director) demonstrates a certain consistency of thematic concerns and visual style—not that it necessarily reflects the "personality" of the creator of those works. To do the type of reading McGilligan advocates—or, for that matter, to take as gospel the comments of a creator about what his or her creation "means"—is to commit what W. K. Wimsatt (in *The Verbal Icon*, 1954) labeled as "the intentional fallacy": the concept that a critic can never fully know what an author intended or what he or she had in mind at the time of fashioning a work and, even if that understanding was possible, that it would not render all other interpretations invalid.[12] Scholars and critics are not psychologists who can climb into the brain of artists to reveal what they were thinking during the time of creation. This is not to say that a creator's commentaries cannot be valuable; Eastwood's own statements about various subjects and his films are sprinkled throughout our anthology. In fact, some of his statements about his own movies are included in this introduction. Many of his observations are interesting and quite helpful tools in digging through his decades of moviemaking, but they are never conclusive, nor do they eliminate other readings.

It is equally true that authors themselves are often the least reliable critics of their own productions, since they may not recognize the multiple meanings spawned by their works or what elements they have unconsciously incorporated within them. It is inevitable that diverse readers and the passage of time will bring different perspectives to any text. Did Shakespeare know that Hamlet had an Oedipus complex? Works of art don't change, but those who read them and the context in which this process of reception occurs do. Did D. W. Griffith think that *The Birth of a Nation* (1915) was racist? Once the work is completed, therefore, its author is just another commentator: he or she can say what was consciously intended, but alternative interpretations never considered by the author are not limited by those personal comments. In fact, an analysis of a work of art often tells more about the reader than the creator, as Dana Spiotta observes in *Innocents and Others: A Novel*: "The immutability of the film (or book or a painting or a piece of music) is something to measure yourself against. That is one of the things a great work of art does. It stays there waiting for you to come back to it, and it shows you who you are now, each time a little different."[13] So then, to make a one-to-one connection between Eastwood's stated political positions and his artistic works is a severely limited auteurist approach that denies the power of Eastwood's artistry, ignores the evolving complexity of his themes, and fails to see his movies beyond a narrowly static concept of his political ideology. All that said, here is our auteurist/genre reading of Clint Eastwood.

Eastwood as Genre Filmmaker

The foundations of genre construction stretch as far back as Aristotle's formal differentiation between the various internal properties of imitative modes (epic, lyric, and dramatic poetry) in the *Poetics* (335 BC). Moviegoers who recognize specific genre categories bring basic expectations to the theater about what they will see on the screen; many arrive with a sense of that genre's history or, at the very least, recollections of particular films they liked or disliked within that genre. As such, they can be delighted or horrified when a filmmaker offers up differences in visual style, narrative patterns, and expected characterizations. Successful genre films, like many of Clint Eastwood's, present audiences with a combination of the fresh and the formulaic, the innovative and the customary. Too many repetitive elements pile up trite clichés that may bore the viewer; too many departures from generic expectations may confuse, frustrate, or even irritate him or her. This tension between new and old is palpable and omnipresent in genre works because their formulations seek a balance between the similarities that align the current piece with the previous works and the individual differences that define a creator's unique contributions.

What is no less impressive than Eastwood's late-career achievements, about which this introduction hardly scrapes the surface, is that as an actor he has appeared in virtually every major American film genre. Though most immediately associated with the Western (he only appeared in ten such films, but he was instrumental in revolutionizing the form) and with the police drama (he made fourteen of these and similarly changed their social value), Eastwood took a turn in many film genres. Three war films, for instance, may be found in his filmography; horror, musicals, adventure stories, military movies, history pictures, road movies, mysteries, thrillers, biopics, science fiction films, spy movies, melodramas, romances, and comedies all provide markers within his career. This breadth across the range of Hollywood genres speaks to a deceptive versatility and one reason for his unprecedented staying power as a box-office giant. While few would claim his acting prowess is the equal, say, of Gene Hackman or Robert Duvall—stars born around the same time as Eastwood—few would deny how much mileage he's gotten out of a handful of facial expressions and a limited amount of dialogue. Yet the enduring influence of his Western and police characters have seared indelible images into the American communal psyche.

As is the case with all genre works, Eastwood's productions are inherently intertextual and, by their very nature, hybrids to one degree or another in that they recall movies from the past and blend elements from various genres. Genre filmmaking and viewing demands knowledge from previous movies, but these categories are not static entities. Quite to the contrary, they always remain fluid, open-ended, and responsive to social conditions, as Eastwood notes in his introduction to Schickel's retrospective of his career: "I'm obviously an American director. Which means that, like my colleagues, my roots are in genre moviemaking. For me, genre conventions add a certain strength to the movies. At the same time, they offer the possibility of creating variations on their basic themes, a chance to refresh the film in question, making it new for the audience and for me."[14] For Eastwood, then, all the components that constitute genres are always in play, always available for revisiting and revising; they provide him with a series of openings to renegotiate societal issues, cultural assumptions, and individual mythologies, while falling within boundaries familiar to a potentially wide range of audiences. Thus Eastwood's genre movies provide conventional options and innovative opportunities by structuring experiences and events within a delicate balance of traditions and modifications that allow him to express particular points of view and viewers to receive them through their personal lenses.

As this book demonstrates, individual auteurs and genre study can occupy common critical ground and deepen an understanding of both the artist and the text. Schickel claims that almost all of Eastwood's films "had lineaments of genre about them . . . The difference now is that they also bear the weight of his years, his hard-won authority . . . taking up sober themes in ways that are largely palatable to a mass audience." As he became a more accomplished filmmaker, continues Schickel, "the line between Clint's genre work and his more overtly aspiring films became more blurred."[15] For some directors, genre expectations limit their sense of total freedom, but Eastwood typically uses these conventions as guiding principles rather than as unbreakable commandments. In his best films, Eastwood imprints personal themes and demonstrates his visual artistry within a particular genre, typifying how genre conventions and individual genius can cohabit the same text and understanding how they can function together to deepen a viewer's appreciation and understanding of the same movie. By so doing, Eastwood throws a spotlight on his particular uniqueness and highlights the distinctive differences he brings to a specific genre. So for example, in his most serious movies, and even some of his less somber ventures, Eastwood peers into the dark corners of characters' lives as they struggle to find a viable pathway toward an ethical life, one that allows them to function meaningfully in an amoral, or even nihilistic, environment with at least a modicum of moral behavior beyond superficial platitudes. No wonder, therefore, that Eastwood seems drawn to stories of revenge and redemption, increasingly complex narratives that provide his characters, who often display a streak of self-destructiveness, with a second chance to correct a wrong or finally set things straight.

Eastwood, as we have noted in our book, has worked within an astounding variety of genres. Writing the forward in Michael Goldman's *Clint Eastwood: Master Filmmaker at Work*, his friend Steven Spielberg observes that "Clint is not only the most emotionally invested filmmaker we have today, but also the most eclectic in his openness in considering all genres. He may have played the same western antiheroes again and again, but as a director, you can never accuse Clint of repeating himself."[16] In our age that creates celebrities seemingly on a daily basis and in a variety of social media platforms, Eastwood's master theme seems particularly relevant: revealing the discrepancies and unpleasant truths inevitably discarded in order to manufacture, mythologize, and ultimately venerate a celebrity-hero. Eastwood films recurrently explore the fissures between cultural commemoration and historical accuracy, intently probing the disparities that emerge between facts and fabrications in the construction of exemplary behavior embodied in an individual.

Eastwood's Method

In his review of our manuscript, Dennis Bingham pointed out that Eastwood's artistry as a director blossomed in almost inverse proportion to his diminishing box-office popularity as a major star. Perhaps one could not have transpired without the other, as he was able to concentrate more fully on his work behind the camera without fearing what audiences might not accept as his persona in front of it. Eastwood's long filmmaking career is characterized by repeatedly working with the same family of loyal craftsman who populate his production company Malpaso, a sort of ministudio composed of skilled collaborators whom Eastwood oversees to formulate his projects. For example, he has had, basically, three cinematographers during his long directing career: Bruce Surtees, Jack Green, and Tom Stern. The same pattern of close-knit colleagues is evident in other technical areas as well: production designers Henry Bumstead and James. J. Murakami; film editor Joel Cox; art director Jack Taylor, and others—including a decades-long association with his agent Leonard Hirshan, which ended only with the latter's death in 2014. Because of his utilization of a crew from film to film who is familiar with his methods, Eastwood has always resisted the label of auteur, instead placing his success on what he calls his "well-oiled machine." As producer Rob Lorenz describes it, "Clint doesn't only cast actors—he casts the crew as well. He intentionally seeks out people who know their jobs and have a lot of experience in their craft, and he then trusts them to do their job . . . And if they do it well, he asks them to keep coming back, and for the most part, that's what they do."[17] Indeed, in accepting his Oscars for both *Unforgiven* and *Million Dollar Baby*, Eastwood thanked his wife and mother, then went on to cite the contributions of his crew.

Upon first encountering an Eastwood film, one is always struck by his use of lighting, among other elements. Already a veteran who remembered the old days of black-and-white cinematography when he first started to work with Eastwood, Bruce Surtees encouraged the director, who admired films by Akira Kurosawa, Carol Reed, Orson Welles, and Don Siegel, to exploit the dramatic possibilities of shooting on the unlit side of his characters' faces, which created a film noirish look with shadows and low-key light for dramatic effect. This type of chiaroscuro lighting endows Eastwood's most powerful movies with shadows across the faces of his lead characters that often bespeak their complex nature. For example, Jack Green explains that in the shoot-out at the end of *Unforgiven*, the saloon was lit entirely with kerosene lamps, perhaps the best example of Eastwood's "abiding and enduring love for deep, rich blacks as the foundation for his imagery." Green continues: "The reason he likes them is twofold. The first reason is that . . . blacks give him, as we describe it technically, a greater dynamic range. And secondly, the more aesthetic

FIGURE 1.4 Noirish chiaroscuro lighting in *Unforgiven* (1992) lends ambiguity to the characters. Frame enlargement.

reason is that blacks are a place of imagination for him—as in mystery."[18] Such a lighting strategy perfectly suits Eastwood's brooding tales filled with morally ambiguous characters and unresolved conflicts.

Eastwood's use of the camera (usually employing a single rather than multiple cameras on the set) brings another vital component to his work, as repeatedly seen in movie after movie. His films, though not static, often resemble carefully blocked stage plays, in that he seems more concerned with the movement of characters within the frame than dazzling the viewer with fancy camera movements or spectacular displays of special effects. Take, for example, the scene of the townspeople watching Little Bill (Gene Hackman) beating up English Bob (Richard Harris) in *Unforgiven* (1992). Eastwood cuts between the horrific, sadistic bashing and the townspeople moving ever so slightly, as if blown by a gentle breeze, in each carefully composed frame—an almost dream-like sequence laced with animalistic brutality.

Most of Eastwood's films depend heavily on the viewer's acceptance of the "reality" of what is transpiring on the screen, and as a result, Eastwood rarely attempts to draw his audience's awareness away from the action by calling attention to splashy displays of visual excess that might induce a less disciplined director to show off his or her skills. The result of this restraint is a series of movies that, at least aesthetically, would fit quite nicely within the Hollywood productions of the studio era, the Warner Bros. of the old days as well as of the Warner Bros. Entertainment Inc. of modern times.

The Anthology

A few decades ago, if someone had prophesized that one day in the not-too-distant future, academic writers would confer upon Clint Eastwood the hallowed status of "auteur" and acknowledge, sometimes quite reluctantly, his membership into the small pantheon of critically respected, commercially popular directors, most scholars would have laughed off the comment as ignorantly absurd. If that person had added, perhaps with a smug smile, that film professors would eventually teach Eastwood's movies and edit anthologies exploring his work, that person would have been asked what he or she was smoking that night. As outlandish as it may have seemed then, you now hold in your hand a book that, among other things, charts Eastwood's improbable journey from TV cowboy to international movie star to celebrated filmmaker. The indisputable substance of Eastwood's work, his ongoing status as a pre-eminent director, and his continued role in our cultural consciousness convinced us to embark upon a project that would offer new insights into his productions and persona from a variety of interdisciplinary perspectives. As evidenced by these original essays, the trajectory of Eastwood's unprecedented career is crammed with contradictions and controversies. Just when you think you have him pigeonholed—he's a fascist, a misogynist, a right-wing ideologue, a libertarian, a gun-toting vigilante, a racist, and so forth—he makes a film that alters your assessment of his work or utters some political statement that seems totally out of character. Sometimes, of course, he says or does things that verify our worst conception of him. Yet whatever we think about Eastwood as a person (and how many of you reading this book actually know Clint Eastwood personally?), his directorial efforts have demonstrated a continued willingness to confront serious issues, to offer a panoply of morally ambiguous characters, and to showcase his undeniable (and seemingly undiminished) talent behind the camera.

Our anthology considers Eastwood's career from two major vantage points: exploring his films within the history and context of the genres within which he works, and scrutinizing a series of complex issues interwoven within the fabric of his films that crisscross the conventional borders of those genres. So in the book's first section, Stephen Prince references Eastwood's work on the *Rawhide* TV series and then compares and contrasts his appearances in films directed by others with those that are self-directed. Lester Friedman explores how Eastwood's war films employ common combat movie tropes but often undercut these conventions to expose the tangled, often brutal, realities that lie beneath them. Jonathan Kirshner's chapter examines the politics of Eastwood's cycle of police movies in the context of Eastwood's stated political views, emphasizing common themes but also engaging with subtleties and enigmas as well. Acknowledging that he is known primarily for his "tough guy" roles, Diane Carson shows how Eastwood embeds melodramatic elements in several of his most important movies, spotlighting the acting choices he utilizes to generate poignant responses from his viewers. The final essay in this first section is David Sterritt's discussion of what he labels Eastwood's "offbeat relationship" with biopics, which focuses on how the director depicts male celebrity figures in his films about fame as both a gift and a burden.

The second section of the book begins with Murray Pomerance's investigation of Eastwood's acting, particularly the ways he structures his scenes for an intensive interplay of the relationship between characters and situations. Lucy Bolton's chapter dissects how Eastwood has related to women in the different phases of his career, while David Desser probes the various ways Eastwood's screen characters acknowledge their aging bodies and what that acceptance means for images of masculinity in a postfeminist society. Noting that race is an important concern in many of Eastwood's movies, Alexandra Keller scrutinizes a range of his movies in which race turns out to be more important than initially evident, as well as those in which race is a central preoccupation. Finally, Charity Lofthouse notes that Eastwood has amassed a sizable, yet largely overlooked, body of work as a film-score composer, devoting her chapter to a musical and intertextual study of Eastwood's often ignored film scores.

Any good anthology shares affinities with a good movie. It is a collaborative effort and casting the right people inevitably makes the difference between success and failure. Here, we gathered together a diverse group of well-respected scholars, asked them to write on specific areas, and turned them loose to investigate the contributions and contradictions that characterize Eastwood's career from his earliest days to the present time. The result is a collection that provides readers with a "holistic" approach, one that features a broad overview of Clint Eastwood—the films he's directed, his star persona, and his career—but also turns a spotlight on areas of his work that have been largely undervalued or ignored. As much as we can resist the obvious choice of words, these writers have probed the good, the bad, and the ugly. We hope, therefore, that our book will find a home among both general viewers who relate to Eastwood's movies and scholars who find significance in his films.

Notes

1 Dennis Bingham, *Acting Male: Masculinities in the Films of James Stewart, Jack Nicholson, and Clint Eastwood* (New Brunswick, N.J.: Rutgers University Press, 1994); Drucilla Cornell, *Clint Eastwood and Issues of American Masculinity* (New York: Fordham University Press, 2009); Marc Eliot, *American Rebel: The Life of Clint Eastwood* (New York: Three Rivers Press, 2009); Leonard Engel, ed., *Clint Eastwood, Actor and Director* (Salt Lake City: University of Utah Press, 2007); Christopher Frayling, *Clint Eastwood* (London: Virgin Books, 1992); Sam B. Girgus, *Clint Eastwood's America* (Cambridge: Polity Press, 2014); Michael Goldman, *Clint Eastwood: Master Filmmaker at Work* (New York: Abrams, 2012); Stuart Kaminsky, *Clint Eastwood* (New York: Signet, 1974); Robert E. Kapsis and Kathie Coblentz, *Clint Eastwood: Interviews, Revised and Updated* (Jackson: University Press of Mississippi, 2013); Laurence Knapp, *Directed by Clint Eastwood: Eighteen Films Analyzed* (Jefferson, N.C.: McFarland, 1996); Joseph McBride, *Searching for John Ford: A Life* (Jackson: University Press of Mississippi, 2011); Patrick McGilligan, *Clint: The Life and Legend*, 2nd ed. (New York: St. Martin's Press, 2002; New York: Or Books, 2015); James Neibaur, *The Clint Eastwood Westerns* (Lanham, Md.: Rowman & Littlefield, 2015); Richard Schickel, *Clint Eastwood: A Biography* (New York: Vintage Books, 1996); Richard Schickel, *Clint: A Retrospective* (New York: Sterling, 2012); Paul Smith, *Clint Eastwood: A Cultural Production* (Minneapolis: University of Minnesota Press, 1993); David Sterritt, *The Cinema of Clint Eastwood: Chronicles of America* (London: Wallflower, 2014); Sara Anson Vaux, *Clint Eastwood: A Biography* (Santa Barbara, Calif.: Greenwood Press, 2014); Sara Anson

Vaux, *The Ethical Vision of Clint Eastwood* (Grand Rapids, Mich.: William B. Eerdmans, 2012).

2 Pauline Kael, *Deeper into Movies* (New York: Warner Books, 1973).

3 McGilligan, *Clint*, 211.

4 Michael Hainey, "Double Trouble: Clint and Scott Eastwood: No Holds Barred in Their First Interview Together," *Esquire*, August 3, 2016, accessed August 12, 2017, http://www.esquire.com/entertainment/a46893/double-trouble-clint-and-scott -eastwood/.

5 Donald Spoto, *The Dark Side of Genius: The Life of Alfred Hitchcock* (Boston: Da Capo Press, 1999).

6 Schickel, *Clint*, 25.

7 Jacob Sullum, "Clint Eastwood's 'Leave Everybody Alone' Definition of Liber- tarianism," Reason: Free Minds and Free Markets, September 19, 2012, accessed August 11, 2017, http://reason.com/blog/2012/09/19/clint-eastwoods-leave -everybody-alone-de.

8 McGilligan, *Clint*, 405.

9 Allen Berra, "Chris Kyle Is a Stand-In for Clint: The Author of Eastwood's Con- troversial Biography on His New Edition, Including *American Sniper* and More," *Salon*, August 10 2015, accessed August 12, 2017, http://www.salon.com/2015/08/ 10/chris_kyle_is_a_stand_in_for_clint_the_author_of_eastwoods_controversial _biography_on_his_new_edition_including_american_sniper_and_more/.

10 Patrick Z. McGavin, "From Clint to Orson: A Conversation with Biographer Patrick McGilligan," RogerEbert.com, July 22, 2015, accessed August 10, 2017, https://www.rogerebert.com/interviews/from-clint-to-orson-a-conversation-with -biographer-patrick-mcgilligan.

11 Joseph McBride, *Searching for John Ford: A Life* (New York: St. Martin's Press, 2001), 565.

12 W. K. Wimsatt, *The Verbal Icon: Studies in the Meaning of Poetry* (Lexington: Uni- versity Press of Kentucky, 1954).

13 Dana Spiotta, *Innocents and Others: A Novel* (New York: Scribner, 2016), 141.

14 Schickel, *Clint*, 8.

15 Schickel, 32, 23.

16 Goldman, *Clint Eastwood*, 15.

17 Goldman, 18.

18 Goldman, 126–131.

Part I

Crosscurrents

• •

2

"I Don't Want Nobody Belonging to Me"

• •

Riding the Post-Leone Western

STEPHEN PRINCE

Clint Eastwood's career in the Western spans four phases and concludes on a curious postscript. Apart from such negligible early films as *Star in the Dust* (1956) and *Ambush at Cimarron Pass* (1958), which were made when he was a bit player in Hollywood, the first phase is defined by the long-running television series *Rawhide*, which was broadcast on CBS for seven seasons, from 1959 to 1966. Eastwood played second lead as the ramrod on a cattle drive, and he chafed at the show's rigid narrative formulas that mandated a clear separation between good and evil and offered tidy resolutions reassuring the families gathered about their television screens that America's frontier enterprise had been a noble and upright undertaking. The moral certainties and complacency that were hallmarks of television in that era, and that also defined many Western feature films, underwent radical changes when Sergio Leone redefined the genre with Eastwood's collaboration in the loose trilogy, *A Fistful of Dollars* (1964), *For a Few Dollars More* (1965), and *The Good, the Bad, and the Ugly* (1966). Eastwood's collaboration with Leone defines the second phase of his involvement in the genre, and this phase proved to be decisive in establishing a moral outlook and type of character to which he returned in his other Westerns. The third phase is a transitional one, occurring after the international success of the *Dollars* trilogy, when Eastwood was working to establish himself as a leading man in Hollywood films. The productions during this period are *Hang 'Em High* (1968), *Two Mules for Sister Sara* (1970), *The Beguiled* (1971), and *Joe Kidd* (1972). The final phase is marked by Eastwood's shift to directing with *High Plains Drifter* (1973), *The Outlaw Josey Wales* (1976), *Pale Rider* (1985), and *Unforgiven* (1992).

As with any periodization, this one rests upon some value judgments. I have, for example, excluded some films that other scholars and viewers might consider as Westerns. In *Coogan's Bluff* (1968), Eastwood is a deputy sheriff from Arizona who travels to New York to extradite a criminal, and in *Bronco Billy* (1980), he plays the proprietor of a traveling Wild West show. Both are modern-dress films, taking place in a story world that is contemporaneous with the years of their production, and thus they cannot be considered true Westerns. The genre is defined by its period setting: west of the Mississippi and roughly between the Civil War and World War I. As Eastwood insisted, Westerns are *period* films.[1] *Paint Your Wagon* (1969) qualifies in that it takes place during the 1850s California Gold Rush, but as a musical adapted from a Broadway play, it is an eccentric entry in the genre, and it was a disaster-ridden production in which Eastwood's creative participation was minimal. It seems reasonable, therefore, to discretely pass it by.

The episode that forms the postscript of his involvement with the genre provides a dramatic illustration of how widely he has continued to be identified as a star of Westerns, long after he ceased to make them. When Eastwood spoke at the Republican National Convention in 2012, he stood before a bigger-than-life image culled from *The Outlaw Josey Wales* (1975). It showed a bearded Eastwood gazing menacingly toward the camera and brandishing a pair of six-shooters. In the context of a political convention, the image evoked ideologies of American empire and American exceptionalism, as these had been encoded by Westerns for generations, and it positioned Eastwood as an avatar of these ideas. A Westerner whose words carried weight and bore listening to—this was the aura the Republican Party was seeking when it invited him to speak. Alas, what ensued when Eastwood stepped to the podium was inconsistent with the ideas evoked by the image of Josey Wales. The iconic avenger in Western dress seemed far removed from the man at the podium. The difference between fact and legend to which John Ford was so attuned and around which he circled in some of his best films, such as *Fort Apache* (1948) and *The Man Who Shot Liberty Valance* (1962), defined this moment of political theater. Candidate Mitt Romney and his party thought they were getting Josey Wales but instead got a senior citizen who seemed unable to focus his thoughts. The cinematic Eastwood depicted in the poster was cool, laconic, and unflappable. The aged man at the podium rambled extemporaneously for a long eleven minutes, speaking in a halting and garbled manner

about politics, President Obama, and conservatives in Hollywood and suc-
ceeded only occasionally in being lucid. Here was a difference between fact
and legend crueler than what Ford had shown: it involved a humbling that did
not stay off-camera like Tom Doniphon's long declension in the backstory of
The Man Who Shot Liberty Valance, which took place after he performed the
titular act. Ford did not show Tom's descent into poverty and neglect; Josey
become flesh did not fare so well.

The selection of the Josey Wales poster image for the evening's event shows
how centrally the Western has performed in the elaboration of Eastwood's
screen persona, which the actor and director has spent many decades assiduously constructing. Yet what is surprising about Eastwood's identification with
Westerns in the popular mind (and this is what the Republican convention
was playing to) is how infrequently he appeared in them once his *Rawhide*
and Leone phases had ended in 1966. At the time of this writing, the Internet
Movie Database (IMDb) identifies Eastwood as a director of thirty-eight films
and an actor in sixty-seven films. Of this feature film output, there are only
eleven Westerns. There are, of course, several hundred episodes of *Rawhide*,
which introduced Eastwood in the genre to national audiences. But arguably,
Rawhide, as a television show, has been a more transient influence than the
international success that he established first with Leone and then with subsequent movies, Westerns or not. Thus the iconic status of Eastwood as a Western star is intriguing, and it raises questions about the role played by Sergio
Leone in helping set a template for a character that Eastwood has remained
comfortable playing and also has enjoyed slyly and gently subverting. These are
questions about influence—how a creative and very ambitious actor/director
used those bequeathed by the Western genre and by his career-burnishing
partnership with Leone—and the uses to which he has put the genre, especially in the wake of the radical surgery that Leone performed on it. Scholars
and critics have written copiously about Eastwood's Westerns. Rather than
seeking to offer new interpretations of films that already have many, I prefer to
offer a forensics on Eastwood's presence in the genre, the uses to which he has
put it, and where he stands in relation to the genre's other stars and directors.

Aspects of Eastwood's screen persona derive from a long tradition in
the Western of focusing on heroes who are lean, soft-spoken, and men of few
words. Robert Warshow perceptively contrasted the figure of the Westerner
with the movie gangster and emphasized that while the gangster was a figure
in constant motion, the Westerner was a figure of repose.[2] Eastwood's slow,
laid-back, seemingly casual screen presence exemplifies Warshow's point, and
his lithe appearance and sparse mannerisms reach back to William S. Hart in
the silent era. Eastwood has identified his screen style with Gary Cooper and
Henry Fonda. About them, he said, "those guys were more laid-back, more
introverted, and you were always leaning forward, wondering what they were

thinking. . . . You were never quite sure with them. They had a mysterioso quality."[3] Cooper and Fonda are important figures in the genre, and it can be instructive, in gaining perspective on Eastwood's place in Westerns, to compare his output with that of other major stars. Of Eastwood's eleven Western feature films, five are classics, a relatively high proportion out of a relatively small number. These five are the three films directed by Leone and two that Eastwood directed, *The Outlaw Josey Wales* and *Unforgiven*.

Other stars worked often in Westerns and consequently appeared in a large number of essential films. Fonda, for example, made twenty-one Westerns, and these included *The Ox-Bow Incident* (1943), *My Darling Clementine* (1946), *Fort Apache, Welcome to Hard Times* (1967), and *Once upon a Time in the West* (1968). James Stewart appeared in twenty Westerns, including *Destry Rides Again* (1939), *Broken Arrow* (1950), *The Man Who Shot Liberty Valance, The Shootist* (1976), and the series of six classic Westerns that he made with Anthony Mann. Gary Cooper appeared in forty Westerns, many during the silent era, which included such essential works as *The Virginian* (1929), *The Plainsman* (1936), *The Westerner* (1940), *High Noon* (1952), *Vera Cruz* (1954), and *Man of the West* (1958). Randolph Scott was in more than sixty Westerns, which comprised the majority of his work as an actor. As Edward Buscombe writes, "1945 must have felt strange to Randolph Scott; it was the only year between 1932 and 1959 that he didn't make a Western. Of all the major stars whose name is associated with the Western, Scott most closely identified with it."[4] Scott's output includes the splendid series of seven films directed by Budd Boetticher, and Sam Peckinpah's *Ride the High Country* (1962). John Wayne appeared in close to ninety Westerns, many of these B-films made during the 1930s, but his career included numerous classics: *The Big Trail* (1930), *Stagecoach* (1939), *Fort Apache, Red River* (1948), *She Wore a Yellow Ribbon* (1949), *The Searchers* (1956), *The Man Who Shot Liberty Valance, Rio Bravo* (1959), and *The Shootist*. In contrast with these actors, Eastwood's career includes long hiatuses from the genre. After the success of the Leone pictures, he worked to establish himself in the American industry and relied frequently on Westerns as a means of doing so, making five Westerns in six years (1968–1973). Thereafter, however, once established as a major box-office attraction in the early 1970s, he strayed from the genre often and for long intervals. A decade separates *Pale Rider* from *The Outlaw Josey Wales*, and another seven years passed before *Unforgiven*, to date Eastwood's last Western. In terms of his overall career, Eastwood did not venture into the genre in a regular and ongoing way.

Moreover, the comparison of Eastwood with other Western stars illuminates an important difference between them. Each of the other stars mentioned above worked with A-list directors (John Ford, Howard Hawks, William Wellman, Sam Peckinpah, Fred Zinnemann, William Wyler) or with idiosyncratic filmmakers (Anthony Mann, Budd Boetticher) with whom they were sympathetic and partnered in creating a large body of interesting work. Eastwood, by contrast, has been relatively unwilling to collaborate with strong directors. Sergio Leone is the only major filmmaker under whom he has worked. Eastwood's ongoing collaborations with Don Siegel are the closest approximations of the Scott-Boetticher and Stewart-Mann partnerships, but Eastwood and Siegel made just two Westerns together, *The Beguiled* and *Two Mules for Sister Sara*. Patrick McGilligan writes "There were many generational differences between Clint and John Wayne. One, not often dwelled upon, is that Wayne subordinated himself to top-ranked directors, working more than once with Raoul Walsh, Henry Hathaway, Howard Hawks and especially John Ford, hardbitten taskmasters who helped mould his image and talent. These associations were part of Wayne's wisdom, accounting in his career for a dozen films that will always be regarded as classics."[5]

A corollary of Eastwood's reluctance to collaborate with strong directors is that he did not appear often on-screen with significant performers. This was a larger problem in his career, going beyond Westerns to affect his films generally. From *Hang 'Em High* onward, the pictures that Eastwood produced through Malpaso tended to feature casts in which second-tier performers took the major roles opposite Clint. This practice certainly had an economic basis. Eastwood was committed to making films quickly and inexpensively, an approach that he thought of as antithetical to major studio productions where inefficiency and waste of resources were normative practices. But such economizing at Malpaso tended to marginalize the productions by excluding top-tier talent from participating. When major talent appears on-camera, it gives a film a level of prestige and visibility that these thrifty Malpaso productions often did not command. It also came to seem like a defensive maneuver by Eastwood, who seemed reluctant to share the screen with major players or perhaps felt himself not quite good enough to hold his own with them. In his biography of Eastwood, Richard Schickel hints at this in his discussion of *The Beguiled*, *Unforgiven*, and *In the Line of Fire* (1993). The practice kept the level of achievement in several films from being higher. The climactic gunfight in *Pale Rider* is weakened by the casting of television actor John Russell as the villainous gunfighter leading a gang of killers against Eastwood. (The gang's members are props who stand there only to be shot down by Eastwood; they never present a credible menace or opposition, a trope that derives from the Leone films.) Russell looks tough enough, but his long association with television (he had his own series in *Lawman* from 1958 to 1962) and B-movies works against his presence as a significant adversary. A strong hero needs a strong adversary, and Eastwood doesn't have it here, whereas in *Unforgiven*, Gene Hackman carries the requisite weight. Richard Dysart and Michael Moriarty also play major roles in *Pale Rider*, and they are fine actors but have worked more effectively on television than in feature films. Eastwood's long association with television seems to have influenced his casting decisions well into his career as a feature film star. In *The Outlaw Josey Wales*, John Vernon plays Josey's main antagonist, Fletcher, his former commanding officer who betrays him to the Union army and sets a band of vigilante Red Legs after Josey to hunt him down. Although he was a prolific character actor who worked prodigiously in television, Vernon never established a strong persona on-screen. This could work for him when he was cast as men who were petty and corrupt, as in *Animal House* (1978), but his character in *Josey Wales* is not scripted as a weakling. Lee Marvin complained about Vernon's difficulties impressing himself on-screen to director John Boorman on *Point Blank* (1967)—Marvin wanted another, stronger actor cast opposite him in place of Vernon.[6] During this period of his career, Eastwood drew repeatedly on a stock company composed of Geoffrey Lewis (cast as the chief bad guy in *High Plains Drifter* but who never seems bad enough), Sondra Locke, Bill McKinney, John Quade, and others drawn from television whom he was comfortable working with and who would not steal a scene or a film from him.

Eastwood's tendency to segregate himself and his work from top-tier actors and directors inhibited critical acceptance of his achievements as an actor and director until late in his career. He could be generous in making room on-screen for dynamic, hugely talented actors, as with Jeff Bridges in *Thunderbolt and Lightfoot* (1973), but this kind of opportunity did not happen very often. Eastwood's self-segregation ended abruptly in 1992 with *Unforgiven*, in which he directed and costarred with heavyweight actors and which was based on a script that Eastwood had held in abeyance for many years. His career was in the doldrums with bad films or tepid box-office performers like *Pink*

FIGURE 2.1 Eastwood mostly avoided working with top-tier actors and directors until relatively late in his career. *Unforgiven* is a Western for the ages in part because of the powerful cast, which includes Morgan Freeman, Gene Hackman, and Richard Harris. Frame enlargement.

Cadillac (1989), *The Rookie* (1990), and *White Hunter Black Heart* (1990), and he seemed to realize that a new degree of effort as a filmmaker and actor was needed. As Richard Schickel writes, "You could see [Eastwood's new ambitions] in his casting of the other major roles. In a typical Eastwood film they would have been played by good, solid, relatively anonymous character men; in *Unforgiven* they were played by Gene Hackman, Morgan Freeman and Richard Harris, stars in their own right."[7] With *In the Line of Fire* the following year, Eastwood agreed to work under another director for only the second time in twenty years, and he did not try to control Wolfgang Peterson as he had done with other filmmakers. He also costarred with an actor, John Malkovich, whose unpredictable improvisations kept Eastwood out of his comfort zone to good effect. These two films rejuvenated his career and launched him on its most prestigious and lauded phase. He didn't look back; he continued on subsequent pictures to work with major talents, including Meryl Streep, Ed Harris, Kevin Costner, Tommy Lee Jones, Hillary Swank, and numerous others. These factors—Eastwood's willingness to share the screen with strong performers, and a new level of critical respect that came his way—are connected, and they coincided with a greater level of care that he took with his films. But in terms of the Western, only one film—*Unforgiven*—is the beneficiary of this turn in his career.

Prior to *Unforgiven*, he had been working variations on the persona that he had developed in Sergio Leone's Euro-Westerns without stretching the template very far. Eastwood's venture to Italy in making *A Fistful of Dollars* was a remarkable gamble. The three films he and Leone made together launched their careers, and it was a creative partnership rife with jealousy and competition. Leone proved to be the most capable and brilliant stylist, and the most ambitious filmmaker, that Eastwood ever worked with, but Leone was not a gracious collaborator and tended to minimize the contributions that others had made to his films. In turn, as Eastwood tells it, he told Leone how the character ought to be played. Eastwood claims that he brought Leone a gift of silence—that is, he schooled the director in the effectiveness of terseness and ambiguity. Eastwood has said that the original script for *Fistful* was very wordy and included numerous passages where his character, a mysterious stranger, made long speeches explaining his past life and his reasons for acting. "The character was written quite a bit different. I made it much more economical. Much less expository. He explained himself a lot in the screenplay. My theory to Sergio was, 'I don't think you have to explain everything. Let the audience imagine with us.' I'd sort of coerce him into going for it on that level."[8] While it may be true that Eastwood shaped the character in this way, coercion seems like a strong claim. As his films demonstrate, Leone's stylistic impulses moved toward extended passages of wordlessness and silence and also toward an audiovisual ostentatiousness in which image and music (sans dialogue) blend to create operatic effects. These elements grow stronger on each successive film, and they suggest that Eastwood's preference for a terse presentation of character melded synergistically with Leone's developing cinematic gifts. Leone, in turn, proved to be a shrewd judge of Eastwood's contribution to the films—he understood the dynamic contrast that Eastwood's sleepy demeanor established in the violent context of the films they were making. He said, "This attitude he had—slow, laidback and lazy—was what he maintained throughout the film, and when you mix *that* with the blast and velocity of the gunshots, you have the essential contrast that he gave us." He added, "Eastwood moves like a sleepwalker between explosions and hails of bullets, and he is always the same—a block of marble."[9] He said that Eastwood as an actor "hurls himself into a suit of armor and lowers the visor with a rusty clang. It is precisely that lowered visor which composes his character." These are perceptive observations for this phase of Eastwood's acting career, and Richard Schickel, in his biography of Eastwood, seems to concur. "The casual and uninflected sobriety with which Joe [Eastwood's character] goes about his deadly business contrasts vividly—and to subtly humorous effect—with the operatic carnage that follows in his wake."[10]

For *Hang 'Em High*, his first American film after the Leone pictures, Eastwood fell back on the professional contacts that television had afforded him. He selected a director, Ted Post, with whom he had worked comfortably on the *Rawhide* series. In an effort to shape his career, Eastwood formed Malpaso, his own production company, which coproduced the film with Leonard Freeman, who also hailed from television and is best known for producing the *Hawaii Five-O* series. Eastwood plays a cowpoke who survives a vigilante lynching and

FIGURE 2.2 As a transitional film in the second phase of Eastwood's Western career, *Hang 'Em High* resembles a television movie in its casting and visual style. Frame enlargement.

subsequently works as a U.S. Marshal for a hanging judge, which gives him the opportunity to track down the men who nearly killed him. The film looks like a television production. The coverage is a conventional mixture of master shots and shot/reverse-shot dialogue scenes, and the exteriors show little of the expansive pictorial qualities that Ford and Leone brought to their work. Eastwood has spoken somewhat disparagingly of Leone's epic pictorial style, but that style is, arguably, a significant element in the popularity and fascination that those films continue to exert. As Jim Kitses wrote of Leone's Westerns, "Few other examples of the genre match the enormous popularity his films continue to enjoy."[11] One consequence of Eastwood's reluctance to work under strong directors, and his preference for working fast and cheap, is that some of his films have a hurried quality that is unlike the careful visual attention that top-tier directors have brought to their work. Eastwood's preference for fast production schedules and an unpretentious visual style has limited opportunities for creating moments of cinematic poetry. In Ford's and Leone's films, one remembers carefully considered, precisely choreographed and designed scenes that are superlative moments of cinematic expression—Ethan Edwards turning away from the open door of the Jorgensen ranch, Wyatt and Clementine walking to Sunday services at Tombstone's first church, Tuco running through Sad Hill Cemetery in a delirium of greed. There are fewer of these in Eastwood's films. As Tom Milne writes, "Eastwood has alternated maddeningly between films that are purely commercial potboilers, and others that constitute an attempt to explore the elements of his success."[12] David Thomson noted, "The most evident streak of Eastwood's hardness, and his greatest limitation as a screen presence, is his unwillingness to push beyond his own gut reactions. If it felt right to Clint, a director might have a tough time going for more takes. Moreover, his briskness onscreen sometimes imparts a feeling that he is not bothering to think too much about a moment or a situation, but just wants to get it done."[13] Describing for Thomson his objectives in forming Malpaso, Eastwood emphasized efficiency and economy of production in an industry where waste of time and resources are prevalent. "We try to organize the films and make them in the least amount of time."[14]

Two Mules for Sister Sara and *Joe Kidd* certainly seem like hurried productions. In the former, the climactic attack by Hogan, the soldier-of-fortune played by Eastwood, and a band of Mexican Juaristas on a barracks full of government soldiers is awkwardly staged, which is surprising in that director Don Siegel elsewhere has staged some of cinema's great action scenes. Both films turn away from the intriguing moral and social issues raised in their narratives. After saving her from a gang of rapists, Hogan travels through the desert with a nun, Sara (Shirley MacClain), who turns out to be a prostitute who has assumed this disguise for the safety that it provides. Hogan lusts after Sara but, out of respect for her, he represses his libido, and the film's emotional climax is not the assault on the barracks but the moment when Hogan, learning the truth about Sara, at last gets into her britches. Eastwood reprises his persona from the Leone films, appearing unshaven and casually gunning down a gang of bandits in the opening scene, as he did for Leone. There is even an Ennio Morricone score. Scripted by Elmore Leonard, *Joe Kidd* deals with a Mexican peasant revolt led by Luis Chama (John Saxon) against white landowners who are seizing Mexican-held property. Joe (Eastwood) is a former bounty hunter who allies himself with professional killers hired to assassinate Chama and his friends. The film glosses over the racial tensions that form the premise of the narrative and Joe's ethical culpability in siding with the killers. Some of the film's unevenness resulted from Eastwood's struggles for creative control with director John Sturges. Glenn Lovell writes, "Sturges saw the protagonist as a bumptious charmer who, when cornered, would rise to the occasion; Eastwood saw him as the Hollywood version of his spaghetti Western persona."[15]

Of all the Westerns that Eastwood made in his transitional period, *The Beguiled* is the most interesting, unusual, and daring. It was his third collaboration with Don Siegel, and it enabled both to step away from action roles and to step into something much more psychological and contemplative. Strictly speaking, the film might not be regarded as a Western, since it takes place in an unspecified Southern location during the Civil War and because the thematic issues and conflicts have little to do with the genre's customary material. Although some viewers may legitimately feel that it lies outside the genre, it might be better conceived as a film that lies on the periphery of the genre. Major encyclopedias of the Western do include it as an important work in the genre.[16] Eastwood plays John McBurney, a Union soldier who is wounded in Southern territory and finds refuge at a girls' school run by Martha Farnsworth (Geraldine Page). Headmistress Farnsworth and her charges have secluded themselves from men as a means of self-preservation during the war, and their levels of sexual frustration, fantasy, and longing run high. Farnsworth is a troubled woman who follows a rigid moral code in her dealings with the students, yet she is stirred by memories of an incestuous relationship with her brother and keeps the letters he wrote her in a bedroom dresser like those from a lover. McBurney comes to regard his convalescence at the girls' school as a vacation in sexual paradise; almost immediately he comes on to several of the women, including the black slave, Hallie (Mae Mercer), who indignantly refuses his advances. She will have no sexual congress with a white man, given the kind of treatment she has known under whites.

McBurney is a character unlike others that Eastwood has played, and while he doesn't quite convey the depths and nuances of the character, this protagonist is part of a most unusual filmic structure. This difference points to some important roads not taken in Eastwood's career and to stylistic alternatives that he mostly eschewed. Wandering away from the school, twelve-year-old Amy (Pamelyn Ferdin), its youngest student, discovers McBurney lying in the woods wounded and barely conscious. As a Confederate patrol passes by, he hides with her in the underbrush and asks her how old she is. When she replies that she is twelve, he tells her that she's old enough to be kissed, which he then does in a lingering fashion, holding the kiss until the patrol has passed by and gone. When he breaks off the kiss, Amy's expression is confused and startled. McBurney's appetites make him a dangerous man; his pursuit of sexual pleasure is heedless and impulsive and brings disaster down on him. Although Amy soon decides that she loves him, his cruel treatment of her pet turtle elicits her wrath, and she becomes instrumental in engineering his death. The sexual affairs he pursues with several women at the school (all of whom are older than Amy) whip up a maelstrom of jealousy and hatred that so disturbs and challenges Farnsworth's repressive reign that she exacts a cruel vengeance. She amputates his leg under the pretext that it has gone to gangrene. Feeling this to be an insufficiently severe punishment, she enlists Amy to pick some poisoned mushrooms, which the group cooks and serves up as part of what they are pretending will be a dinner of forgiveness. The film ends with Farnsworth and her girls sewing his body into a cloth sack and depositing it outside the gates of the school.

Whatever resonances the original script had for Eastwood when Don Siegel broached the idea of making the film, the resulting work departs significantly from the abiding moral point of view that Eastwood's Westerns have instantiated. It is not just that he plays a passive and put-upon character and one that dies at the end. At numerous points, McBurney is held up for criticism, is exposed as a flawed, mendacious, and destructive person. Among the most pointed and cutting scenes are those in which flashback images directly contradict his words and claims about past actions; the intercutting subverts what he is saying. As Farnsworth changes the dressing on McBurney's wounded leg shortly after he arrives at the school, she remarks disdainfully that he probably knows nothing about ethics. He replies that it's because of ethics that he was wounded. He tells her he is a Quaker and carries only bandages into a battle, never a gun. He narrates the events that led him to be wounded, telling her that he saw a Confederate soldier hemmed in by encroaching fire. He says his duty was to stay with his men, but his ethics wouldn't let him, and he went to help the enemy soldier. As he fashions this outlandish narrative, the images show his words as lies. Rather than going to his aid, McBurney shoots the man from the cover of the forest. "I carried that Reb to safety. That's why I got shot," he says, while quick inserts show McBurney shooting another Confederate soldier who has come to help his fallen comrade. Eventually McBurney is shot down by other comrades of the soldier he originally picked off. He tells

Farnsworth that he feels badly because his ethics led him to disregard his duty to stay with his own men. Moved by his account, she gazes at him with empathy and inquires whether his burned hands hurt him much.

The editing places picture and sound into a dialectical relationship that exposes the character's opportunistic nature and frames it in a caustic manner. This critical view distinguishes the film from Eastwood's other Westerns. In them, his characters' behavior synchronizes with the filmic points of view. Leone's sardonic and cynical worldview in the *Dollars* trilogy is consistent with this pattern. Eastwood's character there is as sardonic, cynical, and opportunistic as the world in general. Leone depicts a world of predators, and the Eastwood character is admirable because he is the most cunning and clever of the predators. Even in *Unforgiven*, where Eastwood's Will Munny is chastised and condemned by himself and others as a stone killer, the audience is never made to feel this as a hard and unyielding truth because the filmic point of view belongs to Munny; it doesn't disengage itself from his experiences and perceptions of events. But point of view in *The Beguiled* is distinct from Eastwood's character and subjects him to scrutiny without sentimentality. Eastwood's other Westerns build their worlds as projections of his characters' outlooks, albeit with tentative modifications in *Josey Wales* and *Unforgiven*.

High Plains Drifter and *Pale Rider* exemplify this pattern. In the former, Eastwood again plays a mysterious stranger, unshaven, wearing a duster, and smoking cigars as in a Leone film. He rides into the lakeside town of Lago and proves his deadly skills by gunning down three adversaries in a barber shop (a scene that reprises action from *For a Few Dollars More*), and when he is insulted by Callie Travers (Marianna Hill), a well-dressed woman strolling the main street, he drags her into a barn and rapes her. She responds sexually

FIGURE 2.3 In *High Plains Drifter*, Eastwood borrows numerous motifs from the films of Sergio Leone, including a barbershop ambush in which Eastwood's character guns down a trio of opponents. Frame enlargement.

to the assault, her behavior confirming rape myths that a woman really wants it even if she struggles or says no. Later, Callie pulls a gun on the Drifter and tries to kill him while he's in the bath, but she improbably misses at point-blank range. The Drifter says to the diminutive Mordecai (Billy Curtis), "Wonder what took her so long to get mad." Mordecai replies, "Maybe because you didn't go back for more." When the stranger does go back for more, Callie is willing to comply. The other woman in the film, Sara Belding (Verna Bloom), the wife of the hotel manager, chastises the stranger for being a cruel man, and she regards him with a measure of loathing. Yet her words amount to little because she, too, beds down with him at her first opportunity. The macho point of view offered by these scenes is very different from what *The Beguiled* had shown.

Callie's inability to kill the stranger—she fires directly into the bathtub where he is sitting—lends a supernatural aura to the character. He sinks below the bath water as she fires, and he rises up from the water when she is finished, the bullets having done no damage. It is a resurrection motif, which Eastwood will employ again in *Pale Rider*, and is another reprise from Leone's films. In *A Fistful of Dollars* Eastwood is shot down repeatedly by the film's villain (Gian Maria Volonte) but gets to his feet each time because he's wearing armor under his serape. In *The Good, the Bad, and the Ugly*, his ordeal of torture in the desert at the hands of Tuco (Eli Wallach) ends in a near-death experience from which he recovers. And in that film, the Bad (Lee Van Cleef) describes him as a guardian angel, which is what the Eastwood character becomes in *Pale Rider*. In *High Plains Drifter*, his identity remains anonymous and ambiguous but carries the supernatural aura that an association with resurrection entails. Indeed, one prevalent interpretation of the film is that Eastwood's character is the reincarnation of Marshal Duncan, who was murdered by three outlaws working for the town's mining company, a killing in which everyone in the town was complicit. Eastwood's character materializes out of nothingness in the film's strong, eerie opening shot, and then in its last, he dematerializes back into nothingness, into heat waves hovering in the haze of the desert. The character appears and disappears like an apparition. As Eastwood says, "It was originally written that The Drifter was the brother of the murdered sheriff, but I played it as if it could have been some apparition."[17]

The film's jaundiced view of the town is another lift from the *Dollars* films, where Leone's surgery on the genre entailed cutting the principal characters loose from traditional motivations, such as a hero's intercession on behalf of the weak or in defense of a community that symbolizes social progress and improvement. Before the three outlaws return, the Drifter has the townspeople paint "Hell" over the town's name on the sign marking the main entrance. He wants all the buildings painted red, as in hell, and when the preacher objects that the Drifter can't mean the church too, he replies, "I mean especially the church," reprising the anticlericalism that is a striking feature of Leone's films. Leone's remark about Eastwood being an actor inside of armor is especially apt for this film, since the performance is a rigidly stoic one, lacking the relaxed humor evident in the *Dollars* films. Eastwood's belief that less is more and that it is better to create some mystery than to be unduly literal and explanatory in terms of character histories and motives is exercised here perhaps too strongly because it leaves viewers with little sense about why any of the Drifter's actions have taken place. Since we don't know anything about Marshal Duncan, it's difficult to feel that much is at stake in avenging his murder, and since the town is such an isolated and weird place, it's difficult to feel that retribution for its venality restores a moral balance in the world.

A similar issue affects *Pale Rider*, whose narrative is patterned on George Stevens's *Shane* (1953) and in which Eastwood again plays an avenging angel, this time in a more overtly religious context. In answer to a prayer for help made by fourteen-year-old Megan (Sydney Penny), Preacher (Eastwood) appears on high in snowy mountains and descends, like Shane, to lower ground where a powerful mining company is intent on seizing lands being worked by itinerant prospectors searching for gold. Whereas Shane allied himself with a farming community that was procreative with crops and children, ensuring a productive future, the prospectors whom Preacher aids are a haphazard collection of migrants scratching at rocks for signs of gold. Shane was drawn to help Joe Starrett, his family, and the other farmers because he was moved by what they were trying to achieve and because of unspoken feelings shared between himself and Joe's wife, Marian. Shane respected the fecundity that the farmers represented, perhaps because his own life was barren and a dead end. Preacher is such a stoic, aloof and isolated figure that it is difficult to say why he has come to the aid of the prospectors or what they collectively represent that might be

FIGURE 2.4 The antagonists faced by Preacher in the climax of *Pale Rider* are an anonymous, undifferentiated group of villains modeled on the heavies in Sergio Leone films. Frame enlargement.

worth protecting. Spending all day scratching for gold is a gamble rather than a reliable enterprise. As Patrick McGee observes, "This film expresses little faith in the community itself."[18] Moreover, the delicacy of the unspoken attraction Shane and Marian feel for one another is replaced here by Megan and her mother Sarah (Carrie Snodgrass) both lusting for Preacher. He accepts the mother's offer, thereby cuckolding Hull (Michael Moriarty), a decent prospector who has looked after Sara and wishes to marry her. It's difficult to imagine Shane bedding down with Marian while Joe is away in town. While this distinction provides one measure of how far from classical Westerns Eastwood has traveled, it also suggests that the severe minimalism of the style loses the emotional nuances and resonant themes that operate in *Shane*. Shane fights on behalf of the farmers because important things are at stake. It is hard to know what is at stake in *Pale Rider*, what issues have so roused Preacher that he descends from the realm of demigods to that of human affairs.

The barrenness of the communal life represented by the prospectors in *Pale Rider* is surprising because in *The Outlaw Josey Wales* Eastwood seemed to have been moving toward an acknowledgment of the social world and its importance for the individual. "I don't want nobody belonging to me," Josey says, but in spite of his inclinations, a ragtag band of drifters attaches itself to him. The group includes an old Indian chief and an Indian woman, a dog, and a group of settlers traveling by wagon. Josey leads them to a new home, and the film's ending strongly implies that he will stay to live among them instead of traveling on alone. Yet this is so understated that it remains a minor riff on the persona of the mysterious stranger that Eastwood had been playing since the *Dollars* films. More important, Josey's real family as depicted in the film's initial sequence—a wife and son with whom he lives and farms and who are murdered by Union Red Legs—are little more than props. His life with them and their existence as characters are not taken seriously in the film—that is, are not invested with representational or emotional depth. They exist so that they may be taken away and thereby afford Josey a motivation for his isolation and proficiency with violence. A similar pattern prevails in *Unforgiven*, which finds Will Munny working as a farmer with two children and haunted by the death of his wife. The film's portrait of Will's return to violence is far more convincing than the suggestion that he has been living for some years as a parent with his kids. These films show great difficulty portraying the Eastwood character in domestic circumstances, suggesting that the character has not traveled much distance from the terrain on which he was invented in the Leone films.

Richard Schickel has written that Eastwood's screen character "has taken the American male deeper into the country of disaffection than he has ever ridden before on-screen" and shown "the difficulty men have in making connections—not just with other men, but with communities, with women, with conventional morality, with their own best selves."[19] Schickel's astute observation should be tempered with the provision that the Eastwood Westerns have not gestured very convincingly at the worth of the connections that the character avoids and elides, as other great Westerns have done—*Shane*, *The Searchers*, *The Wild Bunch* (1969). Without some sense that these things may be worthwhile, the narratives are left mainly with situations of isolation represented by the Eastwood character. He exemplifies what D. H. Lawrence wrote—"The essential American soul is hard, isolate, stoic and a killer. It has never yet melted."

This forensics on the Eastwood Westerns leaves us in a perhaps surprising place. As Patrick McGee has written, "The issues raised by Leone's cinema are the ones that continue to haunt Eastwood's imagination."[20] In reworking, reprising, and extending Leone's thematics but not the elaborate stylistic flourishes that distinguished Leone's cinematic approach, Eastwood's Westerns, I am suggesting, can be viewed as a subset of the intervention that Leone made into the genre some fifty years ago. Moreover, because Eastwood worked relatively infrequently in Westerns once he established himself and his production company in Hollywood, he made fewer films than the genre's other stars and with less variety. Of these, two that he directed are classics, others are solid efforts, and many are programmers, made quickly and for a price. As he said, "I never considered myself a cowboy."[21]

These observations challenge conventional notions about the scope of Eastwood's role in the genre. Why then has his identification with it been so extensive and persistent? One answer is that this identification results from the way that Eastwood has sustained the character type that he played for Sergio Leone and from the recognition that Leone's films were instrumental in bringing the genre's modern form into being. Eastwood has benefited from his efforts to extend Leone's imprint, though he would likely disagree that this is what he has been doing. By extending Leone's intervention, Eastwood shared in its magnitude, and audiences have always enjoyed watching Clint gun down his adversaries. Perceptions of Clint Eastwood's place in the genre, then, are conditioned by what Leone had done. By replicating Leone's imprint, Eastwood's Westerns helped make it into an ongoing tradition reaching across several decades. Leone had globalized the Western; Eastwood's periodic Westerns refreshed this project. In this respect, Eastwood has played a key role in the shaping of contemporary Westerns, albeit one that is less original that it might at first appear to be.

Notes

1 Christopher Frayling, "Eastwood on Eastwood," in *Clint Eastwood: Interviews, Revised and Updated*, ed. Robert E. Kapsis and Kathie Coblentz (Jackson: University Press of Mississippi, 2013), 111.

2 Robert Warshow, "Movie Chronicle: The Westerner," in *Film Theory and Criticism*, ed. Leo Braudy and Marshall Cohen, 6th ed. (New York: Oxford University Press, 2004), 704.

3 Tim Cahill, "Clint Eastwood: The Rolling Stone Interview," in *Clint Eastwood: Interviews*, 101.

4 Edward Buscombe, "Randolph Scott," in *The BFI Companion to the Western*, ed. Edward Buscombe (New York: Da Capo Press, 1988), 382.

5 Patrick McGilligan, *Clint: The Life and Legend* (New York: St. Martin's Press, 1999), 268.

6 Discussed in the John Boorman commentary accompanying *Point Blank*, directed by John Boorman (1967; Warner Home Video, 2005), DVD.

7 Richard Schickel, *Clint Eastwood: A Biography* (New York: Vintage Books, 1997), 453.

8 David Thomson, "Cop on a Hot *Tightrope*," in *Clint Eastwood: Interviews*, 67.

9 McGilligan, *Clint*, 136, 159.

10 Schickel, *Clint Eastwood*, 139.

11 Jim Kitses, *Horizons West* (London: BFI, 2007), 282.

12 Tom Milne, "Clint Eastwood," in *BFI Companion*, 339.

13 Thomson, "Cop on a Hot *Tightrope*," 58.

14 Thomson, 64.

15 Glenn Lovell, *Escape Artist: The Life and Films of John Sturges* (Madison: University of Wisconsin Press, 2008), 275.

16 Edward Buscombe, ed., *The BFI Companion to the Western* (New York: Da Capo Press, 1988); Phil Hardy, *The Western* (Woodstock, N.Y.: Overlook Press, 1995).

17 Ric Gentry, "Director Clint Eastwood: Attention to Detail and Involvement for the Audience," in *Clint Eastwood: Interviews*, 46.

18 Patrick McGee, *From "Shane" to "Kill Bill": Rethinking the Western* (Malden, Mass.: Blackwell, 2007), 194.

19 Schickel, *Clint Eastwood*, 496.

20 McGee, *From "Shane" to "Kill Bill,"* 195.

21 Schickel, *Clint Eastwood*, 291.

3

"God/Country/Family"

• •

The Military Movies

LESTER D. FRIEDMAN

Although known primarily through his roles in Westerns and police dramas, Clint Eastwood also has a long history as an actor, director, and producer in a third, equally male-dominated genre, the military movie. The cover of the Warner Bros. celebratory DVD collection of Eastwood's thirty-five years working at the studio, for example, features three iconic images of the actor: as police detective, Western gunslinger, and combat soldier. Indeed, Eastwood appeared in a series of small and often uncredited military roles at the very start of his movie career before his breakout portrayal of Rowdy Yates in the TV series *Rawhide*: *Francis in the Navy* (1955), *Away All Boats* (1956), *West Point* (TV series, 1957), *Escape in Japan* (1957), *Navy Log* (TV series, 1958), and *Lafayette Escadrille* (1958). When his career blossomed after starring as the "Man with No Name" in Sergio Leone's trilogy of hugely popular spaghetti Westerns (1964, 1965, 1966), Eastwood used the Civil War as a backdrop for *The Beguiled* (1971) and *The Outlaw Josey Wales* (1976), World War II for *Where Eagles Dare* (1968) and *Kelley's Heroes* (1970), and the Cold War for *Firefox* (1982). Eastwood later focused on how combat affects men both during the action and after the fighting ceases in four films between 1986 and 2014, one in which he stars and three of which he directs: *Heartbreak Ridge* (1986), *Flags of Our Fathers* (2006), *Letters from Iwo Jima* (2006), and *American Sniper* (2014).

Each of these movies contains Eastwood's particular take on interwoven concepts that inevitably appear in all combat movies. Issues of masculinity, for example, have always been an inherent component of the combat movie, and within current American culture, the battle-hardened soldier has replaced the rugged cowboy as the cinematic representation of masculine behavior when faced with violence and possible death. The soldier, as the man of action, battles bloodthirsty evildoers bent on obliterating humankind's moral values. Blended seamlessly with this hypermasculinity coexists a strand of homo-eroticism and a fetish with the near-naked male body rarely so overtly foregrounded in other genres. Because squad members depend on each other to survive, intense relationships between men under perilous conditions dominate this rigidly gendered genre and make these movies the ultimate "buddy" films. The relentless threat of death that hovers over soldiers endows these tough guys with an intrinsic vulnerability that in turn gives them license to cast off some of the social prohibitions that govern staid civilian life. The combat film, for example, remains one of the few genres in which men can express deep emotional affection for each other while simultaneously displaying extreme physical courage, and the embedded bonds forged between men at war transcend even their intimate connections with their families. At their best, then, combat movies fuse powerful, often disturbing visual spectacles depicting the sweep of history and the heat of battle with intense narratives about the romance of danger, the brotherhood between soldiers, and the cruel necessity to kill for one's country.

Incorporating these components, traditional combat films that depict historical battles reshuffle a series of potent mythologies containing valiant heroes, dangerous quests, malevolent villains, recognizable iconographies, repeated narrative patterns, and recurring conventions into potent allegories that define America's nationalistic ideals. The ubiquitous images of ethnically diverse fighting units that populate historical combat movies, for example, become microcosms of an idealized racial and religious equality. Yet these combat movies inevitably conflate facts and fantasies to fabricate a shared mélange of wartime experiences and fictitious events all situated within dramatic structures. Equally important, the cessation of fighting often signals the beginning of intense clashes about a war's meaning in American culture, generating debates, interpretations, and reconfigurations habitually fought within various spheres of popular culture. We can be reasonably certain about when and where a historical battle occurred, but its meanings ebb and flow with history's tidal currents. Eastwood's quartet of combat movies, as part of our repository of cultural memories, function as significant building blocks that help construct our communal sense of national selfhood by challenging and often undercutting hallowed combat film tropes to expose the tangled realities that lie beneath the surface of a given situation.

Drop Your Cocks and Grab Your Socks: *Heartbreak Ridge*

Heartbreak Ridge (the title refers to the month-long Korean War battle—September 13 to October 15, 1951—in which the main character's bravery earned him the Congressional Medal of Honor) seems like three different movies. In the first segment, the training Gunnery Sergeant Tom Highway (Eastwood) gives his raw recruits—characterized by Highway's incessant series of misogynist insults, homophobic slurs, and verbal invectives—emerges as a parody of previous military movies, in particular John Wayne's hugely popular vehicle *Sands of Iwo Jima* (1949). The second section shows an uncomfortable "Gunny" Highway trying to reconnect with his feisty ex-wife, Aggie (Marsha Mason), and seeking guidance from a series of self-help articles in women's magazines. One never knows how far Eastwood has his tongue buried in his check in these two sections, but he clearly subverts more conventional approaches to these situations. In fact, he claims that the film is "my ultimate statement about macho. He's super macho and he's full of shit—just completely ignorant."[1] Such sentiments encourage an approach slanted toward seeing both the training of the troops and the wooing of the ex-wife through a satiric rather than a serious lens while not denying that both sections contain some sincere elements as well.

The last portion depicts realistic combat scenes using familiar tropes from World War II and Vietnam War movies. Unlike the previous sections of *Heartbreak Ridge*, these dynamic battle segments contain no parodic elements, and one member of Highway's squad dies in the fighting. But skirmishes on a small Caribbean island (Grenada) and a military objective to rescue American medical students who seem in little real danger (one woman casually emerges naked from the shower) undercut some of the firefight heroics. While Eastwood never disparages their bravery, these soldiers risk their lives in a fairly inconsequential invasion with little of value really at stake, allowing the film to present a subtle critique of America's foreign policy. Indeed, many historians regard this invasion as enacted to distract the public from the death of more than two hundred marines in their Beirut compound just two days earlier (October 23, 1983). The divergent tones of these three segments clash with each other, making viewing *Heartbreak Ridge* a rather confusing experience.

Heartbreak Ridge's opening credits, accompanied by militaristic drumming, provide a good example of the film's tonal problems. They begin with black-and-white combat footage from the Korean and Vietnam Wars. About two minutes into the film, we hear twangy banjo music and Don Gibson begins singing "The Sea of Heartbreak," the popular 1961 country and Western song about "lost love an' loneliness." The images now shift to wounded soldiers being helped by their buddies, some limping and some lugged to safety on stretchers. Then fellow soldiers hoist the most seriously wounded into waiting trucks and onto planes, and finally, refugees, mostly children, haul their few belongings along a road crowded with fleeing civilians. The final freeze frame of a crying child dissolves into a black-and-white shot of a massive building complex. The camera takes us inside, a wall calendar identifies the date as July 20–21, 1983 (after the war), and then moves us into a civilian jail cell. How are we to take these distressing images of men and children destroyed by war awkwardly juxtaposed to a self-pitying tune about an abandoned love, the only seeming connection between sound and image being that both contain "heartbreak"—but on a totally different scale from each other.

Throughout his career as a director, Eastwood is as meticulous about his musical choices as he is about his images (see Charity Lofthouse's chapter within this volume), so we can assume the selection of this opening song, a huge hit performed by the original artist, is deliberate and meant to be meaningful. But I find it hard to equate the song's forlorn lover with the wounded and dying soldiers who fill the frames of this sequence. Is the emotional distress of a man feeling "like a lost ship / Adrift on the sea" in any way comparable to the anguish felt by the families of disabled and dead soldiers? "Memories of your caress, so divine" and wishes "you were mine again" pale in comparison to what these men have suffered in battle—and will continue to endure both physically and emotionally for the rest of their lives. On the other hand, I find it equally difficult to conceive of Eastwood consciously denigrating the sacrifices of American fighters in Korea and Vietnam so poignantly rendered on the screen by yoking those images to a song that contains little emotional equivalence. Indeed, the lyrics to "Sea of Heartbreak" would be far more compatible with the sections of *Heartbreak Ridge* where Highway attempts to woo back his ex-wife, but the tune is never heard in the movie again.

The section of domestic squabbling also poses hard-to-resolve questions of tone. The first words in the movie spoken by Highway, while locked in a jail cell for drunk and disorderly conduct, are "I've been pumping pussy since

FIGURE 3.1 One of three distinct modes in *Heartbreak Ridge* (1986): the combat film. Frame enlargement.

Christ was a corporal." That is quickly followed by, "I've gotta tell you, the best poontang I ever paid for was in Da Nang . . . and we got laid in a safe, orderly, proficient, military manner." He expresses similarly crude sentiments throughout the movie, including referring to his squad as "pussies," so when he starts reading articles such as "The Sexual Politics of Living Alone" and "The Big Commitment and You," the viewer feels uncertain about whether this vulgar character's attempt to modify his offensive behavior, and thereby win back the estranged Maggie, is genuine or, as she puts it, just a change in tactics to outflank her. Such confusion escalates when he begins to ask her questions such as "Did we mutually nurture each other and communicate in meaningful ways?" while drinking beer and munching on some chips. One can hear the hint of derision in Highway's tone as he guzzles his beer and crunches on the chips.

As he stumbles toward a basic level of self-realization, Highway seems to recognize that he must change in order to live with Maggie, a decision as pragmatic as it is emotional. Nearing the end of his time in the marines—"there's no room in this man's corps for me now"—Highway has few viable options. But Eastwood utters these pat phrases about relationships with a hint of derision and a wispy smile, the emotional sentiments of a new age man sounding painfully uncomfortable emanating from the mouth of a Neanderthal. Are these sentiments, then, authentic attempts to adjust to altered circumstances or simply poking fun at society's embrace of the modern, sensitive male? By the end of the film, however, these slender gestures are sufficient to convince Maggie to welcome him home from combat, and they walk arm in arm into the sunset. One is left to wonder if Eastwood is trying, in some simplistic way, to respond to the feminist attacks on his work or, perhaps, just deftly satirizing their criticisms of his previous films.

No such ambivalences appear in the final combat section. Although Eastwood called the Grenada offensive a "stupid invasion" and a "mickey mouse operation,"[2] the consequences of a soldier's mistake on this island are as potentially lethal as on Omaha Beach. Bullets kill regardless of political circumstances. Highway's reconnaissance platoon, which he has transformed from a bunch of slackers into a crack military unit, distinguishes itself, liberating the American students at St. George's medical school and outfighting seasoned Cuban troops armed with Russian rifles. The men in Highway's squad initially represent a new breed of undisciplined soldiers, particularly Stitch (Mario Van Peebles), a rock singer with an earring and a defiant attitude, who must learn the ethos of the Marine Corps from this grizzled veteran. Actual combat is their final exam, and they pass with flying colors, Stitch earning a wink of approval from Highway. But like the obsolete Western figures of Ford and Peckinpah, Highway fills no necessary role in the brave new world of modern technological warfare. *Heartbreak Ridge*, with its ambiguous, aging, retrograde protagonist, a fighting man who can teach a new generation valuable lessons but not be part of it, stands as Eastwood first directorial attempt to make a combat movie. As such, it resembles a warm-up, or a practice round, before tackling the far more complicated combat sequences in the next three military films.

"The Right Picture Can Win or Lose a War": *Flags of Our Fathers*

Eastwood's films during the twenty years between *Heartbreak Ridge* and his two Iwo Jima movies provide ample evidence that he had evolved into an increasingly confident, technically skilled, and thematically sophisticated director. As a result, by 2006, audiences expected more than shoot-outs from the man who had directed critically praised work such as *Bird* (1988), *Unforgiven* (1992), *Mystic River* (2003), and *Million Dollar Baby* (2004) during the intervening two decades. First suggested by his friend Steven Spielberg, a film about the fierce battle on Iwo Jima provided Eastwood with multiple opportunities to further develop his artistic style and deepen his thematic complexity. By unpacking the social history of Joe Rosenthal's iconic photograph, *Raising the Flag on Iwo Jima* (taken February 23, 1945), beyond the front pages, Eastwood deconstructs the fundamental assumptions and superficial definitions of aggressive masculinity that define those warriors society elevates into exemplars of bravery during wartime. The entwined spiral of stories concealed behind Rosenthal's famous picture allowed the director to explore, yet again, what can be seen as his master theme: revealing the discrepancies and unpleasant truths inevitably discarded in order to manufacture, mythologize, and ultimately venerate a cultural hero. To that end, Eastwood's films recurrently explore the fissures between communal commemoration and historical accuracy, probing the disparities that emerge between facts and legends and demonstrating how fabrications play a vital role in constructing the persona of heroes.

First, however, a short history lesson. The amphibious invasion of American troops on Iwo Jima, a volcanic island 575 miles from the Japanese coast and only 4.5-by-2.5 miles long, began on February 19, 1945. The battle lasted a bloody thirty-six days, pitting three marine divisions supported by naval and air bombardments against Japanese soldiers hunkered down in thirteen thousand yards of linked tunnels, underground strongholds, caves, bunkers, and camouflaged artillery placements. Of the 30,000 marines and 23,000 Japanese army and navy troops that took part in this strategic battle to establish landing and refueling bases for American planes near the Japanese mainland, 6,800 U.S. Marines and American sailors were killed and another 17,372 were wounded; although a handful of Japanese soldiers were taken prisoner, 18,917 were killed in action. Twenty-seven Medals of Honor were awarded for bravery during the ferocious fighting, more than any other battle in U.S. history. The famous flag-raising atop Mount Suribachi was performed by Corporal Harlon Block, Pharmacist's Mate Second Class John "Doc" Bradley, Private First Class Rene Gagnon, Private First Class Franklin Sousley, Sergeant Michael Strank, and Private First Class Ira Hayes. Strank and Block were killed six days after the flag-raising, the former by a shell from an American destroyer and the latter a few hours afterward by a mortar round. A Japanese sniper shot Sousley twenty days later. Rosenthal's picture won the Pulitzer Prize for Photography, was reprinted around the world, and became the basis of the Marine Corps War Memorial, dedicated in 1954. By some estimates, *Raising the Flag on Iwo Jima* is the most reproduced image in the history of photography.

Delving into the far less glamorous and decidedly more tawdry stories behind Rosenthal's celebrated photo, Eastwood presents viewers with a deeply cynical view of the intimate linkages between war and show business—or, to put it more bluntly, war as show business. In order to raise a desperately needed fourteen billion dollars to fund the war effort, the marine high command transforms the three survivors of the flag-raising into war heroes/celebrities by distorting what actually happened that day—even ignoring that one marine (Gagnon) never fired a shot during the taking of the mountain; withholding that the picture was a second, staged flag-raising; and misnaming one marine. Eastwood's disruptive, nonlinear narrative juxtaposes sham re-creations of the flag-raising with scenes recalling the actual combat (themselves visual compositions), questioning not only the sepia-colored, sentimental images of the homeland (see *Saving Private Ryan*) but also the concomitant "commercialism, materialism, exploitation, and opportunism, all under the guises of involvement in a national war effort."[3] But as Doc Bradley's son, James (Tom McCarthy), comes to understand: "Heroes are something we create, something we need. It's a way for us to understand what is almost incomprehensible: how people could sacrifice so much for us." Ironically, of course, Eastwood's film about this subject is, to some extent, also a participant in this nexus of war and show business, even while simultaneously criticizing it.

The domestic scenes the serviceman encounter while on their tour overflow with crowded images of Americans enjoying themselves on the home front, eating and drinking and laughing while young men risk their lives on a tiny, little-known island in the Pacific Ocean. Even more damaging, however, harrowing combat memories haunt Doc and Ira, even years after World War II ends. In the crucial segment set in Chicago's Soldier Field, Eastwood frenetically cuts between traumatic flashbacks of their frightened struggles to survive on Mount Suribachi and the papier-mâché replica of the mountain decorating the middle of a football field. His images alternate faster and faster between the two sites to visualize the dizzy, disoriented, and emotional responses of Doc and Ira, trapped within both the actual battle and the mock

FIGURE 3.2 *Flags of Our Fathers* (2006): the nexus of war and show business. Frame enlargement.

spectacle that engulfs them. Here, Eastwood and his longtime editor, Joel Cox, delve beneath surface realism to depict the inner turmoil of these two men forever scarred by their wartime actions and, in Doc's case, the recurring nightmares about his failure to rescue his lost friend Iggy (Jamie Bell). Neither man conceptualizes himself as a hero; as Ira puts it, "I know that it's a good thing, raising the money and that, 'cause we need it. But, I can't take them calling me a hero. All I did was try not to get shot. Some of the things I saw done, things I did, they weren't things to be proud of, you know."

Robert Eberwein observes that *Flags of Our Fathers* is "unique in being the first war film to thematize the issue of historical reality presented by war films."[4] By doing so, Eastwood overturns some of the most hallowed conventions of the traditional combat film. Most importantly, his central figure, John "Doc" Bradley (Ryan Phillippe), is not a gung-ho hero cast in the mold of John Wayne's archetypal soldier, Sergeant John M. Stryker, in the classic World War II film *Sands of Iwo Jima*. Unlike Wayne's tough, alcoholic marine sergeant who uses abusive training methods to mold a squad of raw recruits into a brave fighting unit (a forbearer of Gunny Highway), Eastwood's protagonist is a medical corpsman who risks his life to save the wounded and tend to the dying, even when he himself suffers a severe injury. Doc displays courage under fire equal to Stryker, but he exhibits none of the raw masculinity or the harsh bullying that characterizes his cinematic predecessor. War is "one of the most rigidly gendered activities possible," claims Anne Gjelsvik, "an activity that has often served to define manhood itself, where becoming a man often valorizes an aggressive masculinity."[5] Eastwood's Doc Bradley redefines this conventionally unvarnished image of the American soldier, turning him into a caretaker rather than an überwarrior.

Doc, Rene Gagnon (Jesse Bradford), and Ira Hayes (Adam Beach) survive one of the bloodiest battles in history, yet none of them entirely recover from the psychological wounds inflicted by the bond-drive tour that exploits them as its spokesmen. Doc retreats into an isolated silence about his wartime activities, never sharing what he experienced or even his military decorations with his closest loved ones. His son discovers his story only after Doc's death. Although he tries to take advantage of his fleeting heroic status, Rene never manages to capitalize on the business contacts made during his short-lived fame to further his ambitions; he ends his life as a janitor. Ira degenerates into a troubled alcoholic, never able to overcome the jagged memories that torment him; he dies at an early age, a shattered man. Their tour converts them into pitchmen and their actions on Iwo Jima into commodities cynically marketed to mass audiences to inspire them to buy bonds. Sara Anson Vaux argues that *Flags of Our Fathers* "challenges myths about the Greatest Generation and traditional American perspectives on the politics and history of World War II."[6] But she is not totally correct. Eastwood never denigrates or even downplays the heroism of those men who fought on Iwo Jima. His target, rather, is the institutional bureaucracies that exploit those acts of personal courage for their own purposes, even for the necessity of funding the war. As such, *Flags of Our Fathers* acknowledges the real sacrifices made by American soldiers on Iwo Jima while it simultaneously highlights the unbreakable ligature among communal history, personal memory, wartime commerce, and show business. In the final analysis, as Sam Girgus argues, *Flags of Our Fathers*, coupled with *Letters from Iwo Jima*, "revolutionizes the concept of the war film; the films become a consciousness-altering cultural endeavor to suggest the fear and repulsion of the stranger and the other as a source of death and violence."[7] As such, he continues, it directly challenges "the stereotype of Eastwood as a political reactionary."[8]

"Do Not Expect to Return Home Alive": *Letters from Iwo Jima*

Who but Clint Eastwood, despite being the most well-known conservative in Hollywood, would ever even consider making a two-hour-and-twenty-one-minute film that contains dialogue spoken mostly in Japanese (with English subtitles), that is shot in black and white, that possesses no familiar American actors, and that presents a sympathetic, essentially heroic, portrait of Japanese military men? Indeed, no one else in the history of the American cinema provides audiences with such a relentlessly positive portrait of America's Pacific

World War II enemy, not to mention back-to-back movies focusing on the men fighting each other during the same battle. Consequently, while studio executives expressed high expectations for *Flags of Our Fathers*, which opened in 1,876 theaters, they conveyed no such optimism for *Letters*, which premiered in Tokyo and then played in only 781 U.S. theaters. Both films were box-office disappointments: *Flags* had a $90,000,000 budget, returned $33,602,376 in American ticket sales and a total of $65,657,941 worldwide, and received two Oscar nominations; the far cheaper *Letters* cost $19,000,000 to make, generated a feeble $13,756,082 in U.S. ticket sales and a respectable worldwide gross of $67,867,998, and received four Oscar nominations. Surprisingly, then, the more inexpensive gamble outgrossed and out-nominated its far more costly partner movie. Yet embroiled in the seemingly endless Iraq conflict, frustrated and war-weary American filmgoers demonstrated little interest in paying to either explore the morality of wartime propaganda or accept a sympathetic view of former enemy combatants.

Screening *Letters* is a schizophrenic experience, particularly after watching *Flags of Our Fathers*. Prior to the U.S. Air Force's attacks some forty-four minutes into the movie, and then followed by the marines' amphibious assault about ten minutes later, Eastwood depicts the Japanese soldiers in conventional tropes from World War II films about American GIs. They view Iwo Jima as a "sacred" part of their homeland, not just an isolated spit of land in the Pacific Ocean, and accept their patriotic duty to protect their country and loved ones with their lives. As we begin to differentiate between the various officers and enlisted men stationed there, more familiar conventions from American war movies start appearing, such as common soldiers like Saigo (Kazunari Ninomiya) complaining about the island, grumbling about the tastelessness and then the scarcity of food, writing letters home to their families, sharing rumors, suffering in the adverse weather conditions, praying for their survival and the safety of their families, and coming to grips with the "unspeakable things" they must do to survive. One particularly uncomfortable scene shows Saigo, whose actions throughout the movie resemble those of a typical American GI, being assigned to empty the "shit pot" used by the men living mostly in caves and underground tunnels. Although the viewer may initially feel apprehensive about sharing these unique, behind-the-scenes glimpses into the daily lives of our World War II enemies, we soon sink into their everyday reality as they prepare for the coming battle. At times, we may even forget who they are training to kill. Along with these familiar occurrences, the viewer also observes a rigid class system and sadistic officers who literally whip their underlings. But by the time the American and Japanese combatants engage with each other, the viewer is decidedly ambivalent: these American boys charging over the hill, part of the same units we cheered in *Flags*, are killing men we have come to know quite intimately, with families back home who love them as much as those of the Maries firing at them. Surely we cannot root against our own troops, those men we have come to admire for their unstinting bravery in *Flags*. But something in us recoils from the slaughter of these Japanese men, no longer faceless and demonized, who bravely do their duty to their country just as heroically as the men attacking them.

But Eastwood is not content merely to point out the common humanity of men on both sides of the battlefield. He demonstrates the honorable actions of several Japanese soldiers and officers, particularly General Tadamichi Kuribayashi (Ken Watanabe) the commander in charge of defending the island, and Lieutenant Colonel Baron Takeichi Nishi (Tsuyoshi Ihara), a gold medal equestrian in the 1932 Los Angeles Olympics. Throughout the movie, Kuribayashi (the film is based on his book, *Gyokusai soshireikan no etegami* [*Picture Letters from the Commander in Chief*], posthumously published in 2002) exhibits his strategic acumen, treats his men fairly, demonstrates compassion, shares the same rations as his subordinates, and leads his troops into battle. He remains well aware that the American forces possess overwhelming air, sea, and land superiority and that most of his soldiers, and likely he along with them, will die on Iwo Jima. Yet despite it being a suicide mission, the guerrilla warfare he devises using underground fortifications keeps the island from falling to the enemy for thirty-six days, thereby protecting the Japanese mainland from bomb attacks during this period. Eastwood devotes flashback scenes of Kuribayashi's friendships with American officers during his training in the United States, sequences shot with more colorful compositions than the

FIGURE 3.3 *Letters from Iwo Jima* (2006): Japanese soldiers, no longer faceless and demonized. Frame enlargement.

washed out, desaturated images on Iwo Jima. As a parting gift commemorating their comradeship, the Americans give him a 1911 Colt 45, a gun, ironically, he later uses to commit suicide.

For his part, Nishi demands medicine be provided for a fallen GI despite the scarcity of such treatments for his own troops. His final scenes are among the most powerful in the movie. Blinded and unable to continue fighting, he orders his men to abandon him and save themselves; he then commits suicide—off camera. All Nishi's actions demonstrate a fluid grace and the heart of a champion. Rather than suffering the disgrace of being captured, other Japanese soldiers blow themselves up with grenades. Robert Burgoyne argues that these scenes of "honor suicide are the core device through which Eastwood humanizes the characters, the key to the film's tragic tone, and the acts that carry the strongest anti-war charge," This "ethic of self-sacrifice," he continues, acts as "an internal frame to bring issues of history, ideology, and cultural difference into close, microscopic view."[9]

Eastwood shoots the realistic combat sequences in *Letters* from the Japanese point of view; we crouch beside them to view the planes blocking out the sky, the ships cramming the shoreline, and the soldiers securing the beach. In fact, some similar scenes shot from the American point of view in *Flags* now reappear from this opposing perspective. For example, we see the horrible results of the flames the Americans propel into the caves from the Japanese point of view. Ghastly wounds gape open and comrades die in front of friends, but this time, Japanese fighters suffer, and we feel sympathy for the deaths of the same people we hoped our soldiers would kill in *Flags*. Eastwood even muffles the triumphant flag-raising, seen from a distance, a small speck perched atop the mountain, and this time signaling bitter defeat rather than a symbol of victory. By doing so, Eastwood muddies, if not totally confounds, our preconceived notions of bad guys and good guys in a war movie, showing us dramatic examples of both on either side of the conflict. Neither *Flags* nor *Letters* is really about military glory, at least not the John Wayne type characterized by virile masculinity and chest-pounding heroism. Since the battle's outcome is clear in *Letters*, the choice is between suicide and survival, not winning or losing. In his interview with the director, "Clint Eastwood Makes a Huge Anti-war Statement with Iwo Jima," Roger Friedman argued that *Letters* was "the biggest, most propulsive anti-war statement to come out of mainstream Hollywood in years,"[10] but it was *American Sniper* that sparked a far greater firestorm of controversy about Eastwood's prowar vs. antiwar sentiments.

"You Can Only Circle the Flames So Long": *American Sniper*

American moviegoers may have been frustrated and war-weary in 2006, but in 2014, they flocked to see the exploits of a man many characterized as a battlefield hero, a stoic but deeply flawed figure quite different from the World War II combat veteran so often depicted on the screen. Eastwood's filming of Navy SEAL Chris Kyle (Bradley Cooper)—his expert marksmanship, efficiency in dispatching enemy combatants, and subsequent home-life problems, all based on Kyle's memoir, *American Sniper: The Autobiography of the Most Lethal Sniper in U.S. Military History* (2012)—struck an exceptionally resonant chord in the American communal psyche. Although previous films about Iraq, even the Oscar-winning *The Hurt Locker* (2008), failed to achieve box-office success, *American Sniper* became the top-grossing movie of the year, netting a domestic gross of $350,126,372 and foreign sales of $197,300,000 (on a $58,800,000 budget). It developed into the most financially successful war movie of all time, overtaking Spielberg's *Saving Private Ryan* and being nominated for six Oscars.

Perhaps a fearful, confused and anxious public was searching for a way to honor its fighting men and women without necessarily validating the ambiguous reasons the country plunged into war, and Eastwood's movie provided a direct opportunity to do so. The U.S. military involvement in Iraq was officially declared over on December 15, 2011, and, despite a slow but steady increase in American troops, subsequently numbering nearly five thousand, American audiences were clearly receptive to a film that took place within, and maybe even helped justify, a conflict that had a high cost (an estimated two trillion dollars) and death toll (4,491 U.S. service members and between 151,000 and more than 1,000,000 Iraqi deaths). Eastwood's decision to foreground the personal story of one soldier set within a larger historical context made the story relatable to large audiences. *American Sniper*, after all, is a biopic—or, perhaps more accurately, a character study—of a man trained to kill who does so superbly and then regains his mental stability only by becoming a healer for others, doing mentally what Doc did physically for his buddies in *Flags*. Kyle's point of view dominates the narrative, and for most of the film, he devotes himself to fulfilling only one, overriding responsibility: his sacred duty to protect the lives of vulnerable soldiers.

As is the case with almost all combat movies based on actual battles, *American Sniper* ignited controversies about its historical accuracy, personal truthfulness, and most of all, political ideology. After an investigation, for example, the navy determined that Kyle had "overstated" his medal count, ultimately revising his record and eliminating one Silver Star and one Bronze Star Medal.[11] Other commentators pointed out inaccuracies in the movie that ranged from the lies about his rodeo career, his motivation for enlisting, his lack of remorse over shooting the woman (he never shot the child) in the opening scene, the exaggerated roles of Mustafa (Sammy Sheik) and the Butcher (Mido Hamada), and even his legendary status (no bounty of $180,000 was ever placed on him).[12] Some writers attacked the narrative for how easily Kyle shakes off his PTSD symptoms, arguing that the movie presented an unduly simplistic and unrealistic portrayal of the traumas suffered by veterans of Iraq and Afghanistan (particularly in light of a suicide rate 50 percent higher than those who did not serve in the military). Such comments about factual inaccuracies greet every film about historical events, and audiences need to understand that filmmakers habitually heighten, twist, or ignore objective truths to generate more dramatic narrative situations. Despite their ardent claims about authenticity, filmmakers inevitably print the legend, not the facts, and no film can possibly capture the full complexity of complicated events, including battles and wars. That said, however, because movies often become the prism by which large, general audiences view events secondhand, they do have a particular responsibility to attempt to be as authentic as possible. Though they usually cloak themselves in the mantle of "inspired by true events" but are not necessarily always totally faithful to them.

Eastwood claimed that he never intended *American Sniper* to be an apolitical movie. During its theatrical run, he consistently asserted that both he and the movie were antiwar and meant the film to convey that position. Eastwood often commented that he directed war movies because they were inherently dramatic but just as regularly asserted his negative sentiments about America's wars in Iraq and Afghanistan. Later, he spoke specifically about *American Sniper* to a group of students at Loyola Marymount University School of Film and TV: "I think it's nice for veterans, because it shows what they go through, and that life—and the wives and families of veterans. It has a great indication of the stresses they are under. And I think that all adds up to kind of an anti-war message."[13] At the Producers Guild Award Nominees Breakfast that year, he told the group, "The biggest antiwar statement any film can make is to show the fact of what war does to the family and the people who have to go back into civilian life like Chris Kyle did."[14] Scriptwriter Jason Hall made similar comments:

> People see the movie poster, and its [*sic*] got a guy and the American flag, and they know Clint Eastwood—the *Dirty Harry* guy and the Republican convention guy—directed it. So they think it's some jingoistic thing. I would challenge that in a big way. The movie isn't about whether we should have been in Iraq or not. It's about how war is human. I hope every time a politician decides to send us to war, maybe they saw this movie and know the cost of it.[15]

Despite these and a host of other statements about the intentions of the film-makers, critics attacked the movie, the director, the scriptwriter, and Chris Kyle, particularly those who objected to what they perceived as Eastwood making a hero out of someone they considered to be an American psycho, mass murderer, racist, and child killer.

On one level, *American Sniper* reveals, as do so many of Eastwood's movies, the concealed truths that lay behind the public's veneration of a "Legend," which becomes Kyle's nickname due to his 160 confirmed kills during four tours in Iraq between 2003 and 2009. To open the film, Eastwood plucks a chapter out of Leone's cinematic textbook: he sets up a tense situation and, at the moment it must be resolved, cuts away to provide background information that illuminates how we arrived at this decisive point. About two and a half minutes into the movie, Kyle lies hidden on a rooftop; through his scope, he observes a woman and child emerging from a bombed-out building into the rubble-strewn street of Fallujah. By compelling us to share Kyle's point of view, Eastwood implicates us in his lethal decision: we are forced inside the action, not allowed to watch it from the outside as passive bystanders. The woman hands the boy an RKG-3 antitank grenade, and the child begins running toward the American troops. As Kyle's finger slowly curls around his rifle's trigger, we wonder if he will actually kill this youngster and perhaps the woman who put him in harm's way as well.

Just when a decision seems imperative, Eastwood cuts away from this edgy moment; we won't return to Kyle perched on the rooftop until some twenty-five minutes later, and in between, we learn about his childhood, his disappointing rodeo career, the violent anti-American acts that inspire him to join the Navy SEALs, the intensive training he endures, the first time he meets his future wife Taya Renae Studebaker (Sienna Miller) at a bar, the planes slamming into the World Trade Center Towers, his marriage, the enlistment of his young brother Jeff (Keir O'Donnell), and finally, the start of his first tour. After this extended period of cinematic foreplay—which reveals important episodes in the life of the man with his finger on the trigger, who is no longer a stranger to us—Eastwood whips us back to Iraq. Kyle shoots the boy as he runs toward the marines and then kills the woman as she picks up the explosive to finish the task. But despite the fact that his decision and expertise save marine lives, he is clearly troubled by having to make such an emotionally fraught decision, showing a level of overt agitation he will never display in subsequent shootings.

Eastwood's choice to begin the film is this manner proves both technically and thematically significant. No film that opens with an agonizing decision about whether to kill a child and what might well be his mother or risk harm to one's comrades in the field can be easily classified as one-sided or simplistic, as many of the attackers labeled *American Sniper*. Such a choice involves a

FIGURE 3.4 *American Sniper* (2014): the concealed truths that lay behind the public's veneration of a legend. Frame enlargement.

primordial clash between duty to one's group and one's natural moral instincts. Immediately, then, Eastwood generates a psychological burden that will afflict Kyle well beyond his overseas career. A defining moment occurs in a flashback years earlier at the dinner table with Kyle's family, as his father, Wayne (Ben Reed), reveals a philosophy that shapes his son's entire life:

> There are three types of people in this world: sheep, wolves, and sheepdogs. Sheep don't believe that evil exists in the world, and if it ever darkened their doorsteps, they wouldn't know how to protect themselves. Those are the sheep. Then you've got the predators who use violence to prey on the weak. Those are the wolves. And, then there are those blessed with the gift of aggression and the overpowering need to protect the flock. These men are the rare breed who live to confront the wolf. They are the sheepdog. We protect our own.

But as the film later asks, what happens when the sheepdog is without a flock, when the guardian angel of combat soldiers is left alone to wrestle with the demons that plague him?

As in most post–World War II combat movies, including those about the Iraq War, *American Sniper* contains no discussions about whether it is right or wrong that U.S. troops are fighting in Iraq, although history informs us that the government's decision to invade that country as retaliation for the 2,996 people killed and the 6,000 others injured in the September 11 attacks was ultimately a disastrous political choice. Yet no criticism or praise of the overall American mission, or even an articulation of what that is, ever appears. Kyle mumbles vague sentiments about stopping the enemy before he invades the American homeland, but that is about all we hear beyond specific objectives, such as to kill Abu Musab al-Zarqawi, the man responsible for numerous attacks in Iraq. We witness the horrible retribution of the "Butcher," an Iraqi Shia warlord, against an Iraqi family cooperating with American forces, but we also see American soldiers brutalizing Iraqi civilians, and their coerced cooperation results in mutilation or death. Critics like Richard Falk attacked the film for failing "to make any effort at all to understand the experience of this war from the perspective of the Iraqis, creating the absurd impression that the only victims deserving empathy were Americans like Kyle who had endured the torments of warfare and suffered its admittedly disorienting consequences." Such a process, continues Falk, "reinforces the regressive national mood of glamorizing bloody military exploits as the most admirable expression of true patriotism."[16]

Yet Kyle voices no concerns about these or any other moral dilemmas. He carries a Bible from his childhood wherever he goes but is never shown reading it or quoting any of its passages. Rather, as a trained sniper, he skillfully performs inherently repugnant acts necessary to safeguard his buddies. Kyle takes no pleasure in killing the woman and child or exhibiting his marksmanship. When his partner congratulates him, the only response is, "Get the fuck off me!" Yet even toward the end of the film, he expresses no ethical qualms about what he did in Iraq ("I was just protecting my guys, they were trying to kill . . . our soldiers") and conveys confidence about his decisions ("I'm willing to meet my Creator and answer for every shot that I took"). What plagues him is not ethics but regret about, as he tells his psychiatrist, "all the guys I could have saved." Indeed, Kyle only regains a sense of normalcy and is able to get past his PTSD after he decides to help other vets, those missing limbs and suffering psychological problems. The fact that he survives four tours only to be killed by a fellow vet (Eddie Ray Rough) he was attempting to support adds an incredible irony to both his life and his philosophy. His meets his death not at the hands of the "savages" he fights in war-torn Iraq, but rather from one of his band of brothers in Texas.

As if all this was not sufficiently complicated, Eastwood incorporates the figure of Mustafa into the movie, a sniper for the other side with a similar reputation as Kyle—a Syrian doppelgänger whose skill with a rifle rivals Kyle's. He, too, has a family and has even won an Olympic gold medal for his marksmanship, but otherwise he remains a voiceless cipher who functions mostly as a foil and, ultimately, the prime motivation for Kyle to remain in Iraq, despite his wife's pleas for him to come home. He, like Kyle, is ruthlessly efficient in killing the enemy at great distances; he almost kills Kyle and eventually shoots the American's friend Biggles (Jake McDorman). At another time, maybe in another world, Kyle and Mustafa would have been friends. They could well have shared stories and admired each other's skills with a weapon. Maybe they would have competed against each other for a gold medal. In the middle of the Iraq War, however, one must die at the other's hand; which is the patriot and which the killer remains in the eye of the beholder. Finally, Kyle makes a seemingly impossible 2,100-yard kill to take out his doppelgänger, avenging Biggles; this ultimately provides the psychological release he needs to return to his family. Unfortunately, his shot also reveals his squad's position to the enemy, who charge the badly outnumbered American troops.

Not surprisingly for a man so deeply engaged with the Western as both a star and director, Eastwood's *American Sniper* incorporates elements from that genre as well. Kyle's Texas roots, his desire to live as a cowboy, and his reference to the Iraqi fighters as "savages" (his autobiography speaks far more graphically about his hatred of Arab enemies) all bespeak his fascination with the Western's mythology. Indeed, Kyle fulfills the archetypal role of the Western hero, protecting the civilized community from the attacks of bestial barbarians, personified by the Butcher. The final battle with the so-called insurgents amid a sandstorm of Biblical proportions plays out like a modern restaging of the Alamo, the besieged American soldiers surrounded by swarming groups of faceless Arabs and heroically manning their fort. Unlike their Texas counterparts who died rather than surrender, however, the marines ultimately evacuate—almost leaving Kyle behind. In *American Sniper*, as is the case in many Westerns, the gunslinger hero shares traits with the villain—in this case, Mustafa—rather than the peaceful townspeople he risks his life to protect. Thus when Kyle returns home to his wife and children, he fails to find a comfortable place in his new environment, always itching to return to Iraq and his role as the on-high protector of the exposed troops down in the streets. The sheepdog always needs both sheep to defend and wolves to fight. In essence, Kyle is a lone gunman, though not one who faces his opponent at high noon on a dusty street.

American Sniper, then, is not a simplistic movie, despite the commentaries by right-wing pundits who laud it as a glorification of brave men fighting to safeguard America and their left-wing counterparts who deride it as retrograde warmongering. Anyone who is familiar with the recent spate of Eastwood films, or who is reading the essays in this book, would surely be reluctant to argue that he divides up the world into blunt, Manichean black and white. Much to the contrary, his sense of gray overpowers even his most seemingly one-sided movies, and *American Sniper* is no exception. The film is a weird, perhaps even ironic, morality tale, although the central character never explicitly recognizes it as such and does his best to deny anything but his sworn duty. During frightening times like ours, it is, perhaps, tempting to echo the hosannas for an action hero like Kyle who saves the lives of his comrades. But the cost is great on multiple levels, including to Kyle's own psyche, which continues to disintegrate as the movie progresses. The very fact that he breaks down psychologically clearly demonstrates that something within his makeup remains uncomfortable with his actions and simmers just beneath his continual denials and rote answers. Kyle may never overtly question his duty or the circumstances that brought him to that rooftop high about the streets of Fallujah, but Eastwood does.

Notes

1 Richard Schickel, *Clint Eastwood: A Biography* (New York: Vintage Books, 1997), 421.

2 Schickel, 424.

3 Sam B. Girgus, *Clint Eastwood's America* (Cambridge: Polity Press, 2014), 268.

4 Robert Eberwein, "Following the Flag in American Film," in *Eastwood's Iwo Jima: Critical Engagements with "Flags of Our Fathers" and "Letters from Iwo Jima,"* ed. Rikke Schubart and Anne Gjelsvik (London: Wallflower, 2013), 94.

5 Anne Gjelsvik, "Care of Glory? Picturing a New War Hero," in *Eastwood's Iwo Jima*, 103.

6 Sara Anson Vaux, *The Ethical Vision of Clint Eastwood* (Grand Rapids, Mich.: William B. Eerdmans, 2012), 138.

7 Girgus, *Clint Eastwood's America*, 3.

8 Girgus, 4.

9 Robert Burgoyne, "Suicide in *Letters from Iwo Jima*," in *Eastwood's Iwo Jima*, 232.

10 Roger Friedman, "Clint Eastwood Makes a Huge Anti-war Statement with *Iwo Jima*," Fox News Network December 11, 2006, accessed September 9, 2016, http://www.foxnews.com/story/2006/12/11/clint-eastwood-makes-huge-anti-war-statement-with-iwo-jima.html.

11 Tom Vanden Brook, "Navy Lowers Medal Count for SEAL Chris Kyle," *USA Today*, July 8, 2016, accessed September 9, 2016, https://www.usatoday.com/story/news/politics/2016/07/08/navy-lowers-medal-count-seal-chris-kyle/86468402/.

12 Jarvis DeBerry, "Website Reports More Lies from *American Sniper*, Chris Kyle," *Times-Picayune*, May 26, 2016, updated July 9, 2016, accessed September 9, 2016, http://www.nola.com/opinions/index.ssf/2016/05/american_sniper_chris_kyle.html; Anthony Zurcher, "American Sniper: Was Chris Kyle Really a Hero?," accessed September 9, 2016, http://www.bbc.com/news/world-us-canada-30923038.

13 Eliana Dockterman, "Clint Eastwood Says *American Sniper* Is Anti-War," *Time*, March 17, 2015, accessed September 9, 2016, http://time.com/3747428/clint-eastwood-american-sniper-anti-war/.

14 Gregg Kilday, "Clint Eastwood on *American Sniper*'s Biggest Antiwar Statement," *Hollywood Reporter*, January 24, 2015, accessed September 9, 2016, http://www.hollywoodreporter.com/news/clint-eastwood-american-snipers-biggest-766498.

15 Dockterman, "*American Sniper* Is Anti-War."

16 Richard Falk, "Viewing *American Sniper*," *Foreign Policy Journal*, January 30, 2015, accessed September 9, 2016, http://www.foreignpolicyjournal.com/2015/01/30/viewing-american-sniper/.

4

"A Man's Got to Know His Limitations"

• •

The Cop Films from
Nixon through Reagan

JONATHAN KIRSHNER

A cycle of police dramas—from *Coogan's Bluff* (1968) to *The Dead Pool* (1988)—provide the bookends for the middle period Clint Eastwood's career. After a successful apprenticeship in television (*Rawhide*) and popular low-budget spaghetti Westerns, the savvy, curious and ambitious Eastwood took control of his own destiny. In the seventies and eighties, operating from the home base of Malpaso, the production company he established, Eastwood would become one of the biggest and most bankable movie stars in the world, maintaining a tight rein on his films, his image, and, invariably, his budgets.

The period from *Coogan* through *Dead Pool* was also characterized by a distinct political context. It began just as Richard Nixon was about to assume the presidency and concluded in the waning months of Ronald Reagan's second term—years that marked, with Jimmy Carter's four-year interregnum, a sharp conservative turn in American politics. Eastwood's own political leanings, and the politics of the eight films considered in this chapter, were very much in accord with these seismic shifts, attributes that surely resonated with the cultural sensibilities of the time and contributed to their commercial success.

The 1960s and 1970s were characterized by crime rates that were not sim-ply soaring—there were about eight thousand robberies in New York city in 1964 and almost eighty thousand in 1972—they were also suggestive of a violence and chaos that seemed to be out of control, especially in America's big cities, which were also plagued by racially charged riots and other upheav-als. Growing suburbanization and the end of the great postwar economic boom—and, with it, the erosion of blue-collar employment opportunities in traditional industrial sectors—left cities with sky-high expenses, declining public services, and a diminishing tax base, rendering them "ungovernable" in the apt phrase of the time—conditions that contributed to the rise of what Nixon would call a "silent majority" of disaffected middle-class Americans.[1] Majority or not, there were clearly a palpable cohort of citizens, neither rich nor poor, mostly white, feeling increasingly insecure and often resentful of the claims of others and craving the order associated with more tranquil times.

Nixon in 1968 ran a campaign that sought to capitalize on these concerns. Overtly, he placed a central emphasis on "law and order"—that is, getting tough with criminals and rejecting those policies that seemed to coddle them, such as the landmark Supreme Court cases that protected the legal rights for those *suspected* of wrongdoing.[2] Just beneath the surface also lurked the complementary "southern strategy," his party's successful scheme to use race-baiting rhetoric and implicit policy promises in order to flip the South, once held in hammerlock grip by segregationist Democrats, into the Republican column, just as President Johnson had predicted. Nixon also sought to cul-tivate these constituencies by running against the counterculture, castigating what he would summarize as "pot, permissiveness, and protest."

"Dirty" Harry, the protagonist of five of these films, has been recognized by many as the cinematic expression of Nixon's call to arms—and *Dirty Harry* (1971) itself as the ultimate counter-counterculture,[3] law-and-order film.[4] But Inspector Harry Callahan, and Eastwood's middle period cop films more broadly, is not so much about Nixon (that was more of a New Hollywood obsession[5]) as it was engaged with, and a reflection of, the general sociopoliti-cal shifts that characterized these two decades more generally. And if anything, those years, and that movement, were even more essentially embodied by Ron-ald Reagan, who served as governor of California for eight of these years and president for eight more.

Reagan, sitting to Nixon's political right, pushed similar themes and spoke to the same constituencies even more plainly. In 1966, the former actor (Don Siegel directed Reagan's last film performance, *The Killers*, in 1964) running for governor made his promise to "take on the mess at Berkeley" a centerpiece of his campaign. And he would do so just like any good new sheriff in town would: by demanding that the college students of the Free Speech Movement "be taken by the scruff of the neck and thrown out of the university once and for all." He won in a landslide. In 1970, Governor Reagan spoke more bluntly still; weeks before four unarmed students were shot dead and nine others wounded by the National Guard at Kent State, he extended this advice for clearing out student protesters: "If it takes a bloodbath, let's get it over with." He was similarly direct on race. Running for the Republican nomination in 1976, Reagan worked the South by bemoaning the lot of hardworking Americans struggling to make ends meet, suffering the indignity of waiting in line at the supermarket watching some "strapping young buck" use food stamps to buy "T-Bone Steaks." Securing the nomination four years later, for his first speech as the Republican standard-bearer, Reagan choose a spot a few miles from Philadelphia, Mississippi, the infamous town where three civil right workers were brutally murdered in 1964, to offer a ringing endorsement of "states'-rights."[6]

Clint Eastwood's brand of libertarian Republicanism was in several ways very distinct from the ideologies of Nixon and Reagan, but on questions of "law and order," there was little daylight between their respective dispositions. And wherever their differences, Eastwood was an active supporter of each Republican president, and the appreciation was mutual—and public.[7] It is not surprising, then, that some of his films should reflect those underlying sensibilities, which, as I will discuss in this chapter, they do. Unfortunately, they tend to do so crudely, and the majority of these films are not designed to stand up to close scrutiny—they are not, ultimately, the best of Clint. But they were broadly popular, they mattered, and they demand attention.

Coogan's Bluff

Coogan's Bluff (1968) is an effective if formulaic and relatively undistinguished fish-out-of-water-cum-police-drama. Eastwood plays Coogan, an Arizona deputy sheriff sent to the big city (New York) to collect a prisoner wanted back out west. Inevitably, the wanted man is first held up by bureaucratic procedure and then makes his escape, forcing Coogan, alone, to navigate the urban jungle, track down the bad guy, and bring him to justice. Lee J. Cobb is predictably fine as a cynical, world-weary New York police lieutenant; Susan Clark has a trickier role as the social worker/romantic interest in a film that flirts awkwardly with both of those identities; and many of the smaller parts are memorably played. The Big Apple location work is superb, and Coogan even picks up a little humanity in Sin City, pointedly offering a cigarette to his prisoner at the end in direct contrast to his treatment of a not-dissimilar-looking thug taken into custody in the Arizona sequence that opens the film.[8]

Despite its occasional flashes of style and small pieces of humor, *Coogan*, well received at the time and a commercial success, would nevertheless not be especially notable but for the fact that it can be seen as the Rosetta Stone for

Dirty Harry and Eastwood's other cop films in this period. The production brought together contributors who would play essential roles in shaping those future efforts.

Eastwood had tapped Don Siegel to direct *Coogan*, and in addition to serving as the progenitor for Harry Callahan, the film can also be understood as the middle entry in a Siegel cop trilogy, following on the heels of his gently revisionist, New York–infused, similarly themed *Madigan* (1968).[9] Siegel—the liberal-humanist producer-director best known for the prison reform *Riot in Cell Block 11* (1954), the legendary *Invasion of the Body Snatchers* (1956), and the tight, San Francisco–based noir *The Lineup* (1958)—promptly emerged as a crucial mentor figure for Eastwood. On the actor's initiative, they worked together on four films in quick succession (and only conflicting schedules prevented that number from being even higher), culminating in *Harry*. It was Siegel who signed Eastwood's DGA card and then served as an on-set security blanket by taking a small role in Clint's debut effort behind the camera, *Play Misty for Me* (1971). Eastwood valued Siegel's confidence, decisiveness, instincts, and, especially, his no-nonsense economy of shooting.

On *Coogan*, the two men polished multiple drafts of the screenplay before handing it over, on Siegel's recommendation, to Dean Riesner, who would become Eastwood's go-to script doctor. Filling out the family tree, Bruce Surtees operated one of the cameras on *Coogan*, displaying a facility with both action and location work, essential motifs of Eastwood's cop films, here seen most notably in the film's climatic motorcycle chase. Subsequently, as a cinematographer, Surtees would earn the distinction of one of the few top-shelf pros that Eastwood would repeatedly call upon.[10]

The character of Coogan is also recognizable as an early, working version of Callahan. The Arizona lawman is similarly bound by Eastwood's minimalist acting style, but he is a more complex character. Harry is the better cop—he makes fewer mistakes and would certainly never lose a prisoner or his gun, and he doesn't enjoy Coogan's enthusiastic sex drive.[11] But *Coogan* is pregnant with *Harry*, and their respective protagonists are men who live in the same world and see it through similar eyes. Loners and outsiders, they have little patience for courts and procedures and bureaucracy and legal niceties as civilization teeters on the brink of chaos—those are indulgences, even luxuries, in the midst of urban lawlessness, with criminals running amuck only to game the system when caught.

Coogan is more nuanced than the films of the Harry cycle on questions of race, and acknowledging the problematic treatment of racial issues is necessary for any frank consideration of those films. In *Coogan*, the smart black undercover cop clearly reflects Siegel's imprint; it was also on the director's forceful insistence that the early scene with a black doctor who tends to Callahan's leg was included in *Harry*.[12] But even *Coogan* shows its carbon dating with its clumsy portrayals of women and its anachronistic and occasionally embarrassing treatment of homosexuals as exemplars of decadence, camp, and sin, a retrograde awkwardness that is also shared by the early Harry pictures and that cannot be completely explained away by the cultural norms of the time.[13]

Callahan and Coogan also, explicitly, act as vigilantes when the law fails them, ruthlessly applying punishing and gratuitous violence against their adversaries and, quite notably, are commonly pitted against bloodthirsty hippies—a group more typically associated with peace, love, and dope than violent crime. It is not surprising that Dirty Harry, a Nixonian apparition, faces down one set of decadent longhairs after another; less obvious is why Coogan has a dog in that fight. The utterly tone-deaf portrayal of hippie culture in that film most likely reflects the fact that Siegel, born in 1912 and thus in his midfifties at the time, was an old-school liberal on the other side of the cultural divide. Perhaps that liberalism also accounts for why Coogan brings in his nemesis alive—something Harry never does. Ever.

Dirty Harry

Dirty Harry is Eastwood's best film from his long middle period. Much of this has to do with the talent that was attracted to the picture. Siegel was on board as producer-director (as a Malpaso production in partnership with Warner Brothers, Eastwood also had the authority of a producer). Dean Riesner was again called in to polish the screenplay (on both *Harry* and Eastwood's then just released *Misty*, as well as *Coogan*, Riesner's work was extensive enough that it earned a screen credit). And not to be underestimated were the contributions of cinematographer Bruce Surtees, who also shot the crisp monochromatic *Lenny* (1974) for Bob Fosse and the so-dark-you-can-barely-see-it masterpiece *Night Moves* (1975) for Arthur Penn and was known for his ability to push the envelope with darkness and minimalist lighting.[14] *Dirty Harry* features extensive night-for-night shooting, which is perhaps the greatest artistic strength of the picture, notably including but not limited to the "Jesus Saves" stakeout—a remarkable scene that required meticulous and elaborate preparation by the cinematographer (leading to some on-set tension with an impatient star)—and the long, elaborate location-to-location ransom delivery sequence.

It was Siegel's idea to move Harry's location from New York to San Francisco (Seattle was also considered), on "been-there-done-that" logic (*Madigan* and *Coogan's Bluff* had both been shot in the city).[15] But that setting could not have been better chosen for Harry; there was a compelling logic to establishing the icon of the counter-counterculture right in the belly of the beast. As host to the Summer of Love and the Grateful Dead, as well as an epicenter of gay culture, the left coast city was ground zero for pot, permissiveness, and

FIGURE 4.1 A *Dirty Harry* (1971) nighttime set piece staged in the abandoned, floodlit Kezar Stadium. Frame enlargement.

protest—Fun City without the hard hats. And the setting works beautifully for *Harry*, which is two-thirds of a great movie, with Siegel's sense for action and pacing, the majesty of Surtees camerawork, and a decent if off-the-shelf noir plot—a mad sniper terrorizing the city (with interesting shades of Edward Dmytryk's 1952 classic *The Sniper*, also shot on location in San Francisco)—coming together for a tight, imaginative, well-executed thriller.

To a point. And that point takes place about seventy minutes in. Throughout the picture, Harry is something of a loose cannon, to say the least, and his impatience with rules, procedures, and niceties is prevalent from the start—at times, the film pushes further, and more than hints at his barely suppressed rage. Driving through San Francisco's red-light district, Harry, twice surreptitiously peeps at naked women through a window. The second time, during the "Jesus Saves" stakeout, exploring the theme of voyeurism that smartly comes across as an homage to *Rear Window* (1954), Callahan mutters something about how he'd like to "throw a net" over the whole lot of them—anticipating mentally fragile Travis Bickle's premonition that "someday a real rain" will come and clean the streets of the scum in Times Square. Even more subversively, there are moments that suggest an equivalence between Harry and the deranged murderer Scorpio, in particular in the parallel construction of how each man recovers from his wounds following their violent encounter by the giant cross in Mount Davidson Park.[16]

That's the Harry who can track Scorpio down, shoot him as he flees—in another gorgeous nighttime set piece staged in the abandoned, floodlit Kezar Stadium—and then torture him in order to learn the whereabouts of his kidnapping victim. The resort to torture—which, when it occurs is shocking, brutal, unexpected, and not sugarcoated—was Eastwood's idea. And it is to his credit—as he observed, "most actors would not have done that," but he thought it came directly from the character.[17] But the movie chooses not to dive deeper into an exploration of that instinct. And Dirty Harry's enhanced interrogation comes up empty. The girl was already dead, which is just what

FIGURE 4.2 With the Golden Gate Bridge in the background, "Dirty" Harry looks stoically on as a victim's body is recovered. Frame enlargement.

Harry predicted when he initially opposed his feckless superiors' willingness to submit to the ransom demand. From the stadium, we cut to Harry, who, in long shot with the Golden Gate Bridge in the background, looks down stoically as the girl's nude, lifeless body is recovered. Roll the credits there, and the picture ends on a down note, but a thoughtful one: Scorpio is in custody, but given the body count, the victory rings hollow—which would have offered a nuanced consideration of a capacious and well-intentioned but deeply flawed hero of the counter-counterculture.

Unfortunately, the movie does not end there, and the majestic sweep of Surtees's camera pulling back from Kezar Stadium turns out to be not so much the movie's unwillingness to witness more of Harry's brutality as it is the film's withdrawal from any remaining semblance of reality. What was already a deeply dishonest critique of liberalism—we know Scorpio is guilty and a deranged killer, a sadistic embodiment of unmotivated evil with no redeeming qualities, and we could not be more primed to set teeth on edge as he demands his right to an attorney—becomes a completely unhinged right-wing fantasy. For whatever reason, the narrative resumes with Scorpio, sporting his hippie hairstyle and peace-sign belt buckle, walking free and clear of all charges—apparently none of his other murders, including the machine-gunning of a police officer and other various and sundry offenses, are prosecutable, because any evidence turned up during Harry's hot-pursuit search is inadmissible. Even Richard Schickel, in his 550-page mash note in the form of an Eastwood biography, acknowledges the utter implausibility of this legal reasoning.[18] Nevertheless, the district attorney, apparently unconcerned with the consequences, consults on-screen with a judge who teaches a course on such things, at, inevitably, Berkeley, the ground zero of criminal-coddling left liberalism. "That man had rights," they explain to Harry, who is more concerned for the victim: "Who speaks for her?" he wants to know.

Nobody, apparently. Not only is Scorpio free, a freedom he will soon predictably exploit to terrorize a hijacked bus full of small children, but the SFPD can't even be bothered to keep tabs on him. Moreover, aided by an abetting media horde, Scorpio fashions himself a victim of police brutality, as the movie presents a liberal media machine more than eager to portray the police in the most negative light possible without regard for the evidence at hand. The liberal mayor, having apparently forgotten that paying ransom to Scorpio is a fool's errand, tries again to meet the demands of the deranged sadistic serial killer. In the end, of course, it is up to Harry alone, against orders, to do what it takes, save the day, and solve the problem once and for all by blowing Scorpio away with his .44 Magnum.

The politics of this movie are not subtle, and they were not missed. Pauline Kael, who acknowledged that the film was a "stunningly well-made genre piece" nevertheless had little trouble in identifying its central battle between a "hippie maniac" and a police force "helplessly emasculated" by the legal rights "that a weak liberal society gives its criminals." That stacked deck, she argued, yielded "a deeply immoral movie." Roger Ebert concurred, concluding, "The Movie's moral position is fascist. No doubt about it."[19]

Siegel and Eastwood, in contrast, were as they say, shocked . . . shocked by such outrageous claims, and each appealed to the ability of a mature audience to distinguish between fact and fiction. "I don't want my aunt in Des Moines to think I'm a sadist," Eastwood explained. "I give her credit for being intelligent to know I'm an actor playing a part."[20] Siegel, the lifelong liberal, was more defensive, renouncing the very question of such political connections and insistently repeating that his only purpose was "in making a successful picture,"[21] a claim that rings true. Much less convincing are his protestations regarding the distinction between showing a character and condoning that character's behavior. This of course is indisputable, and essential—we can and must distinguish between the philosophy of a given character in a movie and a film's underlying moral grounding. But this is where Siegel's (and Eastwood's) defense comes up so short. The moral content of *Dirty Harry* is not mysterious. Paul Newman, Burt Lancaster, and even Robert Mitchum (who played his share of really bad guys) rejected the role on the grounds of the inherent unsavoriness of the character. Nixon had a different reaction. He screened the picture at Camp David, invited Clint to a reception at the "Western White House" in San Clemente, and appointed him to a six-year term on the National Council for the Arts. Nixon knew what he liked.[22]

Despite its deeply objectionable politics, *Harry* was an excellent film—as noted above, its two-thirds of a great film. Regrettably, it was the last one that could stake such a claim. Eastwood returned to the Harry series when he needed his ticket punched—that is, when he was in need of a sure hit. Moreover, as economy-conscious Malpaso productions—or, more bluntly, as invariably frugal Malpaso productions motivated solely to fill the coffers—top-shelf talent and ambitious production values were assiduously avoided, and those absences are plainly felt. Until late in his career, Eastwood kept his stories very simple and was virtually indifferent to dialogue, and so cheap, adequate screenplays, often from young or unknown writers, would be more than enough for the job at hand. Moreover, following the Keith Richards doctrine ("As far as I'm concerned, Art is short for Arthur"), proficient, workmanlike direction was all that was needed. And since the on-set producer and star knew how to direct, the path of least resistance was to hire journeymen directors, who, under Eastwood's watchful eye and authority, could be counted on to shoot it simple and shoot it fast. *Magnum Force* (1973) set the template for all that would follow.

Eastwood took on the *Dirty Harry* sequel after a few commercial misfires. The most important of these was his director-only effort *Breezy* (1973), a May-December romance featuring William Holden and Kay Lenz from a screenplay by Jo Heims, who had written *Play Misty for Me*. A thoughtful, interesting, understated film with something to say, its most novel insights are not about the unsustainable romance itself but in the personal politics between members of Holden's generation, and it considers those confrontations with a judicious, observing perceptive. Feminist film critic Molly Haskell offered qualified praise, calling it his "most accomplished directorial job so far" and "a love story in which almost everything works." But the film was both a critical and a commercial failure.[23]

Magnum offered a sure thing, and would indeed be an enormous hit. Written by John Milius (*Apocalypse Now*), who was just starting out, and Michael Cimino (*The Deer Hunter*), Eastwood raised eyebrows by hiring television director Ted Post over Don Siegel, who would have seemed the natural choice. But Eastwood had outgrown Siegel—or, more pointedly, had little interest in having an accomplished, reputable, feisty pro around who might have preferences of his own. Although Eastwood always acknowledged his great debt to the director, wrote a generous introduction to Siegel's memoirs, and prominently dedicated *Unforgiven* (1992) to both Siegel and Sergio Leone, forceful talent was not what he was looking for. After their intimate flurry of collaborations at the turn of the 1970s, the two men only worked together one more time, for *Escape from Alcatraz* (1979), during which, predictably, the two robust egos clashed.[24]

From *Magnum Force*, the Harry films would become a virtual genre unto themselves, with the predictable pattern of and structure as entries in the James Bond franchise. One or two preliminary episodes open a Harry picture, featuring light humor followed by the blood-soaked execution of violent rescue from an impossible situation by a just-happened-to-be-there Callahan, who kills all the sadistic, malevolent bad guys and saves the innocent. Promptly, however, he is called on the carpet for excessive use of force and disregard for property and criminals' rights[25] by obtuse, scum-coddling liberal brass with eyes for nothing but celebrity and political patronage. Put on leave or bound to a desk job, Harry is soon called back by the desperate hypocrites, who are facing an enormous crisis with which they cannot deal and so willing to look the other way while Callahan does what everybody knows is necessary to get the job done. This, of course, is the implicit articulation of an authoritarian ideology that prioritizes stability over civil liberties. The films also suggest an anxiety about female sexuality—topless women and/or those expressing an uninhibited and enthusiastic sexuality inevitably meet with a terrible, violent fate; another common if dispiriting element is the way that Harry's efforts usually involve the ritual sacrifice of his (typically minority) partner. In sum, if you've seen one, you've seen them all.

Magnum Force is interesting, if at all, for its direct pushback against the charges of vigilante fascism leveled at *Dirty Harry*. The film opens with the requisite stacked-deck critique of liberal "justice," with an obviously guilty mob kingpin striding out of court a free man, his acquittal due to a legal technicality. This travesty, one character explains, "happened before and will happen again," thus setting in motion a nominal story: a death squad of young cops takes to meting out the justice that the system is incapable of providing. *Magnum* aspires to position Harry somewhere between the caricatured liberals and these cartoonish storm troopers, cops who kill fellow officers in cold blood and machine-gun a swimming pool full of nubile beauties who are either collateral damage in a necessary war or simply receiving their just deserts for consorting with gangsters. Positioning Harry in the middle ground between these unpalatable extremes, the move allows him to mutter unconvincing speeches about working within the system. Of course, Harry says it's "not too hard to understand how [a squad of blindly violent vigilante cops] happens" and, naturally, reminds his timid superiors that "nothing's wrong with shooting as long as the right people get shot." But when told by the young storm troopers who idealize him, "Either you're for us or you're against us," Harry chooses the law.

Once again, it was Pauline Kael who saw right through this half-hearted head fake: "Despite the superficial obeisance to the rule of law, the underlying content of *Magnum Force*—the buildup of excitement and pleasure in brutality—is the same as that of *Dirty Harry*, and the strong man is still the dispenser of justice, which comes out of his gun." David Denby assessed the film to be "vile"; Gene Siskel saw a "mediocre sequel" about "the supreme delight of holding one's quarry at bay while challenging him to make a move so you can have an excuse to blow his head off." Nora Sayre in the *Times* got straight to the point, opening her review with "let's hear it for hypocrisy."[26] Refreshingly, the remaining sequels didn't pussyfoot around with such questions of Callahan's moral standing. Regrettably, they didn't get any better.

Following the commercial failures of *Thunderbolt and Lightfoot* (Michael Cimino's debut effort) and the (Eastwood-directed) *Eiger Sanction* (1975), Clint again turned to Harry. For *The Enforcer*, Malpaso hired first-time director James Fargo, whose appeal was summarized by one Eastwood biographer as "someone who would not challenge his opinion, would not screw with his themes, and would get the film done quickly and within budget."[27] The first draft of the screenplay was purchased from two film students and handed over to prolific Hollywood pro-for-hire Sterling Silliphant, then polished by Riesner, who shared the principal writing credit with Silliphant.[28]

The Enforcer is paint-by-numbers Harry, and takes its shots against the usual suspects: uptight tsk-tsking spinsters in authority; wild-eyed, trigger-happy hold-up men; still more sadistic hippie killers; hypocritical police brass; media-hungry local politicians; and, of course, misguided liberals everywhere. Among this latter group, in a head-turning and once again unmistakably politically charged choice, is a liberal priest, a characterization that seems to implicitly align Harry with the bloodthirsty dictators of Central America. As if checking off a right-wing enemies list, in a clever a twofer, one chase sends Harry crashing through a skylight into the midst of a porn film production where the fictional crew's union flag is proudly displayed. More generally, the usual (non)subtleties hold—another partner is cut down, and at his deathbed, his widow shares this thought: "It's a war, isn't it? I guess I never really understood that."

The Enforcer boasts two notable novel attributes, neither distinguished. First, and contra the half-hearted protestations of *Mangum*, here Harry is plainly an extralegal executioner. As Eastwood explained in a 1978 interview, "I was one of the people who took the hero further away from the white hat." This, of course, is suggestive of the welcome new sophistication in American film that followed the end of the old censorship rules.[29] But much depends on just how far away from that white hat one wants to go—there is a difference between trafficking in moral ambiguity and celebrating the morally repugnant. In contrast to the old days of "Hayes office rules," Eastwood continued, "if some guy is trying to kill the character I'm playing, I shoot 'em in the back."[30] Or even, it turns out, if "some guy" is just running away. In the opening sequence of *The Enforcer*, Harry shoots a fleeing, unarmed suspect in the back, apparently clipping his genitals from behind as a bonus, a choice that could be interpreted as charged with the most ominous of racial overtones and inaugurates a disturbing thread that weaves its way throughout the Harry films. Second, Callahan is here saddled with a female partner, leading to a battle of the sexes that was simplistic even by the standards of 1976 and is little more than embarrassing today. Tyne Daly (Kate) does a fine job with a thankless role, and the actress fought to shape and defend the character during production. Kate ultimately saves Harry's life, twice (once by icing a fake nun in cold blood) before being cut down by the hail of bullets that were meant for Harry.

All in all, however, *The Enforcer*, another big success at the box office, does not offer much substance to consider. The plot is wafer thin, even by Harry standards, and it is hard to recall a memorable shot (first-time cinematographer Charles Short would enjoy a long career in television). David Sterritt, in his careful study *The Cinema of Clint Eastwood*, devotes two paragraphs to *Magnum Force* and one to *The Enforcer*, which seems about right. Even Clint seemed to have had enough of Harry—it would be seven years and seven films before he agreed to the next installment.

The Gauntlet

The Gauntlet (1977) was the cop film that freed Eastwood from the rigid confines of the Harry franchise—Callahan has no flaws, no backstory, no friends—and Clint took on the directing himself as well. But despite these opportunities, at this stage of his career, Eastwood seemed simply unwilling to invest in the idea that the story might matter and remained content with journeyman writers-for-hire. Worse, even free of Harry, Eastwood here hangs on to his standard tropes: corrupt brass, an incapable DA (who "couldn't convict Hitler"), a seemingly respectable killer with embarrassing sexual proclivities to conceal, the exogenous appearance of hippie bad guys—solely there to deliver gratuitous beatings—and, most egregiously, the painfully predictable, utterly arbitrary ritual sacrifice of partner, in this case narratively unmotivated and inserted unnecessarily at the very end. Also, as in all the Harry films, even in the end, justice is administered extralegally, execution-style, with the killing of the two principal villains in turn, both unarmed. *The Gauntlet* also withholds sex from Ben (Clint), as it tends to with Harry[31]; it also pulls the *Magnum Force* fast one, introducing a character whose sole purpose is to spew forth an endless stream of raw-sewage misogynist rage in the direction of Ben's prisoner, Gus (short for Agustina), a hooker with a heart of gold played by Sondra Locke, Clint's then girlfriend. Thus the movie gets to vent its spleen and then some, but our hero is positioned on the right side of the argument.

Ultimately, *The Gauntlet* is a long chase scene in search of a movie (there's nothing wrong with that—*Midnight Run* [1988], for example, did it brilliantly), and its ending is, plainly, ridiculous. Certainly we go to the movies to escape, but at some point, logic, physics, and plausible expectations of human behavior must at least be acknowledged, if at a distance, and the long, long, climactic shoot-out simply fails to do so. Vincent Canby saw in the film "a kind of violent grace," but it is hard to disagree with his conclusion that "it is a movie without a single thought in its head."[32] In the context of Eastwood's police films, however, glimmers of growth can be discerned. Ben is a much more flawed character than Harry—a bit of a renegade, yes, but less successful and a drunk—and this allows for greater dramatic possibilities. He is also indeed a different character: more soft-spoken, comparatively passive, and at times uncertain as to what to do next—this is not just Harry under another name. In fact, for a movie with a cartoonish level of gunplay, Ben himself does very little shooting at all. Finally, although *The Gauntlet* would never be mistaken as a feminist tract, it is notable that Gus is clearly smarter than Ben and one or even two moves ahead of his thinking every step of the way. Modest steps forward perhaps, but it could have been worse.

Worse, indeed, took the form of *Sudden Impact* (1983), which scrapes the bottom of the Harry barrel in search of box-office gold. Not much by way of praise can be said about this one other than that it is a pleasure to welcome back Bruce Surtees, whose signature nighttime exteriors bring a visual ambition to the proceedings not seen since *Harry*. Surely the best moments in the film—the climatic carousel sequence (spatial continuity errors aside), a well-executed homage to Hitchcock's *Strangers on a Train* (1951)—were possible because he was on the set. Other than that, the principal motivation for this film was that, once again, Clint was in need of a hit, and again Harry delivered. Schickel, a reliable source for Eastwood's point of view, reports that he had mixed feelings about the project, which had its "impetus in a marketing survey" that suggested there remained a potent consumer demand for yet another sequel. Still, it "took a few Fridays to come up with a story he liked."[33] A few more Fridays might have been in order. Again content to lean on near-novice (and low-rent) screenwriters, the plot of *Impact* looks like something that was dragged out of the shallow end of the *Death Wish* (1974) pool. (The catatonic rape-surviving relative seems directly lifted from *Death Wish II*, which came out the previous year.) Not even Riesner's script doctoring, this time uncredited, can breathe life into this turkey.

Directed by Eastwood with his midperiod workmanlike efficiency, the prefatory set piece established one of the key lines of Reagan's America: "Go ahead, make my day." Indeed, the most notable aspect of *Impact* is that it exposes, without even pausing to contemplate second thoughts, the darkest corners of the Nixon/Reagan law-and-order doctrine. Jennifer Spencer (Sondra Locke) takes the law into her own hands—she's not a rogue cop, but a rape victim, and has taken to executing her previous tormentors one at a time. Two moves here have an especially sharp political edge. First, although, as necessary for a Harry picture, most of the bad guys are sadistic, irredeemable longhairs, one member of the gang has fallen out with that crowd, set his life straight, and is tormented by the guilt of his actions a decade previously. Confronted by

Spencer, he shares his remorse and begs for his life. She kills him in cold blood. Second, after all is said and done, Harry abets in the confusion of evidence that will pin all the murders on the main bad guy, as Harry (and, more to the point, the film—and the audience as well, which is rooting for her), explicitly endorses her crime-fighting (well, crime-avenging) strategy. This is another Harry movie pitched in opposition to civil liberties and due process. Consider the assessment of the *Time Out* film guide, searching for something nice to say about *Magnum Force*: that film, which in the end "fails to convince," at least is ultimately "far less objectionable than the later *Sudden Impact*."[34]

Before the film is over, *Sudden Impact* will have dutifully hit all its marks: a female judge tossing a case due to an illegal search with barely restrained glee, long speeches about the rigged system, a double serving of moments where the reading of rights is ridiculed, and, dispiritingly, the black sidekick/buddy who comes for a visit and gets his throat slit for his troubles. But ultimately, despite Reagan's embrace, *Sudden Impact* does not flash the same sharp political edge of its predecessors, *Harry* in particular. Most likely, with its egregiously clunky dialogue ("People have a nasty habit of getting dead around you") and action sequences that finally veer into self-parody, the film simply isn't good enough to sting. Even the cheerleading Schickel, who for some reason thought the basic premise clever, nevertheless laments that "the film does not execute it as crisply as crisply as it might have."[35] There wasn't much left for Harry to do, and Eastwood seemed plainly bored with the character.

Tightrope

Seemingly in response to the dead-end frustration of playing Harry, Eastwood would resurface within a year, playing by far his most complex and ambiguous cop yet, an experience that must have been liberating. *Tightrope* arrives as a breath of fresh air, easily Eastwood's most interesting and ambitious film since *Dirty Harry*, showcasing, again, the fine work of cinematographer Surtees at the top of his night-for-night game. Unfortunately, the film still suffers from Malpaso's penny-pinching. *Tightrope* was the debut (and only) original screenplay of Richard Tuggle (his first credit was for the adaptation of *Escape from Alcatraz*), and Clint signed him on to direct as well, though by all accounts, Eastwood's influence on the direction was even more overt than usual in such situations, to say the least—an interpretation buttressed by the observation that Tuggle would get only one more crack at directing: the universally derided *Out of Bounds* (1986). And the traditional weak spots seen in previous efforts are again plain and exposed: wooden dialogue, plot points in turn obvious and implausible, voluminous body count, ritual sacrifice of a valued companion, clichéd characters, rote denouement.

But let's not quibble. *Tightrope* is an interesting stretch for Clint and for his interpretation of the lawman. It is a film with some notable strengths and even, remarkably, of thoughtful introspection—attributes prominent even now and that were especially notable in the context of its time. The year 1984, after all, was the height of Reagan's feel-good, can-do, "morning in America," "my country right or wrong" popularity. (Reagan's historic landslide reelection a few months after *Tightrope*'s release was the high watermark for these sentiments; a stubborn recession proved costly at the ballot box in the 1982 midterm elections, and the Republicans lost control of the Senate in 1986, after which the president would begin his long, slow fade toward the sunset.) *Tightrope* looks all the more impressive, and daring—which it was—in the context of that historical moment; it was a year when John Milius's ludicrous, reactionary propaganda piece *Red Dawn* could both pass as entertainment and score big at the box office. The three biggest hits of the year were less objectionable but nevertheless paragons of moral certainty: *Indiana Jones*, *The Karate Kid*, and *The Terminator* all of which pitted noble underdogs against various forces of evil.

Tightrope, in contrast (and contra the core ethos of midcareer Clint) is an exercise in uncertainty and moral ambiguity. And as with the torture scene in *Dirty Harry*, Eastwood is doing things no other movie star of his stature and reputation would consider doing—most notably with the on-screen penchant of his character (Wes Block) for edgy bondage sessions with prostitutes picked up in the seamiest corners of New Orleans's pansexual red-light district. As David Denby subsequently observed, "Here was the biggest star in the world implicating himself in the kind of pathologies that his earlier characters had scornfully eliminated."[36]

Wes is no Harry. Flawed, compromised, and vulnerable, he is also—and this more than anything is impossible to imagine in Harry's universe—a family man. Not only is he the single father of two daughters; the film even hints at, if you are looking for it, some slight creepiness in his relationship with the older

FIGURE 4.3 In *Tightrope* (1984), Eastwood's character indulges in some of the pathologies that his earlier characters had scornfully eliminated. Frame enlargement.

child[37]—a daring and complex choice unthinkable within the confines of the Harry franchise. Moreover, his wife was not, as cliché would demand, murdered or even tragically lost; rather, she left Wes because she thought she could do better. And despite the standard-issue "women with jobs annoy me" meet-cute with new love interest Beryl (Geneviève Bujold), who is also saddled with clunky lines, the movie positions her as a real character who more or less holds her own. In fact, *Tightrope* would have probably worked extremely well as a silent movie, which would retain the essence of that relationship and if anything enhance the film's best qualities: several suspenseful set pieces, and the movie's central conceit, that only a razor's edge of barely contained self-control distinguishes Wes from the hooker-killing sadist he finds himself playing cat and mouse with.

This essential dualism was Eastwood's intention: "I stressed that even more in the film than the screenplay," he explained to David Thomson, "I liked the parallel between he and the killer, and I liked the not knowing." Clint even looped some of the villain's dialogue in an early scene to subtly nudge the audience in that direction. The viewer knows all too soon that Wes is not the killer, but Eastwood makes the compelling and perhaps deeper argument that even "when you know it isn't him," you realize that "it could very well have been him."[38] Well played, these qualities were noticed at the time and remain worthy of consideration. In an uncharacteristically insightful review from the preternaturally ill-mannered John Simon—although still inevitably condescending, mean-spirited, and (here properly) critical of the film's too-easy flirtation with softcore pornography, implausible thriller tropes, and routine ending—he calls attention to Wes's own "demoralization" as he comes to recognize his similarities with the serial killer, and Simon observes that "*Tightrope* makes some pertinent comments tersely and devastatingly."[39]

The Dead Pool

Whatever *Tightrope*'s limitations, it looks like *Citizen Kane* in comparison to *The Dead Pool* (1988), the last film in the Dirty Harry cycle, released just as Reagan was getting ready to head west into his senescence. It was written by amateurs, three friends of Clint who would share their only writing credit, and to direct the picture, Eastwood flipped the keys to his longtime stuntman/stunt coordinator Buddy Van Horn (another relationship that traces to *Coogan's Bluff*). Van Horn would direct once more, Eastwood's *Pink Cadillac* (1989), before returning to stunts.

It is tempting to say that Eastwood phoned this one in, but that would have required lifting the receiver, more effort than he appears willing to take on in support of the film, which is a lazy retread, often literally. The credit sequence (nighttime helicopter shots of San Francisco) repeats that of *Sudden Impact*, and both films, if for ever-so-slightly different reasons, feature four men with machine guns taking Harry by surprise and spraying endless streams of bullets in his direction—to no effect. If *Dead Pool* has any pulse at all, it's in its sense of humor, as it (at times knowingly) flirts with self-parody: the movie within a movie allows for pontificating speeches about movie violence, a critique of commercial/video tie-ins takes place in the context of its own commercial/video tie-in, an amusing if physically impossible car chase offers a toy car homage to *Bullitt*, and a copycat killer in a copycat movie gets to plunge a knife into the heart of a famous female film critic. Other than that, it is yet again paint-by-numbers Harry, hitting the usual marks from start to finish. The final chase scene is suggestive of the series' closure, as it is the bad guy who holds the empty .44 magnum. And as if to prove that despite all the levity, Harry is still the vigilante executioner, he harpoons his defenseless prey through the heart, case closed. Eastwood's main objective in returning to Harry one last time was to provide some commercial cover for his ambitious Charlie Parker biopic, *Bird* (1988), which is an understandable business move. But as for *Dead Pool*, if he doesn't care why should we?

Coogan's Bluff and *The Dead Pool* mark the territory of Eastwood's midcareer. After a long apprenticeship, he emerged as a major movie star, and one with a serious interest in both the commercial and the artistic aspects of his career. But with the exception of a few experiments along the way, it was not until he was pushing sixty that Clint would let art rival commerce for his affections. The potential to make serious films was long visible—*Play Misty for Me* and *Breezy* each flashed real promise and ambition; it was the commitment that lagged. Norman Mailer, in a very favorable feature and interview for *Parade* in 1983, assessed Eastwood an important artist and called him out for squandering his talent and failing to try "hard enough for what's truly difficult." Mailer was especially dismissive of the Dirty Harry films, "movies made to manipulate audiences and satisfy producers."[40]

By the close of that decade, as if Mailer's message finally had time to sink in, Eastwood decided to put away childish things. *Bird* and *White Hunter Black Heart* (1990) were serious, reaching explorations about the self-destructive nature of artists and the enigmatic relationship between art and life. And in an even more remarkable volte-face, Eastwood seemed to come to acknowledge and embrace the sharpest critique of his most bitter nemesis: "With a Clint Eastwood, the action film can—indeed, must—drop the pretense that human life has any value," Pauline Kael charged in 1974. His films offer "an impersonal, almost abstract excuse in brutalization." In contrast to the "strong, quiet man of the action film," Dirty Harry is "emotionally indifferent."[41] With his mature films—including notably *Unforgiven* (1992) and *Mystic River* (2003), each of which were serious (and top shelf) ruminations on violence and its consequences (the latter in particular)—Eastwood clearly took these criticisms to heart. He will be remembered as a major American filmmaker. But that reputation will rest largely on the achievements of the final decades of his long career.

Notes

1 Political scientist Ted Lowi urged Mayor Lindsay to declare New York City "ungovernable" and propose a radical reorganization of political arrangements. See Theodore Lowi, "Dear Mayor Lindsay," *Nation*, December 8, 1969, 626; see also Vincent Cannato, *The Ungovernable City: John Lindsay's New York and the Crisis of Liberalism* (New York: Basic Books, 2001).

2 *Suspected* is a crucial word here. In the world of Eastwood's cop films, liberal reforms seem designed to protect the guilty, not the accused, an important political move those films managed to slip by.

3 Defining Harry as an expression of the "counter-counterculture" was a productive theme of conversations I had with a former undergraduate student of mine, Peter Cohl.

4 J. Hoberman, *The Dream Life: Movies, Media and the Mythology of the Sixties* (New York: New Press, 2003), 321–325.

5 Jonathan Kirshner, *Hollywood's Last Golden Age: Politics, Society and the Seventies Film in America* (Ithaca, N.Y.: Cornell University Press, 2012).

6 W. J. Rorabaugh, "The FSM, Berkeley Politics, and Ronald Reagan," in *The Free Speech Movement: Reflections on Berkeley in the 1960s*, ed. Robert Cohen (Berkeley: University of California Press, 2002), 515; see also Gerard J. De Groot, "Ronald Reagan and Student Unrest in California, 1966–1970," *Pacific Historical Review* 65, no. 1 (Feb. 1996): 107–129.

7 Marc Eliot, *American Rebel: The Life of Clint Eastwood* (New York: Three Rivers Press, 2009), 113, 202.

8 Coogan mistreats a Native American prisoner in Arizona, humiliating him and tying him to a post. His contrasting final gesture is suggestive of a type of progressive liberal humanism that is associated with Siegel.

9 *Madigan* features a tough cop (Richard Widmark) working outside the rules in desperate search for a killer and a morally compromised police commissioner (the iconic Henry Fonda, in a subversive bit of casting).

10 David Sterritt, *The Cinema of Clint Eastwood: Chronicles of America* (New York: Wallflower, 2014), 56, 58, 60, 75; Don Siegel, *A Siegel Film: An Autobiography* (London: Faber and Faber, 1993), 300; Eliot, *American Rebel*, 91, 98, 125.

11 Harry's muted (repressed?) sexuality is another important element of that character; its fraught with meaning in a decade during which gender roles were being reassessed.

12 Siegel, *A Siegel Film*, 369–370, reports that the studio wanted to cut the scene.

13 Even Tony Rome, the tough-guy masculinist cop portrayed in 1967 by rat-packer Frank Sinatra—who at one time was slated to play Harry—seems more tolerant of alternative lifestyles and social change.

14 The ever budget-conscious Eastwood also highly valued Surtees's "gift for frugal improvisation." Margalit Fox, "Bruce Surtees, Oscar-Nominated Cinematographer, Dies at 74," *New York Times*, February 28, 2012; Eliot, *American Rebel*, 136.

15 Siegel, *A Siegel Film*, 358; see also 369–370 for Siegel's defense of the film's racial politics.

16 Dave Kehr pushes this observation even further in his capsule review for the *Chicago Reader*, arguing that "Eastwood's renegade detective" is "in the usual Siegel fashion . . . equated visually and morally with the psychotic killer he's trampling the Constitution to catch." Dave Kehr, *"Dirty Harry,"* review of *Dirty Harry*, directed by Don Siegel, *Chicago Reader*, https://www.chicagoreader.com/chicago/dirty -harry/Film?oid=1069848. See also Roger Greenspun, who notes that the film "fails in simple credibility so often and on so many levels that it cannot even succeed (as I think it wants to succeed) as a study in perversely complimentary psychoses." Roger Greenspun, "Dirty Harry," *New York Times*, December 23, 1971.

17 David Thomson, "Cop on a Hot *Tightrope,*" *Film Comment* 20, no. 5 (1984): 65.

18 Richard Schickel, *Clint Eastwood: A Biography* (New York: Knopf, 1996), 269–270.

19 Pauline Kael, "Dirty Harry," *New Yorker*, January 15, 1972; Roger Ebert, "Dirty Harry," *Chicago Sun-Times*, January 1, 1972.

20 Thomson, "Cop on a Hot *Tightrope.*"

21 Siegel, *A Siegel Film*, 373, 495.

22 Mark Feeney, *Nixon at the Movies* (Chicago: University of Chicago Press, 2004), 280; Eliot, *American Rebel*, 133, 139.

23 Molly Haskell, "Breezy," *Village Voice*, November 29, 1973, 86.

24 Eliot, *American Rebel*, 148–149; Schickel, *Clint Eastwood*, 302.

25 Again, crucially, these films elide the distinction between criminals and suspects, a politically charged and consequential move that can serve to rally the audience to the side of "law and order."

26 Pauline Kael, "Killing Time," *New Yorker*, January 14, 1974; David Denby, "Law and Disorder," *Harpers*, March 1974; Gene Siskel, "Law and Order on Film," *Chicago Tribune*, February 17, 1974; Nora Sayre, "Review: *Magnum Force*," review of *Magnum Force*, directed by Ted Post, *New York Times*, December 26, 1973.

27 Eliot, *American Rebel*, 163, 172.

28 Schickel, *Clint Eastwood*, 340. Silliphant won an academy award for *In the Heat of the Night* (1967) and also wrote *The Lineup* (1958) for Don Siegel and seventies-cop-under-siege *New Centurions* (1972) with George C. Scott and Stacy Keach (more thoughtful than Harry but still middling); but he could also reliably crank out assembly-line work on demand, including *The Poseidon Adventure* (1972); the third installment of the Shaft franchise, *Shaft in Africa* (1973); and *The Towering Inferno* (1974).

29 On this point more generally, see Kirshner, *Hollywood's Last Golden Age.*

30 Richard Thompson and Tim Hunter, "Clint Eastwood, Auteur," *Film Comment* 14, no. 1 (1978): 75.

31 Women are attracted to Harry, and very occasionally, if safely offscreen, he does sleep with them.

32 Vincent Canby, "The Gauntlet," *New York Times*, December 22, 1977. Roger Ebert, who was often generous to a fault in his praise for mindless films, was kinder, reporting that the film "tells a cheerfully preposterous story with great energy and a lot of style." Roger Ebert, "The Gauntlet," *Chicago Sun-Times*, January 1, 1978.

33 Schickel, *Clint Eastwood*, 385; see also Eliot, *American Rebel*, 206, 208.

34 G. A., "*Magnum Force*," review of *Magnum Force*, directed by Ted Post, TimeOut, accessed December 21, 2015, https://www.timeout.com/london/film/magnum-force.

35 Schickel, *Clint Eastwood*, 385.

36 Denby, "Law and Disorder."

37 Played by Eastwood's own daughter Alison, then age twelve, in her first screen credit.

38 Thomson, "Cop on a Hot *Tightrope*," 65, 66, 67; see also Christine Holmlund for a discussion of the movie's ambiguous position on women, its parallel constructions of cop and killer, and her observation that *Tightrope* undermines "the usual Hollywood alignment of a stable masculinity." Christine Holmlund, "Sexuality and Power in Male Doppelganger Cinema: The Case of Clint Eastwood's *Tightrope*," *Cinema Journal* 26, no. 1 (Fall 1986): 32.

39 John Simon, "Film: Dark Crannies," review of *Tightrope*, directed by Clint Eastwood and Richard Tuggle, *National Review*, October 5, 1984, 56; similarly, Sterritt assesses *Tightrope* as "hardly an essay in depth psychology, but it delves more deeply into hidden strata of American masculinity than previous Eastwood films, or most previous Hollywood films for that matter." *Cinema of Clint Eastwood*, 129.

40 Norman Mailer, "All the Pirates and People," reprinted in *Mind of an Outlaw: Selected Essays*, ed. Jonathan Lethem (New York: Random House, 2013), 398.

41 Kael, "Killing Time"; Sterritt also dates Eastwood's artistic maturity to *Bird* and *White Hunter Black Heart*. *Cinema of Clint Eastwood*, 3.

5

"I'm Not So Tough"

• •

Melodrama and Performance in the Later Films

DIANE CARSON

Although melodrama is not often associated with the iconic persona of Clint Eastwood or his films,[1] for the four and a half decades of his directing and acting work since 1971, elements of melodrama have fortified and buoyed his narratives. In fact, the stereotypical association of Eastwood with a "tough guy" is a macho veneer that facilitates the acceptance of his melodramatic infusion, making it more palatable than overplayed sentimental appeals by directors with reputations for more emotionally indulgent storylines. As significantly, Eastwood's predominantly quiet, measured presentation of unsettling emotions delivered through controlled, subdued performances encourages viewers to embrace his melodramatic touches. In his last two decades, Eastwood has appealed more directly to emotions than his previous popular persona or directorial reputation suggests.

Melodrama

As Barry Keith Grant writes about this "somewhat indistinct genre that refers to films about familial and domestic tensions," historically *melodrama* "referred to stage plays that, beginning in the late eighteenth century, used music to emphasize dramatic or particularly emotional moments."[2] In the cinematic world, "more recently the category refers to narrative in any popular form that seems contrived or excessive in emotion and sentimentality."[3] This has led to negative estimation, as Marcia Landy notes, because of "its identification with mass, or what has been termed 'low culture' . . . identified with escapism, vulgarity, sensationalism, excess, and exaggeration."[4] In particular, some critics have regarded melodrama's association with a demonstrative over-indulgence in emotion as an undesirable, superfluous appeal to viewers' heart-strings, eliciting undesirable tears or the struggle to suppress them.

The different, even dichotomous, emphasis of male-oriented versus female-oriented films has led to a devaluing of narratives in which the protagonists (usually women) indulgently suffer rather than stoically withstand misfortune, react to tribulations rather than confront difficulties, and succumb to adversity rather than triumph over it. Further denigrated as appealing primarily to women, melodrama has often been relegated to a lesser cinematic cultural status than gangster, film noir, or Western genres. And yet with several iconic melodramas such as *Stella Dallas* (1937), *Mildred Pierce* (1945), and *All That Heaven Allows* (1955) dominated by female protagonists (Barbara Stanwyck, Joan Crawford, and Jane Wyman respectively), feminist analysts have reclaimed and redefined this filmic subset of "women's weepies" as a positive challenge to a patriarchal industry's values and attitudes toward what is stereotypically regarded as the female domain—what today might be called, in equally derogatory fashion, the "chick flick."

Reconsidering the melodrama genre as an opportunity for oppositional interpretations, reading, as Lucy Fischer notes, "against the grain," Thomas Elsaesser argues that melodrama functions "to formulate a devastating critique of the ideology that supports it."[5] In fact, as Christine Gledhill adds, "Melodrama addresses us within the limitations of the status quo, of the ideologically permissible. It acknowledges demands inadmissible in the codes of social, psychological or political discourse."[6] We may therefore regard melodrama, especially family-anchored melodramas, as "prosocial pablum for passive, naïve audiences [or] as subtle, self-conscious criticism of American values, attitudes, and behavior."[7]

Broadening the restrictive definition of melodrama in her anthology, Gledhill explains the critical reappropriation of this "cross-cultural form with a complex, international, two-hundred-year history," that "as a mode melodrama both overlaps with and competes with realism and tragedy" exploring issues of class, ethnicity, and bourgeois values in provocative ways.[8] Further expanding our consideration of this genre, Landy notes that "melodrama traverses a number of genres—romances, narratives of crime and espionage, thrillers, and historical narratives."[9]

With this in mind, Eastwood's films provide a less surprising arena for considerations of melodramatic features than a quick assessment might suggest.

Moreover, in this regard, Eastwood's "tough guy" persona may provide a disarming cover for a riot of demonstrative emotion infrequently considered integral to his work. I argue that his films' enduring and extensive appeal includes and relies on his complex integration of melodramatic features. Vitally, Eastwood's ability to elicit nuanced performances from a diverse group of actors, sometimes within one film, distinguishes his work, and nowhere as much as in melodrama does acting carry the burden of success or failure. As Richard De Cordova argues, "Performance is perhaps the principal critical standard by which audiences have judged films, and there is little doubt that melodrama, in its emphasis on acting as expression, has provided the ideal object for the application of such a standard."[10] In addition, he observes that "it is clear that certain melodramatic scenes are written as showcases for performance . . . Suffering, hysteria, and madness not only become topics of melodrama; they also mark out a highly conventionalized space within which the scene of performance can unfold."[11]

Especially in his more recent work, Eastwood merits a reevaluation of his strategies for such successful dramatization. Sustaining a formidable undercurrent of melodrama, expertly guiding actors through demanding performances, and foregrounding characters' inner turmoil, director and actor Clint Eastwood defies simplistic "macho" classification. Instead, he integrates a multivalent world of psychologically conflicted characters. If I wanted to be more provocative, I might go so far as to argue that he reminds me of "woman's director" George Cukor who, according to Christoph Huber, "prized a 'detached' quality, yet was able to imbue his films with nuanced observations and scenes of sudden, overwhelming intimacy."[12]

Given Eastwood's economical, even austere, stylistic approach to the character-driven stories in the four films examined here, analysis of acting proves illuminating. In agreement with Andrew Klevan, I will treat performance as one element of the totality of film style and explore "the achievement of expressive rapport."[13] As Cynthia Baron and Sharon Marie Carnicke explain, "Films use lighting, setting, costuming, camera movement, framing, editing, music, and sound to give audiences privileged views of characters' inner experiences."[14] Even so, "the research in mirror neurons suggests that audiences do not respond directly to framing and editing choices but instead to gestures and expressions that serve as the locus of meaning," or, put another way, "the connotatively rich features of actors' performances."[15]

By studying the nonverbal acting choices in four of Eastwood's films, Laban Movement Analysis offers "a conceptual framework that facilitates observation and analysis of human movement."[16] This useful framework offers a rubric for identifying critical performative details because Laban pinpoints direction and speed of movement, as well as the performers' degree of control. It is worth considering that "through study, Laban and his collaborators located eight basic efforts: pressing, thrusting, wringing, slashing, gliding, dabbing, floating, and flicking."[17] Analysis directs our attention to and accounts for a range of variations: for example, a movement's weight or weakness and whether the movement is sustained. Using this methodology, we see that Eastwood's actors rely more often on "Light and Indirect" and "Light and Direct" movements such as float, stroke, pat, and glide, thereby giving his melodramatic elements a unique signature. Eastwood's choices as an actor and as a director convey a quiet, unfussy, softer appeal punctuated only at decisive, dramatic moments by more direct, sharp movements that gain impact because of their judicious use. In addition to helping explore actors' complex and complicated choices, Laban analysis illuminates how a good director generates our affective involvement and provides a sense of narrative momentum in ways that extend beyond editing rhythm and the contributions of music and sound.

Clint Eastwood, Laban, and Melodrama: Four Case Studies

Steering a complex approach to ideas and performance, Clint Eastwood has masterfully interwoven melodrama with social criticism in the four films examined here: *The Bridges of Madison County* (1995), *Mystic River* (2003), *Million Dollar Baby* (2004) and *Gran Torino* (2008). In dramas, characters get angry and act. In melodrama, characters suffer and react.

The Bridges of Madison County (1995)

Among the most pervasive melodramatic stories is the fated, lost love between a man and woman. *The Bridges of Madison County* qualifies as Eastwood's entry in romantic yearning and heartbreaking separation. In the eighteenth feature film he directed, Eastwood transforms a story from Robert James Waller's 1992 novel. Eastwood told Iain Blair that someone gave him the novel, he read it and thought, "There's a good idea here but it's written rather flowery. How do we pare it down into a screenplay?"[18] Told from the woman's point of view, the story follows *National Geographic* photographer Robert Kincaid (Eastwood) who arrives at Francesca Johnson's (Meryl Streep) farm shortly after her husband and their son and daughter have left for the Iowa State Fair. Kincaid is looking for the Roseman Bridge that he is tasked with photographing, and Francesca agrees to show him the location. Over the next four days, they experience deep, passionate love. Though Kincaid wants Francesca to leave with him, she regretfully but wisely realizes the impossibility of walking away from the family to which she has devoted her life.

Taking Richard LaGravenese's screenplay based on Robert James Waller's 1992 novel, Eastwood engineers an elegiac, conflicted love story suffused with suffering and suppressed passion, sacrifice, and self-denial. Evoking the longing for the perfect connection with another person, the notion that "this kind of certainty comes only once in a lifetime," as Robert Kincaid says to Francesca, Eastwood indulges in intensely melodramatic appeals. Few will resist shedding their own tears along with Robert and Francesca.

Two scenes illustrate the performance choices Eastwood the director and Eastwood the actor marshal in his emotional appeal: their dance in the kitchen and Robert's departure from the Johnson home. Experienced, expert actors know that within a scene between two characters, to maximize the impact, mirroring the temperature of the other's emotional state is less powerful than operating in a contrasting, or at least moderately different, register. Throughout *Bridges*, Streep and Eastwood perform a pas de deux of strikingly complementary design without replicating each other's choices. In Laban terms, if one actor expresses his character's state with indirect and light gestures and movement, the second actor would more wisely answer with direct, strong movements. In fact, this variation in acting expression best describes Francesca's and Robert's preferences in their initial interactions.

In their first meeting, Robert's movements are light and indirect. He moves slowly, he flows forward, he stands still as he repeats Francesca's directions to the Roseman covered bridge. By contrast, Francesca opts for direct, strong, sudden gestures. She's fussy, seems nervous and uncomfortable in scenes even before he arrives, and her sudden, flicking movements increase after he appears. As Robert drives up the long gravel driveway, Francesca is beating a throw rug against the porch post with sudden, whipping action. She drops it when she spies Robert's truck, hesitates, folds her arms, and unfolds her arms as she picks up her tea, which she sips and puts down, all within several seconds. Her choices involve quick, flicking movements when she slides her left hand up her right arm, gestures in the general direction of the bridge, plants her hand on her right hip and just as quickly raises it and awkwardly steps down off the porch.

She jabs and points, scratches her head, wrings her hands, and continues this busy pattern. Robert steps slowly to the front of his truck, tucks his hands in his jeans' pockets, calmly repeats her words, and amicably accepts her help. The weight of Eastwood's gestures is light, the force minimal, his movement deliberate and unhurried. By contrast, Streep's gestures are sudden, sharp, and quick, conveying the impression of an impulsive, self-conscious woman, nervously fluttering her arms and hands. She has difficulty keeping her hands or head still; he watches quietly, apparently almost amused at times.

Throughout succeeding interactions, Francesca's gestures remain characteristically sharp as established in the early scenes, while Robert's movements continue to contrast with hers. However, in the kitchen dance scene, they come the closest to mirroring each other's movements, gestures, and reactions—an appropriate occasion for their synchronization, since it is in this scene that they achieve perfect harmony, a harmony that will be irretrievable in subsequent interactions. But they will move gradually toward this unity in gesture and movement, beginning with their more characteristic preferences yielding to harmonious union.

This scene of Francesca and Robert's most hypnotizing accord occurs at the halfway point of the two-hour, fourteen-minute film, as Francesca and Robert dance in the kitchen, leading up to their first kiss. In these suspended moments, they fall in love. In earlier interactions between them, Francesca has flirted self-consciously, unsure of herself but responsive to Robert's attention and interest. As they move together in their intimate dance, Streep drastically slows down Francesca's tempo, aligning it with Robert's rhythm. These two characters now mirror each other. After Francesca enters the kitchen in her new dress, she turns her head, he turns his. She sighs, he sighs. She parts her lips, he parts his. Sentimental in the extreme, the music reinforces and intensifies the mood, eliciting in most viewers a poignant yearning and intense emotion—that is melodrama writ large.

After the telephone interruption, the camera cuts back to a long shot and they dance slowly, wordlessly, as a couple. They flow, embrace, and enjoy the moment as they begin, stop, then begin to kiss again. They have become two people in love, both smiling, kissing, gliding, moving slowly through dissolves to a fade to black. Daughter Carolyn's reading of Francesca's description interrupts the progression to Francesca and Robert's lovemaking. After a brief pause that elides their sexual union, the scene rejoins them, naked, embracing and kissing some more.

The melodramatic progression of their relationship will reach its most profound and powerful moment again in the kitchen, an hour and a half into the

FIGURE 5.1 Francesca (Meryl Streep) and Robert (Clint Eastwood) mirror each other in harmony—*Bridges of Madison County*. Frame enlargement.

film, when Francesca turns on Robert, accusing him of being "a hypocrite" and "a phony," someone who dabbles in emotion and affairs, needing no one. Streep again chooses sharp and sudden, strong and direct movement to express Francesca's disturbed state while Eastwood continues to interpret Robert with quiet, indirect, light gestures complemented by a still comportment.

The scene starts with Francesca questioning and challenging Robert about their and his previous relationships, his "routine" with other women. Streep retrieves the tilting of her head, the sudden sweeping action of her arms, the fussing with her hair, and sudden, direct, flicking motions. Eastwood reacts to her charges, while maintaining physical control, remaining still even as his voice rises in anger. Francesca beats Robert's chest and retreats. Robert stands, turns, and glides to the sink, in profile to the camera, his back to Francesca. He speaks quietly, slowly, baring his heart and soul, breathing deeply but physically still. When he turns to her, choking back his tears as one runs down her face, they embrace and kiss. Francesca is sobbing when her neighbor Madge pulls into the yard to interrupt them. Robert turns slowly, clearly having cried (though it is withheld from our direct view), brushes a tear from his eye, and walks out of the kitchen.

After a fade to black, Francesca joins Robert as he lies in bed, saying, "Come away with me." Her packing and a candlelight dinner follow, and Robert knows: "You're not coming with me, are you?" Again, he sits still even as he counters her reasons. She shrugs, looks up, sits up straight, folds her hands, props her chin on them, and shakes her head. He fondles her arm as she pulls back, fidgets more with her arms and hands, and articulates the sacrifices she makes as a mother and wife. They embrace as he says, "Don't throw us away." At this moment of their painful parting, as he expresses hope that she'll change her mind and she sobs, Robert slowly walks toward the door. He purposefully turns to step from darkness into the light and says, "I'll only say this once. I've never said it before, but this kind of certainty comes but just once in a lifetime." As Francesca sobs, bent over in grief, the music swells and viewers, male and female alike, cry with her as Robert drives away, so successful has the emotional manipulation been.

This dichotomy in Streep's and Eastwood's acting choices in both kitchen scenes maximizes the melodrama, adding layers of emotional conflict. The contrasting acting choices described using Laban's rubric add another dimension to the melodrama—that is, because of Streep's and Eastwood's divergent choices, except in their dance of perfect harmony, we feel the conflict on a performative level. In terms of classic melodrama, it is the woman's passion and her emotional excess that cause problems for which she must suffer and be contained. In this regard, Francesca's multilayered and conflicted emotional state complicates her newly discovered and overwhelming desire.

The physical ecstasy leads to jealousy and fear, while her longing for such rapture traps her in a crisis of conscience along with the realization that, probably as with her current marriage to Richard, such bliss cannot endure the daily routine. But in a palpably and intensely emotional reply, in a move that is unusual for conventional melodrama, Robert expresses and shows his excruciating pain, caused by both Francesca's insulting accusations and her retreat from his protestations of unexpected and unprecedented love. As Philippa Gates writes, assessing Eastwood's persona in his later films, "Eastwood's tough-guy past is tempered, and his image is aligned with contemporary ideals of masculinity as physical and heroic but, simultaneously, sensitive and romantic."[19] Ironically given his "Man with No Name" fame, Eastwood says, "For the first time in my life, I feel like I'm just portraying myself."[20]

Discussing this second kitchen/separation scene in their commentary on the DVD of *Bridges*, veteran Eastwood director of photography Jack N. Green and veteran Eastwood editor Joel Cox call it their favorite scene. As the relationship matures, Green notes, they begin increasing the intensity of the lights, making Francesca's and Robert's faces warmer. Cox notes, "The shots get closer." The technical elements, therefore, invite, even encourage, our greater emotional involvement. Assessing Eastwood's performance, both Green and Cox agree that "it was as far as I've ever seen him in a scene allow his emotions to really fall out."

They had never seen Eastwood so emotional in a scene.[21] "It's in his eyes, you can see he really got into that scene." They add that this one scene when Eastwood "really let it go" was in the film's first cut but removed in further edits. Pursuing the impact of this scene, Cox notes that men with emotions who always felt they had to hide them felt free to acknowledge and address them because of Eastwood's choices in this scene. In fact, they explain that Streep implored Eastwood to use another take of Robert's reaction at the sink, so powerful was his summoning of tears, but Eastwood kept the take with Robert in profile and seen from the back. Though Eastwood has said audiences do not want to see him cry, I believe he also realizes that the reserve shown in understating Robert's agony invites our own involvement and elicits an even stronger response.

What is most unusual for melodrama, and a pattern that will recur in other films directed by Eastwood, is the shared torment because of their ordeal. Typically, the woman must be recuperated into patriarchy, but for director Eastwood, the transgressive male will suffer for his equally powerful, albeit illicit, passion.

Mystic River (2003)

Clint Eastwood's twenty-fourth directorial project, *Mystic River*, dramatizes the heartbreaking story of several friends in East Buckingham, Boston. Although described by Robert Merrill and John L. Simons as "virtually the only film in which Eastwood strives for tragic effects, classical or otherwise"[22] and debated as either transcending or succumbing to detective novel genre conventions, my concern is not to delineate the pure or modified genre features but to consider the ways melodramatic touches confer powerful jolts at critical junctures in the story.

The film begins in 1975 with three eleven-year-old boys—Dave Boyle, Jimmy Markum, and Sean Devine—playing street hockey in their Irish Boston neighborhood. Two pedophiles, impersonating police officers, lure Dave into their car and lock him in a cellar where they sexually abuse him until, four days later, Dave escapes. Twenty-five years later, Dave (Tim Robbins), Jimmy (Sean Penn), and Sean (Kevin Bacon) still live in Boston's working-class Flats area. Jimmy, an ex-con, runs the Cottage Market corner grocery store; Sean has become a homicide detective in the Massachusetts State Police; and Dave works as a handyman while also caring for his son.

After Jimmy's nineteen-year-old daughter Katie is murdered, Sean and his police partner Whitey Powers (Laurence Fishburne) become the primary investigators, with Dave among the suspects. He returned home late the previous night, shaken and bloody, telling his wife Celeste (Marcia Gay Harden) that he fought off a mugger. Celeste, cousin to Sean's wife Annabeth (Laura Linney), becomes increasingly skeptical of Dave's story. After Katie's funeral, she tells Jimmy, who is convinced of Dave's guilt and, with his two friends the Savage brothers, entices Dave to a local bar, takes him out back, and cold-bloodedly kills him.

Mystic River was released in October 2003, with its premiere as the prestigious opening film for the New York Film Festival. With an estimated budget of thirty million dollars, *Mystic River* proved successful at the box office, making approximately ninety million dollars in its first seven months of release.[23] Professional critics peppered their mostly positive reviews with telling comments about the film's emotional appeal and impact. For example, Roger Ebert wrote, "The movie uses a group of gifted actors who are able to find true human emotion in a story that could have been a whodunit, but looks too deeply and evokes too much honest pain."[24] Peter Travers in *Rolling Stone* wrote, "There's nothing ordinary about the way Eastwood merges all the elements into a movie of startling power and intimacy."[25] Writing for the *New York Times*, A. O. Scott explained, "What gives the movie its extraordinary intensity of feeling is the way Mr. Eastwood grounds the conventions of pulp opera in an unvarnished, thickly inhabited reality. There are scenes that swell with almost unbearable feeling, and the director's ambitions are enormous, but the movie almost entirely avoids melodrama or grandiosity."[26] The uniform acknowledgment of *Mystic River*'s affecting power derives from the universally praised acting on display in two pivotal scenes that punctuate the narrative. In them, showing his directorial expertise, Eastwood uses very different ways to convey intense emotion: hysteria and silence. Because of their superb performances, both actors won Academy Awards: Sean Penn for Best Actor and Tim Robbins for Best Supporting Actor. The first of these momentous scenes belongs to Jimmy Markum (Penn) as he moves from sickening suspicion to dreaded confirmation that Katie has been murdered, her body discovered by the police searching in Pen Park.

Thirty-two minutes into the film, just after Jimmy and wife Annabeth attend their younger daughter Nadine's first communion, Jimmy realizes something is amiss when Katie fails to arrive. Sean, Whitey, and other state police have already discovered Katie's car and body in scenes intercut with the church ceremony. With sirens blaring, as police cars race down the street, Jimmy, his family, Val and Nick Savage, and other congregates watch from the church steps. The crosscutting between Pen Park and the ceremony recalls original sin and the brutality still present. With the police on the ground and in the air, the camera moves fluidly, searching, probing, moving forward as it tracks, pans, and in aerial shots pivots in circular reframing. The helicopter glides over the river, bridges, houses, fields, and swivels 180 degrees over the abandoned car. The communion service contrasts with the park scene in music and sound, shallow focus and primarily static shots in the church versus sweeping camera movement for the park. The divergent content and stylistic choices between the church and the park increase the tension.

As in *Bridges of Madison County*, Eastwood relies on this dissimilar pattern to increase, even unconsciously on the part of the viewer, an uncomfortable friction. At twenty-six minutes, in the dominant foreground screen right position, in medium close-up, only Jimmy and Annabeth are in focus as they sit at the end of their pew. Eastwood cuts to a shot of the ground as the camera then tilts and cranes up—a state policeman putting a piece of torn clothing in a jar. The camera gliding and panning with him, Sean walks from the pit toward a lake as he requests scuba divers. Continuing the crosscutting, we next see Jimmy in medium close-up, shot from the back. He turns his head to look around as the camera creeps in to a close-up with shallow focus. The effect of continuing this crosscutting, which extends over the next few shots, is to contrast, in Laban's terms, smooth, gliding, direct, and light movement for the police versus Jimmy's irregular, jagged, temporal movements as he turns with a more direct, slightly sudden tilt of his head toward the camera. Jimmy's constrained versus Sean's freer movement "highlight[s] the expressive qualities of actors' choices that are revealed by the relationship of expressions, gestures, and movement to space, time, weight, and flow."[27]

Consistently, inside his market or the church, compositions trap Jimmy in space, hold him still in time, heavy in weight, and abrupt in his flow. As this scene builds and Jimmy recognizes Katie's car, Sean learns of the situation. The tempo and movements shift to strong, sudden, and direct. Advancing quickly, shoving, poking, and throwing elbows in sharp, quick movements, the Savage brothers abruptly and rudely push their way through the onlookers as Jimmy waits. In a conventional shot/reverse shot, Sean and Jimmy briefly talk and Jimmy plans how to get into the park. With shots of the victim confirmed as Katie by Sean, sentimental music plays, setting up the emotional register for what follows as the most sustained, strong, sudden, and direct action in the film: a melodramatic immersion in hysteria. As David Edelstein asserts, "Eastwood has never shot anything with the sustained emotional power of the sequence in which Katie's body is found."[28] Dennis Rothermel calls it "Jimmy's Promethean struggle" and describes how he "writh[es] inexhaustibly but futilely . . . his face of agony, grief, and anger surrounded by the sea of dark uniforms that engulfs him."[29]

For thirty-two seconds (from 33:13 to 33:45 in the film[30]) Sean's calm, quiet, controlled energy deepens as Jimmy's unhinged physical reaction escalates to a terrifying, animalistic, screeching protest against the agonizing, incomprehensible truth of Katie's murder. Jimmy's naked pain is so unbearable, so excruciating that Eastwood cuts twice to a wordless, motionless Sean, a surrogate for our stunned reaction as well as a brief respite from news too heartbreaking and a performance so raw it sears right through us. Jimmy's thrashing, howling response to what he dreads crashes in on us because Sean's light, direct movement has lulled us into its calm flow just as Jimmy's strong but brief gestures of minimal weight have not foreshadowed his explosive force. Moreover, Jimmy's screeching, unearthly vocalization articulates and amplifies his horror as he confronts the unbearable recognition of the discovery of his daughter's body. From an overhead perspective, the camera pulls back, and Jimmy continues to thrash in the policemen's arms, screaming "Oh, God." The scene concludes with majestic music swelling, a dissolve to the bear pit, and a tilt up to the heavens from which no mercy has descended and no peace will be found.[31]

The second most melodramatic scene in the film occurs as Jimmy and Dave interact on Jimmy's porch after Katie's wake. Wisely, instead of attempting to match the histrionic impact of Jimmy's earlier action, Eastwood swings the pendulum to the other end of the emotional spectrum. In this scene, forty-seven minutes into the film, the painful state of Dave's and Jimmy's lives is encapsulated in their exchange on the porch. The implosive, disturbing texture of this scene contrasts dramatically with Jimmy's explosive force in his moment of realization of Katie's murder. Psychologically authentic and emotionally compelling for the characters' states in both instances, these two scenes further illustrate how the actors' choices convey the depth of their mental and physical agony, a depth that again intensifies a visceral assault on the viewer's emotions.[32]

Dave walks onto the porch for a cigarette. Sitting quietly in a chair in the corner, Jimmy gives Dave a jolt when he quietly says, "Hey, Dave." Dave's sudden, quick flick of the match pack, his shake of the match and his turn toward

FIGURE 5.2 Jimmy's (Sean Penn) thrashing, feral, screeching protest to his daughter's murder—*Mystic River*. Frame enlargement.

Jimmy yield to a medium long shot of an immobile Jimmy, arms crossed, legs open. Dave rocks back and forth slightly, ducks under the clotheslines, and sits after Jimmy points with a light, indirect gesture toward a plastic chair. In the three-minute exchange that follows, Dave remains, for the most part, stock-still. With the exception of several minimal looks from Dave to his hand (about which Jimmy asks), Dave listens but makes no other sustained, noteworthy movement of direct or indirect energy.

Jimmy guides the scene, but with closed, contained movements. He has turned inward, his grief subsumed under a mantle of guilt. Arms crossed across his diaphragm, Jimmy gestures with a light, brief nod toward the house, turns his head toward the street and back toward Dave, moves his legs in and out with small readjustments, and briefly raises and lowers his shoulders. As this scene progresses, the light, indirect quality of Jimmy's movements changes as the camera moves in to a medium close-up. Jimmy moves his head and shoulders with a more direct, stronger shudder, uses his facial muscles to crease his eyes and cheeks, and jerks his hands up into the frame, eventually placing one hand over his nose and eyes.

Dave's answering shot is a medium close-up, an asymmetrical match to Jimmy's close-up, thereby adding emphasis to Jimmy's strong emotions. In this close-up, Jimmy moves with stronger, more direct, sustained shakes of his head, punctuated with strong vertical jerks of his hand. His stillness has transitioned to pokes and thrusts and the crossing of his arms, with the timbre of his quivering voice expressing the pain his upper body conveys. Sean Penn's and Tim Robbins's nonverbal choices define the scene as it builds to express Jimmy's ineffably agonizing trauma and Dave's pent-up and conflicted but suppressed torment, caused by both his past abuse and the recent murder of the pedophile he stumbled across in the car outside the tavern.

Though both are sitting, Dave quietly, Jimmy's use of his hands, the turning of his head, the tension in his neck and his shoulders—all his acting choices declare his tortured state. In response to his protest that he can't even cry over his daughter, Dave says, "Jimmy, you're crying now." This fails to stop Jimmy's erratic, inelegant movements and visible facial pain. His anger informs his naked suffering, presented without any music. Indeed, none is needed and would only seem extraneous to Penn's gut-wrenching performance.

Cataloging the minutiae of these performances reveals the significant choices that accumulate to produce a profound effect. Melodrama depends on the ability of actors to elicit emotional reactions or at least to produce a palpable, emotional impact, and these choices are critical to building the effect desired. Moreover, melodrama feeds on such moments to maximize viewers' emotional investment, and it is difficult for me to imagine viewers anything but deeply moved, even painfully so, by the two scenes noted here.

Million Dollar Baby (2004)

Perhaps finding the tragic melodrama appealing, Eastwood followed *Mystic River* with *Million Dollar Baby*, his film that received the most prestigious awards. It won four 2005 Academy Awards, including Best Picture, Best Director, Best Actress for Hilary Swank, and Best Supporting Actor for Morgan Freeman. The Academy also nominated it for Best Adapted Screenplay, Best Achievement in Film Editing, and Best Performance by an Actor in a Leading Role for Eastwood. In addition, it won the 2005 Golden Globe Best Performance by an Actress for Swank and Best Director for Eastwood, as well as numerous other awards. We also love to watch people suffer, especially women, hence the lasting appeal of melodrama and its infusion into numerous genres parading under different flags. In the films examined here, Eastwood is immensely more evenhanded than most directors, with a more equitable attention given to male and female suffering.[33]

The emotional facets of *Million Dollar Baby* make it excruciatingly painful. The film focuses on Maggie Fitzgerald (Swank), a down-and-out woman determined to succeed as a boxer, and her initially reluctant trainer, Frankie Dunn (Eastwood), and his assistant, Eddie "Scrap-Iron" Dupris (Freeman), who narrates the story. After a disastrous bout in which Maggie's opponent knocks her down after the bell, Maggie ends up in a hospital, her career and normal physical life over. She begs Frankie to end her life, and he does.

As noted by John M. Gourlie, "A few reviewers find the emotions and dramatic elements of the film to be sentimental and hackneyed."[34] For example, David Edelstein wrote in *Slate*, that Maggie's role "is grotesquely sentimental."[35] In that vein, writing for *Salon*, Charles Taylor wrote, "A compendium of every cliché from every bad boxing melodrama ever made, *Million Dollar*

Baby (written by Paul Haggis from stories by F.X. Toole) tries to transcend its cornball overfamiliarity with the qualities that have long characterized Eastwood's direction—it's solemn, inflated and dull," further noting "Eastwood's cheap grab at audience sympathy by playing up Frankie's aches and pains."[36] And A. O. Scott wrote: "*Million Dollar Baby*, with its open-hearted mixture of sentiment and grit, might almost be mistaken for a picture from the studio's 1934 lineup that was somehow mislaid for 70 years," adding that "when, late in *Million Dollar Baby*, Frankie sheds tears, the moment brings a special pathos, not only because we're unaccustomed to seeing Mr. Eastwood cry, but also because we might have doubted that he had it in him."[37]

Principally sentimental music (composed by Eastwood) deepens the melodramatic appeal. Given Eastwood's established persona, I can't help but feel that the negative critiques to this and other Eastwood films spring, to some extent, from the broader cultural resistance both to embracing stories that prompt tears and to redefining Eastwood as a director who evokes such a response.

As standard with Eastwood and firmly in his comfort zone, the actors establish complementary qualities. Again in Laban terms, Frankie adopts the repressive, stoic persona characterized by constrained, implosive force; strong but slow, even cramped movements; and the feeling of a heavy, difficult-to-summon energy in his verbal and nonverbal responses to Maggie. By contrast, she exhibits an uninhibited, explosive vitality; quick, impetuous physicality; and a barely controlled fury to prove herself and succeed.

After Maggie's expressive vitality has been crushed, that Frankie euthanizes her is a profoundly moving tragedy. The events leading up to it are distinctly melodramatic in their presentation. One such illustrative scene occurs as Frankie trains Maggie thirty-five minutes into the two-hour, twelve-minute

FIGURE 5.3 A tearful Frankie—Eastwood as seldom presented—*Million Dollar Baby*. Frame enlargement.

film. With the backdrop of a sentimental score that weaves its way through the entire film, Frankie, who comes most alive in the ring, advises Maggie. Framed in long shots and in close-ups, alone and with Frankie, she is in near constant motion. Even when Maggie knocks out her first opponent in the gym match, Frankie minimizes the expression of his satisfaction. Often mirroring his low-key energy, Scrap (Freeman) further reinforces the dichotomy between the trainers and Maggie. Most surprisingly, rather than resisting the melodramatic indulgence of the story, Eastwood embraces and champions its appeal. The pattern of his emotional pas de deux carries the day here as in *Bridges of Madison County* and *Mystic River*.

Gran Torino (2008)

Though for me a less accomplished narrative than those in the other Eastwood films examined here, *Gran Torino* received numerous award nominations and won AFI's Movie of the Year, primarily, I surmise, for its admirable cross-cultural examination and endorsement of humanitarian values. It proved popular with audiences as well, with an estimated box-office gross of $148 million and a $33 million estimated production budget.[38] Heavy-handed in its presentation of two-dimensional characters, the story presents no complexity in its presentation of good versus bad. However, as John M. Gourlie and Leonard Engel point out, "Eastwood has built the family into a dramatic center of meaning in recent films, such as *Mystic River* and *Million Dollar Baby*, and *Gran Torino*[, which] fall into this pattern."[39] They add that he makes his characters in these films elicit greater "emotional depth than he was able to in the past," particularly in contrast to his loner, "acting for the most part out of pure self-interest and self-preservation."[40]

In *Gran Torino*, Korean War veteran Walt Kowalski lives next door to the extended Hmong family, initially greeting them with racial insults. As the personal and the political collide in a series of encounters, the most significant over Walt's 1972 prize Gran Torino, a connection develops between a reluctant but increasingly paternalistic Walt and Hmong teenagers Thao and his sister Sue. After Sue is beaten and raped by local Asian gang members and Thao burned with a cigarette and robbed of his work tools (bought for him by Walt), Walt realizes and tells Father Janovich, "You know, Thao and Sue are never gonna find peace in this world as long as that gang's around, until they go away, you know, forever." Walt locks Thao in the basement, confronts the gang members, and invites their gunfire, sacrificing himself before numerous witnesses as the police arrive and promise to send the gang members to prison.

As with *Mystic River* and *Million Dollar Baby*, what pushes *Gran Torino* into melodrama is not only the sentimental focus on a natural or surrogate family but the way details and scenes engineer and elicit an indulgent emotional response. Most obvious in this regard in *Gran Torino* is the shameless melodramatic use of Walt's dog, Daisy, in the moments before he leaves for his certain death. Daisy has been present in several scenes throughout the film: when Walt is reading his horoscope on his front porch and watching the Hmong family (38:36[41]), sitting on his steps when the grandpa and youngest girl ask Walt to have Thao clean out the wasp nest under the porch (59:36), watching a baseball game on television just before the gang shoots up the Hmong house (1:26.10), and lying smoking in the bathtub, cleansing before his final move (1:35.18). Having made several digs about the Hmongs not eating Daisy, at 1:41.45 Walt surprisingly takes Daisy to Grandma, tells her that he needs her to watch "my dog," secures Daisy to the chair, and pets her, saying "Bye-bye, sweetheart. Take it easy. Her name is Daisy."

As Walt leaves, we watch Daisy walk after him to the top of the stairs. The camera cuts to behind as she lies down, whimpering, with the next cut to a shot of her with her left front paw hanging over the stair, head down and whimpering for three seconds before a cut to the next scene of a phone ringing next to Sue's bed. From Rin Tin Tin in silent films from 1922 on, to *Lassie Come Home* (1943) and *Old Yeller* (1957), to name just a few, writers and directors have milked the sentimental, melodramatic possibilities of dogs in peril or pain. If the sadness and dread of anticipating Walt's imminent death and the assaults on Thao and Sue have not stimulated a sympathetic response, Daisy's whimpering surely will, intensifying the already excessive indulgence in tearful appeals.

Throughout these concluding moments, Daisy displays and invites the emotions that the stoic Walt represses. She becomes our surrogate through whom we can vicariously experience our pain. Moreover, she is a counterpoint to an angry Thao, who wants to accompany the deliberate, calm Walt in his sacrificial confrontation as he tricks the gang into murdering him. Again, Eastwood uses counterpoint—the loud, aggressive behavior of the gang set against his still, controlled presence—to invite and add to emotional involvement.

FIGURE 5.4 A whimpering Daisy left by Walt—*Gran Torino*. Frame enlargement.

Conclusion

The addition of the emotional register in *Gran Torino* and in the previous three films discussed here invites the viewers' empathy as much as it taps into archetypal themes and historical myths. Through a diverse range of emotional appeals, from music to acting choices to plot devices, Eastwood engages the viewer through techniques and tactics that credit him as a mature, masterful director. Writers analyzing Clint Eastwood's films seldom mention melodramatic elements, yet he is long overdue for receiving credit for his multilayered interlacing of the full spectrum of intellectual and emotional elements. I hope more critics pursue his work with a more expansive perspective.

Notes

1 A random survey of seven books devoted to Clint Eastwood by authors Drucilla Cornell, Leonard Engel (two anthologies), Howard Hughes, Robert Kapsis and Kathie Coblentz, Laurence F. Knapp, and Paul Smith shows not one index reference to "melodrama." All address issues of masculinity. See Drucilla Cornell, *Clint Eastwood and Issues of American Masculinity* (New York: Fordham University Press, 2009); Leonard Engel, ed., *Clint Eastwood, Actor and Director: New Perspectives* (Salt Lake City: University of Utah Press, 2007); Leonard Engel, ed., *New Essays on Clint Eastwood* (Salt Lake City: University of Utah Press, 2012); Howard Hughes, *Aim for the Heart: The Films of Clint Eastwood* (London: I. B. Tauris, 2009); Robert E. Kapsis and Kathie Coblentz, ed., *Clint Eastwood: Interviews, Revised and Updated* (Jackson: University Press of Mississippi, 2012); Laurence F. Knapp, *Directed by Clint Eastwood: Eighteen Films Analyzed* (Jefferson, N.C.: McFarland, 1996); Paul Smith, *Clint Eastwood: A Cultural Production* (Minneapolis: University of Minnesota Press, 1993).

2 Barry Keith Grant, *Film Genre: From Iconography to Ideology* (London: Wallflower, 2007), 75.

3 Grant, 75–76.

4 Marcia Landy, ed. *Imitations of Life: A Reader in Film & Television Melodrama* (Detroit, Mich.: Wayne State University Press, 1991), 16.

5 Lucy Fischer, *Cinematernity: Film, Motherhood, Genre* (Princeton, N.J.: Princeton University Press. 1996), 11; Thomas Elsaesser, "Tales of Sound and Fury: Observations on the Family Melodrama," in *Imitations of Life*, 85.

6 Christine Gledhill, ed., *Home Is Where the Heart Is: Studies in Melodrama and the Woman's Film* (London: BFI, 1987), 38.

7 Thomas Schatz, *Hollywood Genres: Formulas, Filmmaking, and the Studio System* (New York: Random House, 1981), 225.

8 Gledhill, *Where the Heart Is*, 1.

9 Landy, *Imitations of Life*, 15.

10 Richard De Cordova, "Genre and Performance: An Overview," in *Film Genre Reader*, ed. Barry Keith Grant (Austin: University of Texas Press, 1986), 136.

11 De Cordova, 137.

12 Christoph Huber writes about this label MGM's publicity department "cooked up" after Cukor's "successes like *Camille* (1936) and the all-female cast of 1939's

The Women." Christoph Huber, "George Cukor: A Master (of the) In-Between," *Cineaste* 39, no. 2 (Spring 2014): 14.

13 Andrew Klevan, preface to *Film Performance: From Achievement to Appreciation* (New York: Wallflower, 2005).

14 Cynthia Baron and Sharon Marie Carnicke, *Reframing Screen Performance* (Ann Arbor: University of Michigan Press 2011), 39.

15 Baron and Carnicke, 59, 58.

16 Baron and Carnicke, 190.

17 Baron and Carnicke, 190.

18 Iain Blair, "Clint Eastwood: The Actor-Director Reflects on His Continuing Career and New Film, *Absolute Power*," in *Clint Eastwood: Interviews*, 228.

19 Philippa Gates, "A Good Vintage or Damaged Goods?: Clint Eastwood and Aging in Hollywood Film," in *New Essays on Eastwood*, 169.

20 Knapp, *Directed by Clint Eastwood*, 195.

21 Both Green and Cox know Eastwood well. Green worked as director of photography on *Unforgiven* (1992), *The Rookie* (1990), *White Hunter Black Heart* (1990), *Pink Cadillac* (1989), *Bird* (1988), *Pale Rider* (1985), *Sudden Impact* (1983), *Honkytonk Man* (1982), *Bronco Billy* (1980), and *Every Which Way but Loose* (1978). Cox edited *A Perfect World* (1993), *Unforgiven*, *The Rookie*, *White Hunter Black Heart*, *Pink Cadillac*, *Bird*, *Heartbreak Ridge* (1986), *Pale Rider*, *Sudden Impact*, and *Honkytonk Man*.

22 Robert Merrill and John L. Simons, "*Mystic River* as a Tragic Action," *New Essays on Clint Eastwood*, 205.

23 Hughes, *Aim for the Heart*, 153, 155.

24 Roger Ebert, "*Mystic River*," review of *Mystic River*, directed by Clint Eastwood, RogerEbert.com, October 8, 2003, accessed February 3, 2016, http://www.rogerebert.com/reviews/mystic-river-2003.

25 Peter Travers, "*Mystic River*," review of *Mystic River*, directed by Clint Eastwood, *Rolling Stone*, September 25, 2003, accessed February 3, 2016, http://www.rollingstone.com/movies/reviews/mystic-river-20030925.

26 A. O Scott, "Dark Parable of Violence Avenged," *New York Times*, October 3, 2003, accessed February 3, 2016, http://www.nytimes.com/2003/10/03/movies/03MYST.html.

27 Baron and Carnicke, *Reframing Screen Performance*, 192.

28 David Edelstein, "Youth and Consequences: Three Men Fight Off the Past in *Mystic River*," *Slate*, October 8, 2003, accessed February 3, 2016, http://primary.slate.com/articles/arts/movies/2003/10/youth_and_consequences.html.

29 Dennis Rothermel, "Mystical Moral Miasma in *Mystic River*," *Clint Eastwood, Actor and Director: New Perspectives*, 219–220.

30 *Bridges of Madison County*, directed by Clint Eastwood (1995; Warner Bros. 2010), DVD.

31 An anecdotal story about Sean Penn recounts that he asked Eastwood how many men would be holding him. Eastwood replied, "Four or five." Penn reportedly said, "That won't be enough."

32 There are special moments in very few films that rise to the level of a transcendent experience. For me, Penn's performance as Jimmy, reacting to learning of Katie's murder, is one of those rare moments.

33 However, to truly evaluate the progressive presentation, or lack thereof, the most revealing shift is to reverse the sex of all characters involved along with the gender

characteristics. Few mainstream American films can sustain that kind of scrutiny and still qualify as progressive.

34 John M. Gourlie, "*Million Dollar Baby*: The Deep Heart's Core," in *Clint Eastwood, Actor and Director: New Perspectives*, ed. Leonard Engel (Salt Lake City: University of Utah Press, 2007), 249.

35 David Edelstein, "Punch Drunk," *Slate*, December 15, 2004, accessed February 26, 2016, http://www.slate.com/articles/news_and_politics/reel_time/2004/12/wings _of_desire.html.

36 Charles Taylor, "*Million Dollar Baby*: Clint Eastwood's Boxing Movie Floats like a Lead Balloon and Stings like a Dead Bee," *Salon*, December 15, 2004, accessed February 28, 2014, http://www.salon.com/2004/12/15/million_dollar/.

37 A. O. Scott, "3 People Seduced by the Bloody Allure of the Ring," *New York Times*, December 15, 2004, http://www.nytimes.com/2004/12/15/movies/3-people -seduced-by-the-bloody-allure-of-the-ring.html.

38 *Gran Torino*, IMDb, accessed February 24, 2016, http://www.imdb.com/title/ tt1205489/?ref_=nv_sr_1.

39 John M. Gourlie and Leonard Engel, "*Gran Torino*: Showdown in Detroit, Shrimp Cowboys, and a New Mythology," in *New Essays on Eastwood*, 266.

40 Gourlie and Engel, 266.

41 *Gran Torino*, directed by Clint Eastwood (2008; Warner Bros. 2010), DVD.

6

"Heroes Are
Something We Create"

· ·

The Biopics

DAVID STERRITT

Clint Eastwood has cultivated an offbeat relationship with the Hollywood biopic. Of more than three dozen films directed by the iconic auteur, ten can fairly be called "biopics"; yet only half of those films fully exemplify the possibilities of the genre by tracing the experience of a notable personality over a significant span of time with attention to both individual psychology and sociohistorical context. Eastwood's interest in biopics and quasi-biopics has grown over the years; he made twelve films before undertaking his first effort in the genre, then made two in the 1990s and two in the early 2000s and directed no fewer than four between 2011 and 2016. Although his public image will always be connected most closely with Westerns and action pictures, his varied exploration of the biopic is a noteworthy facet of his career that deserves more attention than it has generally received.

Not surprisingly, given Eastwood's gifts as a jazz musician, his most widely acclaimed biopic is *Bird*, a 1988 study of saxophone legend Charlie Parker that fulfills all qualifications for the genre by focusing on a key period in the protagonist's life and fleshing this out with flashbacks and reminiscences. Eastwood's other biopic in the classic mode is *J. Edgar*, his 2011 portrait of Federal

Bureau of Investigation chief J. Edgar Hoover, whose history unfolds when an agent prompts him to reflect on his long career for a biography. In the underrated 2014 film *Jersey Boys*, about the rise of the Four Seasons to pop-culture fame, Eastwood expands his conception of the biopic by combining it with the musical genre and dealing with a group rather than an individual. On a very different note, the 2014 drama *American Sniper* taps into questions about the morality of war in general and the Iraq War in particular, but much of the film's emotional heft comes from its treatment of the protagonist's early years and emotional conflicts, and critics strongly disagree as to whether Eastwood appropriately balances the personal and political aspects of the narrative. His most recent film to date, the 2016 release *Sully*, again explores linkages between the public and private personae of its main character, a commercial pilot who safely lands his damaged plane in the Hudson River.

Those five films are Eastwood's true biopics, and another five are semi- or quasi-biopics, centering on real-world protagonists in oblique or unconventional ways: *White Hunter Black Heart* (1990), in which Eastwood's character is a thinly veiled version of John Huston, a Hollywood actor and director who made some quasi-biopics himself; *Midnight in the Garden of Good and Evil* (1997), which revolves around a reporter and a wealthy man charged with murder, both drawn from life; the great World War II diptych *Flags of Our Fathers* (2006) and *Letters from Iwo Jima* (2006), the former probing the experiences of the men pictured in the famous Iwo Jima flag-raising photo of 1945, the latter viewing the Battle of Iwo Jima through the eyes of the general who commanded the Japanese garrison; and *Invictus* (2009), in which the South African leader Nelson Mandela and the South African rugby captain Francois Pienaar are the main characters.

Celebrity

As early as the dawn of the talkie era, movie industries around the world started pursuing what film scholar Ian Christie calls "a concerted project of 'national biography' through cinema."[1] This undertaking flourished in the Hollywood studios, where biographical pictures—or *biopics*, a term dating from the middle 1940s—became a staple in the early sound-film era and have continued to thrive ever since, usually focusing on famous or infamous figures already embedded in the popular imagination via literature or other media. The nature and characteristics of celebrity have been steady preoccupations of the genre, which has repeatedly applied its energies to more or less heavily fictionalized accounts of the triumphs and travails traversed by national rulers, corporate titans, canonical culture heroes, and others with lives deemed dramatic enough to captivate audiences at home and abroad.[2] Given the longtime partnership between Eastwood and Warner Bros., it's worth noting that Warners became the studio most closely associated with the biopic during the genre's classic era.[3]

It is also noteworthy that Eastwood's biopics invariably center on men, all of whom (the main characters of *Midnight in the Garden of Good and Evil* excepted) qualify as public personalities to one degree or another. Eastwood's own history as a world-class celebrity is a probable factor in his gravitation toward male-oriented biopics—and toward biopics in general—and it is telling that his involvement in the genre has become strongest in the latter decades of his career, when his iconic status has been most powerful. As film scholar Dennis Bingham points out, biographical movies about women tend to be burdened by "myths of suffering, victimization, and failure perpetuated by a culture whose films reveal an acute fear of women in the public realm," whereas those about male figures occupy a more varied spectrum ranging from "celebratory to warts-and-all to investigatory to post-modern to parodic."[4] Eastwood's male-oriented biopics fall easily into these categories. *Bird*, *Invictus*, and *Sully* are celebratory—it may not be coincidental that their single-word titles have the mnemonic snappiness of memes, mantras, or cheers—while both World War II films are investigatory and *J. Edgar* presents its subject with warts galore, as does *Bird*. Warts also abound in the parodic *Midnight in the Garden of Good and Evil* and *White Hunter Black Heart*, and the metacinematic reflexivity of the latter places it under the postmodern rubric as well. *Jersey Boys* and *American Sniper* are harder to label, but the former manages to combine warts with celebration and the latter might be called "investigative" if it weren't bound to a memoir that's a vanity publication at heart.

Casting

Effective casting is essential to effective cinema, and biopics arguably have an added responsibility in this area, for while a fictional character must be played more or less *persuasively*, a character drawn from life must be played more or less *accurately* as well, assuming that the filmmakers want to keep at least a modicum of grounding in the real world that their movie claims to represent. As a leading actor-director with a substantial record of box-office success, Eastwood has made good use of his ready access to the industry's A-list, populating his biopics with Hollywood stars whose physical traits, behavioral mannerisms, and professional skills are well suited to the accuracy and persuasiveness required by the genre.

As film scholar James Naremore has observed, however, biopics tend to be "crucially dependent upon an interaction between mimicry and realistic acting that can become threatened when a major star undertakes an impersonation."[5] Eastwood has occasionally fallen afoul of this hazard, as with Leonardo DiCaprio's makeup-caked impersonation of Hoover in the old-man scenes of *J. Edgar*. Still, this has generally not been a big problem for him, in part because his biopics often deal with people whose exploits have achieved some renown—army sniper Chris Kyle and airline pilot Chesley Sullenberger, for instance—but whose faces and voices are not especially familiar to large numbers of people.

As a major star himself, moreover, Eastwood has refrained from playing the protagonist in any of his biopics except *White Hunter Black Heart*, where main character John Wilson makes a uniquely good match with his own looks, demeanor, and screen image. Naremore rightly regards *White Hunter Black Heart* as one of Eastwood's most underrated films but criticizes his decision to cast himself as the character based on John Huston, saying that his accurate imitation of Huston's slow, mannerly speech is "slightly disconcerting" because when "an iconic star in the classic mold" makes a "basic change in . . . voice and persona," the result is "bizarre, almost as if he had donned a wig or a false nose."[6] In a parenthetical aside, Naremore allows for the possibility that Eastwood might know exactly what he is doing here, deliberately using the dissonance between his own persona and that of Huston to create an "intentionally alienating" effect. Given the thematic sophistication of *White Hunter Black Heart*, an understated satire of show-business glamour and cosmopolitanism, it is indeed likely that Eastwood saw his performance as a conscious contribution to an enjoyably "alienating" conceptual mix. Usually, of course, the lead performances in Eastwood biopics are more conventionally conceived, and for the most part they strike artful balances between imitation and interpretation, producing reality-based portraits that are biographically plausible if not always as psychologically rounded or dramatically compelling as one might wish.

Style

By the time he entered the biopic arena, Eastwood's visual style had become more varied and expressive than was evident in, say, the relatively heavy pyrotechnics of the high-octane thriller *Play Misty for Me* (1971) and the allegorical Western *High Plains Drifter* (1973). His approaches to montage and mise-en-scène in the period starting with *Bird* could still indulge the hyperbolic violence of *The Gauntlet* (1977) and the macho heroics of *Heartbreak Ridge* (1986), but they were also capable of bringing out the milder moods of a *Bronco Billy* (1980) and a *Honkytonk Man* (1982) via colorful, almost comicbookish aesthetics in the former and dusty Depression-era drabness in the latter. Broadly speaking, Eastwood's first biopic marked the beginnings of his full maturity as an artist.

A major contributor to Eastwood's early style was director of photography Bruce Surtees, one of two cinematographers (the other was Gordon Willis) known in Hollywood as a "prince of darkness" because of his fondness for shade and shadow. Surtees's successor as Eastwood's most frequent cinematographer, Jack N. Green, brought similar skill with low-key tones and pools of dimly illuminated space. Green set the tenor for his collaboration with Eastwood in *Bird*, a movie full of nighttime scenes and smoky dives, and tempered variations on that visual theme enhanced the darker portions of their subsequent films together, including *White Hunter Black Heart* and *Midnight in the Garden of Good and Evil*.

Eastwood's other biopics have all been photographed by Tom Stern, and while Stern's flexible approach does not lend itself easily to generalities, the deliberately depressed tones of *Flags of Our Fathers* and *Letters from Iwo Jima* carry the legacies of Surtees and Green to Eastwood's later films. A largely subliminal factor in Eastwood's best work is the immediacy produced by his penchant for speedy shooting with minimum fuss, and Stern is clearly able to oblige. Film editor Joel Cox and production designer James J. Murakami have also worked on a large number of Eastwood films, enabling the director to develop and sustain his increasingly distinctive style. Since no particular visual stylistics are inherent to the biopic as a genre, the eclecticism of Eastwood and his most frequent collaborators has served these movies well.

Bird

There's going to be a Birdland in every city one day.
—Charlie Parker

Eastwood's first biopic was written by Joel Oliansky, who based the screenplay in part on *My Life in E-flat* (1999), a then unpublished memoir by Chan Parker, the protagonist's common-law wife. *Bird* posed an interesting challenge insofar as Charlie "Bird" Parker was a toweringly brilliant and profoundly troubled African American jazz artist whose tumultuous life "played out every cliché of the self-destructive-celebrity life," in the words of film critic Jay Scott, who nonetheless called the film a "marvel that avoids every cliché of the self-destructive-celebrity biography."[7] Eastwood solves the problem inherent in telling Parker's story—how to make a fresh, surprising narrative from a life that followed all-too-familiar patterns of jazz-world excess—by tempering biopic realism with offbeat structural maneuvers and touches of poetic, even dreamlike action, as in the opening scene, where a dramatic moment in Parker's early career is related in a bravely nonlinear fashion.

Eastwood first heard Parker play in 1946, and he remembered the experience as an "overwhelming" one. His intention was to "pay tribute" to Parker via the biopic format, employing a seemingly intuitive yet carefully calculated style to capture the contradictions he saw as integral to an artist who "could be very charismatic and sweet, and . . . could be mean and very undisciplined." Parker's excesses were "enormous," he told me in a 1988 interview, "but when it came to his music, he switched into another kind of mode."[8] Blending its unusual elements with standard Hollywood devices, *Bird* chronicles the basics of Parker's career from start to finish, depicting his childhood love of jazz and his rapid ascent as a player and bandleader, his rapport with other musicians, his relationship with his white common-law wife, his alcoholism and addiction to heroin, and ultimately his death in 1955 at age thirty-five, so devastated by liver disease, heart disease, and a bleeding ulcer that the physician inspecting his corpse initially estimated his age at fifty or more.

To reproduce the power of Parker's playing, Eastwood needed to consider both visual and aural matters. The former depended to a large extent on casting, and Forest Whitaker is a gifted actor whose resemblance to Parker makes him a persuasive surrogate. To convey the specific qualities of Parker's sound, Eastwood had to choose between recording a Parker imitator, which would diminish the authenticity quotient of the film, or putting Parker's own recordings onto the soundtrack, which was problematic because his studio recordings generally have longer durations and more audio-engineered sheen than his live performances. While pondering this dilemma, the filmmakers unexpectedly came upon a trove of Parker tapes that had never been transferred to disc and released. Since the piano, drum, and bass sounds came across poorly on the tapes, music supervisor Lennie Niehaus recruited a recording engineer to isolate and extract Parker's saxophone lines, whereupon new backup tracks were recorded with a top-flight jazz crew (including trumpeter Red Rodney, a character in the film) and string section. This was an ingenious solution to a problem that biopics about musicians (and about artists in other fields, mutatis mutandis) often face: how best to represent the work of the biographical protagonist when the work is unavailable in a readily employable form.

Critical responses to *Bird* as a biopic have varied. In his *Washington Post* review, Desson Howe wrote that Eastwood's respect for Parker "runs so deep it disappears underground; and only the faintest signature arises from those devotional depths."[9] The jazz-savvy film critic Jonathan Rosenbaum had a different view, asserting that despite "legitimate quibbles that must be made—about substituting new accompanists, short-shrifting the issues of racism, and muddling certain musical and biographical facts—the man and his music almost get the canvas they deserve."[10] The critical consensus on *Bird*

FIGURE 6.1 Forest Whitaker plays saxophone giant Charlie "Bird" Parker in *Bird* (1988). Frame enlargement.

inclines toward the latter view, consolidating its status as one of Eastwood's most broadly successful biopics.

White Hunter Black Heart

Hollywood is just a place where they make a profit.
—John Wilson

Eastwood made his second venture into biographical territory with his very next film: the 1990 quasi-biopic *White Hunter Black Heart*, based on Peter Viertel's 1953 novel about working with director John Huston on the screenplay of *The African Queen*, the 1951 classic starring Humphrey Bogart and Katharine Hepburn as an extremely odd couple surviving harsh conditions and personality clashes during a harrowing African journey. In one of his most audacious performances, Eastwood plays the semifictional Huston surrogate John Wilson, whose film-within-the-film doesn't get started until after Eastwood's actual film has ended. The reason for the delay is Wilson's obsessive wish to hunt and shoot an African elephant, and if puttering around in the bush looking for a target jams the gears of the film production that brought him to Africa in the first place, this is a price he is willing to pay. In his autobiography, *An Open Book*, Huston admitted that he never managed to kill an elephant when *The African Queen* was in production; the same happens in Eastwood's film, where he faces the elephant but doesn't pull the trigger. "I prefer . . . that the obsession come to an end" without the killing, Eastwood told an interviewer. "The obsession driving him

FIGURE 6.2 John Wilson (Clint Eastwood) aims at the elephant in *White Hunter Black Heart* (1990). Frame enlargement.

to the brink [and causing the death of a guide] is bad enough to give him the guilts."[11]

Eastwood portrays Wilson as a narcissistic bon vivant and swaggerer. What injects uncommon boldness and novelty into his performance is the decision to make Wilson a grinning, garrulous, chain-smoking imitation of the real John Huston, whose voice and mannerisms are well known to moviegoers (especially in 1990, only three years after his death) from his appearances in such major Hollywood productions as Roman Polanski's *Chinatown* (1974) and Otto Preminger's *The Cardinal* (1963), which brought him an Academy Award nomination. Eastwood surely realized that Huston's persona was distinctive and familiar enough to make a purely imitative portrayal seem derivative, unimaginative, and perhaps ridiculous. But a deeper strategy underlies his approach. The key can be found in Oscar Wilde's famous claim that he put only his talent into his art, putting his genius into his life. Although the swashbuckling, speechifying Wilson is ostensibly in Africa to put his talent to work on a movie, he is putting whatever genius he can muster into a self-appointed effort to be more of an adventurer and daredevil than his limited supplies of courage and concentration can ever allow. Eastwood's portrayal is a walking, talking metaphor for Wilson's ill-fated attempt to be what he clearly is not, a job he botches so badly that his art *and* life come perilously close to collapsing.

One of Eastwood's motivations for making *White Hunter Black Heart* was his longtime interest in obsessive characters, but he took the project's biographical properties no less seriously. The costumes draw on photographs published in Hepburn's book about the production, Wilson's crew members wear khaki outfits like those of the actual technicians, and their on-screen camera equipment is of authentic 1950s vintage.[12] These and other details confirm Eastwood's commitment to basic principles of the biopic, even in an obliquely constructed one where the spirit of the breed is respected but the laws are bent with abandon.

Midnight in the Garden of Good and Evil

This place is fantastic. It's like *Gone with the Wind* on mescaline.
—John Kelso

Seven years elapsed before Eastwood returned to the biographical field with *Midnight in the Garden of Good and Evil*, based on a best-selling nonfiction novel by John Berendt, a journalist and editor. Berendt's book chronicles the murder trials of Jim Williams, an antiques dealer who became a leading light of Savannah, Georgia, by virtue of his successful business, his restoration of a historic house in the city, and his munificence as host of a Christmas party held annually in the refurbished manse. Although the narrative's dramatic impact derives chiefly from the legal process, both the book and Eastwood's screen adaptation—written by John Lee Hancock, who had scripted *A Perfect World* for Eastwood in 1993—surround the main action with colorful and idiosyncratic characters. The primary figures are Williams (Kevin Spacey) and journalist John Kelso (John Cusack), a fictional visitor from New York who

FIGURE 6.3 Journalist John Kelso (John Cusack) and accused killer Jim Williams (Kevin Spacey) take a stroll in Savannah, Georgia, in *Midnight in the Garden of Good and Evil* (1997). Frame enlargement.

adds psychological warmth to the detached, observational tone of Berendt's account. Among the Savannah citizens are Billy Hanson (Jude Law), the druggy, bisexual murder victim; Minerva (Irma P. Hall), a voodoo priestess; Joe Odom (Paul Hipp), a house sitter and party-giver; Sonny Seiler (Jack Thompson), a defense attorney; Lady Chablis (Lady Chablis), a drag queen; and Mandy Nichols (Alison Eastwood, the director's daughter), a Savannah woman who gets romantically involved with Kelso.

Eastwood was attracted to the project by its arresting title, its Southern setting, and his increasing realization that stories driven by plot, action, and sensation now held less interest for him as a director than "character studies" centered on psychology and personality.[13] Hancock's original draft pared away parts of the book that Eastwood asked him to replace, including an alternative account of the killing that Williams came up with in jail, contradicting parts of his initial statement. This reminded Eastwood of Akira Kurosawa's *Rashomon* (1950), a classic exploration of the slipperiness of truth. "I like that ambiguity," Eastwood said. "Williams tells us two different scenarios. . . . It leaves Kelso in a quandary, but life is like that." Elusiveness and ambiguity are the main concerns of the film, along with the importance of open-mindedness and acceptance. The movie is about "tolerating other lifestyles," Eastwood said in 1998, "learning to be less judgmental."[14]

Midnight in the Garden of Good and Evil is as much a courtroom drama as a quasi-biopic, but the latter aspect gains in importance through Eastwood's decision to condense the multiple trials that Williams actually went through into a single proceeding. Although streamlining the story in this way has the effect of downplaying bigotry and other factors that skewed the judicial process as described in Berendt's account, it sharpens the movie's narrative thrust and the focus on its biographically based protagonist. Since the city's moods and flavors are atmospherically captured by Jack N. Green's cinematography and further evoked on the soundtrack via songs by local luminary Johnny Mercer, the film can also be seen as a quasi-biopic of Savannah itself.

Flags of Our Fathers and *Letters from Iwo Jima*

Heroes are something we create, something we need. It's a way for us to understand what's almost incomprehensible: how people could sacrifice so much for us.
—James Bradley

A day will come when they will weep and pray for your souls.
—General Tadamichi Kuribayashi

Eastwood's two movies of 2006 are distinctive achievements in every respect, including their approach to the quasi-biopic subgenre. The first to be released was *Flags of Our Fathers*, a film about war but not a film *of* war. The title alludes to the raising of an American flag on the Japanese-held island of Iwo Jima by five marines and a navy corpsman who became famous when the federal government turned an Associated Press photograph of the event into a public-relations tool, using it to rally Americans in support of the war effort. Three of the men subsequently died in combat. The others, who were brought home and sent on tour to promote war-bond sales, are the film's central characters: John "Doc" Bradley (Ryan Phillippe), the quietest and most equable of the three; Ira Hayes (Adam Beach), a shy and vulnerable Native American; and Rene Gagnon (Jesse Bradford), a jaunty and genial type. A profound irony that sets the intellectual and emotional tone of the picture is the fact that the six men in the photo were not the first to raise an American flag on the Mount Suribachi site—a smaller flag had been planted earlier by another team, then taken by a souvenir-hunting naval officer—but were hailed as unique, trailblazing heroes by a public under the thrall of a devious advertising ploy.

The screenplay by Paul Haggis and William Broyles Jr. is based on the eponymous best-selling book by the corpsman's son, James Bradley, and Eastwood used it to develop the ideas about violence and mortality that were increasingly on his mind. He also regarded the narrative as a cautionary tale about the hazards of celebrity, a recurring concern in the history of biopics. The famous flag-raisers didn't feel heroic, he noted, however brightly the unsought and unwanted spotlight glared upon them. Treated like stars and courted by powerful people, they were more dazed and confused than thrilled or excited, as the film shows in harrowing detail. Such matters are a world away from the Hollywood pyrotechnics of earlier military movies that Eastwood had starred in and/or directed. *Flags of Our Fathers* is an exemplary portrait of three overlooked historical figures.

Letters from Iwo Jima, made immediately after *Flags of Our Fathers*, focuses on Tadamichi Kuribayashi, the Imperial Army general who commanded the Japanese forces on Iwo Jima before and during the battle that ended with their utter defeat. Written by Iris Yamashita from a story she crafted with Haggis, the screenplay had two principal sources: *Picture Letters from the Commander in Chief*, a collection of letters written by Kuribayashi in the late 1920s and early 1930s, and a book by Kumiko Kakehashi about the Iwo Jima battle based on letters Kuribayashi wrote on the island. Eastwood recruited the samurai-film specialist Ken Watanabe to play Kuribayashi, a venturesome figure who inclines toward intuition and experience where others rely on protocol and tradition. The literate and introspective Kuribayashi is the story's biographical center of gravity, and the chief supporting character is Saigo (Kazunari Ninomiya), a rank-and-file soldier excruciatingly aware that fate is inexorably closing in.

Apart from sequences with explosions and the like, Eastwood and cinematographer Tom Stern shot both *Flags of Our Fathers* and *Letters from Iwo Jima* in starkly desaturated color, aiming to convey a "non-comfortable" sense of war.[15] More boldly still, Eastwood presented the Japanese-language dialogue in *Letters from Iwo Jima* in Japanese with English subtitles for English-speaking audiences. Since major American distributors regard subtitles as commercial poison, no filmmaker lacking Eastwood's industry clout could have managed this extraordinary feat. *Flags of Our Fathers* was Eastwood's least financially successful film in years, earning back only about two-thirds of its ninety-million-dollar budget. *Letters from Iwo Jima* fared even worse in American markets, freighted as it was by subtitles, a color-drained appearance, and a reverse perspective on what Hollywood customarily depicts as a virtuous battle fought by a greatest generation of American warriors. But the latter's dismal domestic returns (less than fourteen million dollars on a twenty-million-dollar investment) were outbalanced by almost fifty-five million dollars overseas, most of it in the Japanese market. In the end, Eastwood's experimental war picture paid gratifying dividends in both aesthetic and financial terms.

Invictus

People don't realize that I played rugby myself when I was a student. . . . It is a very rough game, almost as rough as politics.
—Nelson Mandela

Invictus takes its title, a Latin word meaning "unconquered," from the 1888 poem by William Ernest Henley that concludes with the often-quoted couplet, "I am the master of my fate: / I am the captain of my soul." During his twenty-seven-year imprisonment by South Africa's notorious apartheid government, the revolutionary leader and future president Nelson Mandela recited it to others incarcerated with him. Eastwood's film begins with Mandela, played by Morgan Freeman in a case of incontestably ideal casting, attaining his long-delayed release from prison in 1990. From the window of the car carrying him to freedom, he sees South African racial divisions personified by two everyday athletic matches alongside the road: on one side, whites playing rugby on a carefully maintained field; on the other, black children playing football on a patch of uneven ground. The scene is a précis of the movie's main concerns: racial separation and the power of sports to divide people in such circumstances and unite them in others.

The film then fast-forwards to 1994, when Mandela is elected as South Africa's first black president, facing the task of ameliorating the country's seemingly intractable racial animosities. Sports reenter the picture when he attends a rugby march and sees black South Africans cheering for England instead of for the Springboks, their own rugby union team. Meeting with Francois Pienaar (Matt Damon), the Springboks' captain, Mandela exhorts him to make an all-out effort in the World Cup competition their country will be hosting soon, reasoning that if blacks can be persuaded to overcome their hostility toward a team they associate with white privilege and domination, shared enthusiasm for victory on the rugby field will spur healing and reconciliation throughout the land. Pienaar and his players train for the tournament, reach out to black communities, defeat the Australian and French teams, and prepare for the decisive match with the All Blacks from New Zealand, their archrivals.

Eastwood and Freeman had worked together well in *Unforgiven* (1992) and *Million Dollar Baby* (2004), and Eastwood liked the idea of Freeman playing Mandela in a quasi-biopic crystallizing a decisive moment in the struggle to bring about black-white rapprochement. It is likely that Eastwood's conservative politics were an additional factor when he took on the project. Barack Obama had become America's first black president a few months before shooting began, and although Eastwood said when the film opened that he "wasn't trying to sell any American politics in the thing," he added that Obama had not inspired him with confidence thus far. Obama was "a charismatic young man," he told an interviewer, "and he did talk about change and all this kind of stuff that sounded great. . . . Whether he's able to deliver the goods or not is another thing."[16] This comment lends piquancy to an early moment in *Invictus* when the newly elected President Mandela sees an Afrikaans newspaper headline reading, "He Can Win an Election but Can He Run a Country?" The thing might contain American politics after all.

Directorial touches aside, Anthony Peckham's screenplay for *Invictus* is based on John Carlin's 2008 book *Playing the Enemy: Mandela and the Game That Made a Nation*, an account that has been accused of treating Mandela too uncritically and deferentially. Rather than refute the charge, Carlin has pleaded nolo contendere: "It's difficult not to do a hagiography. Mandela is to politics what Mozart is to music. He is the Abraham Lincoln of our times. And the great good fortune of my working life has been to know him."[17] Eastwood and Peckham fall into the same pitfall, if pitfall it is, and their consistently reverent film sparks less excitement than one might wish from a fact-based movie about sports and politics, the key competitive areas of our age.[18] Its message of racial union and understanding is thoroughly sincere, however, and its heart is in the right place even when its art wanders elsewhere.

J. Edgar

What's important at this time is to reclarify the difference between hero and villain.
—J. Edgar Hoover

Eastwood's politics may also inform *J. Edgar*, his first full-fledged biopic since *Bird* almost a quarter century earlier. Famous in all circles and infamous in many, longtime FBI chief J. Edgar Hoover was regarded by countless critics as the embodiment of clandestine power, conspiratorial maneuvering, ideological blackmail, and moral turpitude—the very forces that his public persona purportedly opposed throughout his seemingly interminable career. But moviegoers looking for a sensational exposé did not find it in Eastwood's film. What they did find was a reasonably well-balanced account of Hoover's bull-in-a-china-shop tactics juxtaposed with his passionate friendship for deputy and companion Clyde Tolson (Armie Hammer), the sexual undertones of which rumble steadily in the movie's id. Melodramatics erupt when Hoover's fantasy of marrying a Hollywood actress elicits an overwrought response from Tolson, culminating in a knockabout fight, an unwelcome kiss, and a lingering fog of fiercely repressed yearnings. The men's situation is pitiable and inescapable save through growing estrangement, disharmony, and ultimately Hoover's lonely death.

As film scholar Douglas McFarland observes, Eastwood's right-wing views might have encouraged an aspiration to "restore Hoover's reputation," and the participation of screenwriter Dustin Lance Black, a prominent gay-rights advocate, opened the possibility of a "sympathetic perspective" on Hoover's compulsively closeted homosexuality. In the end, McFarland concludes, Eastwood and Black steered between the overheated and the understated, examining "a life enmeshed in the interwoven complexities of familial, ethical, social, psychological, and political forces."[19] This is a fair assessment. Eastwood's libertarian leanings had inflected his approach to homophobia and heteronormative hypocrisy in *Midnight in the Garden of Good and Evil*, and the same propensities are evident in *J. Edgar*, which limns an absorbing portrait of a top-grade Eastwood protagonist: a Dirty Harry who has a whole police force in his pocket but is burdened to his depths by anger, shame, and desperately denied desire.

Jersey Boys

They ask you, "What was the high point?" Hall of Fame, selling all those records . . .
it was all great. But four guys under a streetlamp, when it was all still ahead of us,
the first time we made that sound, our sound. . . . That was the best.
—Frankie Valli

Eastwood's next film was the second of four consecutive biopics. *Jersey
Boys* is also the first out-and-out musical he has directed, leaving aside the
music-laced melodramas *Bird* and *Honkytonk Man* (1982) and the documentary *Piano Blues* (2003). Again placing celebrity into the foreground,
Jersey Boys is a lively ramble through the collective career of Frankie Valli
and the Four Seasons, beginning with early iterations of their act, when
they went by names like Frankie Valli and the Four Lovers, and passing
through the usual pop-group succession of renown and riches, jealousies
and rivalries, and disillusionments and breakups, ultimately yielding the
nostalgic glory of induction in the Rock & Roll Hall of Fame, the 1990
event that climaxes the film.

The characters are standard-issue Joisey boys one and all: lead singer Valli
(John Lloyd Young), née Castelluccio; bandmates Tommy and Nick DeVito
(Vincent Piazza, Johnny Cannizzaro), Bob Gaudio (Erich Bergen), and Nick
Massi (Michael Lomenda); Gyp DeCarlo (Christopher Walken), a mob-
ster who serves as Valli's mentor; Bob Crewe (Mike Doyle), a gay recording
entrepreneur and songwriter who fuels the group's success; and Norm Wax-
man (Donnie Kehr), a loan shark you wouldn't want to mess with. Even more
familiar are the more-or-less golden oldies that pepper the soundtrack, ranging
from the 1962 chart-toppers "Big Girls Don't Cry" and "Sherry" to the more
mature "My Eyes Adored You" (1974) and "Grease" (1978), number one hits
for Valli as a solo performer.

Jersey Boys came into existence as a stage musical that opened on Broadway in 2005, with a book by Marshall Brickman and Rick Elice, music by
Gaudio and lyrics by Crewe, all of whom make the same contributions to
Eastwood's adaptation. Like the theatrical work that inspired it, the film
has an episodic structure and a presentational acting style whereby characters periodically speak to the camera, passing the narration from one
person to another in a relay-race manner that lends fresh life to an old
convention.

As with *Bird* some twenty-six years earlier, Eastwood faced the question of how best to present the music so essential to the tale, and as before,
he took an unusual option. Normally music and vocals are prerecorded
before shooting begins and the actors mime (or sing and play along) while
the recordings are played back, aware that no sounds made on the set will

be heard on the film's soundtrack. Eastwood made two unexpected choices. First, he decided not to replace the stage show's main performers with actors more experienced in movie roles, reasoning that they had "done 1,200 performances: How much better can you know a character?"[20] And second, he and his sound engineers recorded the vocal and instrumental performances live while the camera rolled. This is not a new methodology, but Eastwood uses it skillfully, producing a seamlessness and spontaneity that serve the biopic well.

Few suspected that the jazz-loving Eastwood harbored a yen for jukebox sounds, but his feel for the Four Seasons rings true, and he spices the story's well-worn ingredients with the spirited textures, tones, and moods that distinguish the period's best popular music. *Jersey Boys* is a worthy addition to the honor roll of rock-and-roll biopics.

American Sniper

There are three types of people in this world: sheep, wolves, and sheepdogs.
—Chris Kyle

Eastwood's biopic of 2014 is based on *American Sniper: The Autobiography of the Most Lethal Sniper in U.S. Military History*, a memoir written by Navy SEAL Chris Kyle with Scott McEwen and Jim DeFelice; published in 2012, it stayed on the *New York Times* best-sellers list for more than nine months and sold more than a million copies in its first three years in print. The popularity of the film, starring Bradley Cooper as Kyle, was no less phenomenal: racking up the highest worldwide earnings of any 2014 release, it became the biggest grosser of Eastwood's career and the highest-grossing war film (unadjusted for inflation) of all time. It also received Academy Awards nominations for Best Picture, Best Actor (Bradley Cooper), Best Adapted Screenplay (Jason Hall), Best Film Editing (Joel Cox and Gary Roach), Best Sound Mixing, and Best Sound Editing. A stellar showing indeed.

And a troubling one. Kyle's very personal, very action-packed book can be read as an avowal of patriotism, a celebration of self-sacrifice, and a candid memoir of what it's like to wage war in the Middle East when you could be living an ordinary, contented life. But it can just as easily be read as the self-justifying confession of an unreflective man who enlists in an elite military branch for valid personal and patriotic reasons, then discovers he has a natural talent for shooting and, deep-down, a taste for killing that finds an ideal outlet for expression amid the violence-ridden chaos produced by the American-led invasion of Iraq in the early 2000s.

Kyle's musings are invariably trite. On Islam: "The people we were fighting . . . wanted to kill us, even though we'd just booted out their dictator, because we practiced a different religion."[21] On rules of engagement: "Picking apart a soldier's every move against a dark, twisted, rule-free enemy is more than ridiculous; it's despicable."[22] On the pleasure of killing: "It was like a scene from *Dumb and Dumber*. The bullet went through the first guy and into the second."[23] "I had been trained to kill. . . . And I liked doing it. A lot."[24] "I wondered, how would I feel about killing someone? Now I know. It's no big deal. . . . They all deserved to die."[25]

The interesting thing about Kyle's book is not his hackneyed thinking but rather the fact that it attracted Eastwood, whose treatments of violence, vengeance, and death had been deepening with the passage of time, as the contrast between, say, the Dirty Harry films (1971–1988) and the clumsy yet humane *Gran Torino* (2008) illustrates. Here he bypasses nuanced thinking to produce a hard-fisted biopic organized mainly around action and suspense. After sketching out Kyle's all-American upbringing, youthful stints as a ranch hand and rodeo cowboy, and marriage to a (usually) patient wife, the movie depicts his military enlistment and training, multiple deployments to the Middle East, success as a sharpshooter, temporary addiction to combat-induced adrenaline—a theme more powerfully explored in Kathryn Bigelow's *The Hurt Locker* (2008)—and finally his departure from the service and volunteer work with wounded veterans. The film ends with a brief, elliptical account of Kyle's death at the hands of a marine veteran with post-traumatic stress disorder, who killed him at a shooting range where they had gone for an informal therapy session.

Critical opinions about Eastwood's film have been diverse, but the overall tone has been positive, with praise going to Cooper's acting, to Eastwood's success at humanizing the rifle-toting protagonist, and to the film as an extension of Eastwood's decades-long fascination with gunslingers and their guns. Eastwood himself says he makes war movies "because they're always loaded with drama and conflict" but adds that by showing the stresses undergone by veterans and their families, *American Sniper* "adds up to kind of an anti-war [message]."[26] This writer is not convinced, finding *American Sniper* to be a guts-and-glory drama that adds no luster to Eastwood's filmography. What value it has derives from its credentials as a topical biopic, not as a study of war and its horrifying human consequences.

Sully

Everything is unprecedented until it happens for the first time.
—Chesley Sullenberger

The protagonist of *Sully* is Chesley "Sully" Sullenberger, a U.S. Airways pilot who was hailed as a hero in January 2009 after taking his abruptly disabled Airbus A320 from a height of some 2,800 feet to an emergency landing in the Hudson River, having made an instant judgment that the nearest airports were too distant for the incapacitated craft to reach. There were no significant injuries, but Sullenberger was profoundly shaken by the experience, which he kept reliving in flashbacks and nightmares. Todd Komarnicki's screenplay takes an unexpected route into these events, organizing the narrative around an investigation by the National Transportation Safety Board, which has data suggesting that Sullenberger (Tom Hanks) and First Officer Jeffrey Skiles (Aaron Eckhart) did have sufficient power for a return to New York's LaGuardia Airport, whence the flight originated, or a landing at New Jersey's Teterboro Airport, fairly close and undoubtedly safer than setting down on a river. Following a great deal of technical debate, ethical discussion, and review of high-tech simulations executed by test pilots, the inquiry concludes that Sully and Skiles made the only decisions that could have worked under the circumstances, thereby saving their reputations and careers.

The portions of *Sully* that show Sullenberger's private life—learning to fly in the past, reassuring his wife in the present—qualify the film as a biopic rather than a fact-based drama revolving around a single headline-grabbing

FIGURE 6.4 Airline pilot Chesley "Sully" Sullenberger (Tom Hanks, right) and first officer Jeff Skiles (Aaron Eckhart) prepare to land their disabled plane in the Hudson River in *Sully* (2016). Frame enlargement.

occurrence. Its main liability is the by-the-numbers neatness of its construction, which proceeds from thought-provoking questions—perhaps the lifesaving feat was not a marvel of quick thinking under pressure but a potentially disastrous instance of bad judgment—to a series of exculpatory scenes that hammer home the hero's professional purity with diagrammatic precision, elbowing moral and psychological complexity off the screen. On another front, the film's skeptical take on the NTSB has been accused of propagandizing for Eastwood's antigovernment politics, a plausible charge that seems rather flimsy in this context.

The limitations of Komarnicki's screenplay are counterbalanced by Hanks's richly three-dimensional performance—his work as chief of a hijacked ship in Paul Greengrass's biopic *Captain Phillips* (2013) erased any hesitations about his ability to make vulnerability and emotional damage seem achingly real—and by Eastwood's directing, which is less surprising in cinematic terms than on the level of old-fashioned storytelling but unfailingly fluid, eloquent, and engaging nonetheless. Again reaching an enormous audience and profits to match, it is another worthy milestone in his worthy career.

Epilogue

At this writing, Eastwood is eighty-six years old and still hard at work, with yet another biopic in the making. Trade publications report that the new project is based on *Impossible Odds: The Kidnapping of Jessica Buchanan and Her Dramatic Rescue by SEAL Team Six*, a 2014 memoir in which Jessica Buchanan and her husband Erik Landemalm recount the events of three months in 2011 when she and another American aid worker were kidnaped in Somalia and held captive in the desert while Landemalm worked with various agencies to effect a rescue. Freedom finally arrived when President Obama approved the engagement of a SEAL team that parachuted in, killed the land pirates, and extracted the prisoners. The screenwriter is Brian Helgeland, who penned Eastwood's *Blood Work* in 2002 and the stunning *Mystic River* a year later.

Eastwood's late-career stock-in-trade is primarily modern Americana, whether with a military-political or pop-culture twist. If and when *Impossible Odds* comes into being, six of his seven films since 2009—the exception is *Hereafter* (2010), made between *Invictus* and *J. Edgar*—will have been biopics, underscoring the importance of this supple, adaptable genre to one of Hollywood cinema's key chroniclers of the American scene.

Notes

1 Ian Christie, "A Life on Film," in *Mapping Lives: The Uses of Biography*, ed. Peter France and William St. Clair (New York: Oxford University Press, 2002), 292.

2 William H. Epstein, "Introduction: Strategic Patriotic Memories," in *Invented Lives, Imagined Communities: The Biopic and American National Identity*, ed. William H. Epstein and R. Barton Palmer (Albany: State University of New York Press, 2016), 11.

3 Christie, "A Life on Film," 291.

4 Dennis Bingham, *Whose Lives Are They Anyway? The Biopic as Contemporary Film Genre* (New Brunswick, N.J.: Rutgers University Press, 2010), 10.

5 James Naremore, "Film Acting and the Arts of Imitation," *Film Quarterly* 65, no. 4 (Summer 2012): 40.

6 Naremore, 41.

7 Jay Scott, "*Bird*," *Globe and Mail*, October 14, 1988, Toronto edition, C1.

8 David Sterritt, "Hollywood Players Who've Made a Difference: Cassavetes, Eastwood, Martin, Nicholson," in *Guiltless Pleasures: A David Sterritt Film Reader* (Jackson: University Press of Mississippi, 2005), 38.

9 Desson Howe, "*Bird*," review of *Bird*, directed by Clint Eastwood, *Washington Post*, October 14, 1988, accessed August 12, 2017, http://www.washingtonpost.com/wp -srv/style/longterm/movies/videos/birdrhowe_a0b1cc.htm.

10 Jonathan Rosenbaum, "The Ten Best Jazz Films (1999 List)," JonathanRosenbaum .net, June 4, 1999, accessed October 9, 2013, http://www.jonathanrosenbaum.net/ 1999/05/the-ten-best-jazz-films-1999-list/.

11 Jane Perlez, "Clint Eastwood Directs Himself Portraying a Director," *New York Times*, September 16, 1990, accessed August 18, 2017, http://www.nytimes.com/ 1990/09/16/movies/film-clint-eastwood-directs-himself-portraying-a-director .html?pagewanted=all.

12 Perlez.

13 Michael Henry Wilson, "Truth, like Art, Is in the Eyes of the Beholder: *Midnight in the Garden of Good and Evil* and *The Bridges of Madison County*," in *Clint Eastwood: Interviews, Revised and Updated*, ed. Robert E. Kapsis and Kathie Coblenz (Jackson: University Press of Mississippi, 1999), 173.

14 Wilson, 171.

15 Terry Gross, "Eastwood's *Letters from Iwo Jima*," in *Clint Eastwood: Interviews*, 211.

16 Scott Foundas, "Eastwood on the Pitch: At Seventy-Nine, Clint Tackles Mandela in *Invictus*," in *Clint Eastwood: Interviews*, 243.

17 Ellen Cheshire, *Bio-Pics: A Life in Pictures* (London: Wallflower, 2015), 102.

18 David Sterritt, *The Cinema of Clint Eastwood: Chronicles of America* (London: Wallflower, 2014), 202.

19 Douglas McFarland, "J. Edgar: Eastwood's Man of Mystery," *Invented Lives, Imagined Communities: The Biopic and American National Identity*, ed. William H. Epstein and R. Barton Palmer (Albany: State University of New York Press, 2016), 146.

20 Ramin Setoodeh and Scott Foundas, "Should *Jersey Boys* Have Cast Movie Stars?," *Variety*, June 19, 2014, accessed August 19, 2017, http://variety.com/2014/film/ features/clint-eastwood-jersey-boys-movie-broadway-1201223827/.

21 Chris Kyle with Scott McEwen and Jim DeFelice, *American Sniper: The Autobiography of the Most Lethal Sniper in U.S. Military History* (New York: Harper, 2013), 80.

22 Kyle, 151.
23 Kyle, 289.
24 Kyle, 316.
25 Kyle, 370–371.
26 Ben Beaumont-Thomas, "Clint Eastwood: *American Sniper* and I Are Anti-War," *Guardian*, March 17, 2015, accessed August 18, 2017, https://www.theguardian.com/film/2015/mar/17/clint-eastwood-american-sniper-anti-war.

Part II

Controversies

● ●

7

"I Am a Camera"

• • • • • • • • • • • • • • • • • • • •

The Performative Gaze

MURRAY POMERANCE

> Some day, all of this will have to be devel-
> oped, carefully printed, fixed.
> —John Van Druten

The conceit that a movie star might be classified and categorized in terms of one single predominating characteristic is longstanding in the history of motion pictures and indeed suggests a way of thinking about and remembering figures that is not so very different from people's general approach to one another in everyday life. However much a cluster of attributes and tendencies is perceived by audiences, the "personality" (as we name it) can always be cumulated under one marquee aspect, a feature that makes possible nicknames, advertising, and caricature. With stars we have, for example, "plainspeaking" Barbara Stanwyck, "suave" Cary Grant, "innocently seductive" Marilyn Monroe, "homey" Jimmy Stewart, or "frenetic, explosive" Al Pacino. The headline does not fully describe the star, or point us in every direction necessary for understanding his or her complex body of work, but as a way of mnemonically encapsulating, packaging, and disseminating an image, it works, more or less, once it has been collectively applied.

The Seer

Not because I intend to conceive of his work as falling entirely under an abbreviating rubric in this way, nor forgetting that when one comes to write about Hollywood it is difficult to see anything very clearly—"Much of what is written about pictures and about picture people," writes Joan Didion, "approaches reality only occasionally and accidentally"[1]—I propose to suggest that Clint Eastwood can be understood as, above all else, "scrutinizing" or "perceptive," a kind of seer. As he enters fictional worlds as a character or creates them as a filmmaker, he spies out, surveys, and surveils. Standing far back from analysis, Amy Taubin labels Eastwood's gaze a "signature squint."[2] It is narrowed for improved focus, unblinking, unswerving. Bob Rubin, who worked as assistant director on *Dirty Harry* (1971), recollected to me the spontaneous "naturalness" of the Eastwood gaze, as much a part of the man off- as on-camera:

> It was part of his whole expression of being a fierce guy. . . . His eyes were a whole part of that, as was his mouth when he gritted his teeth. His teeth were a big part of that as well. . . . His eyes show grit, tremendous determination. He gets very serious. He had an intensity that every bit of that picture was important to him, every frame was important to him. . . . I don't think he was a fun guy to work with. That posture was one of taking charge off-camera, on-camera. He was the money. He was tough. He was not exactly a lot of laughs. You could tell in his eyes whether this was the right time to ask him about something.[3]

As to the "tremendous determination" behind the Eastwood gaze, one may think of Freud's reminder that obsessive visual images may be accompanied by obsessive thoughts.[4] The Eastwood character sees fully, truly, accurately, unrelentingly, and not rarely out of the back of his head. But is his vision affirmative and accumulating, or inquisitive? Guy Davenport reflects on his own childhood, "The purpose of things ought perhaps to remain invisible, no more than half known. People who know exactly what they are doing seem to me to miss the vital part of any doing."[5] For dramatic purposes, he can see other characters' depths before the film viewer does and thus leap into actions that are for us surprising and explosive (expectedly and relentlessly so). The Eastwood gaze, in fact, prepares audiences to enter a state of generalized readiness for surprise and explosion: because he gazes, he detects, and because he detects, he readies himself to act. If at some times he is a detective on-screen, he is always a camera.

Further: Eastwood tends toward *squinting*, a technique that leads to increased depth of field and the opportunity for distal focus. Not only does Eastwood see well; he sees at a distance, sees what is coming well before it is upon him, predicting or at least gleaning hints of what the future holds. One of the pleasures of watching and admiring Eastwood's screen work lies in our sense of repose: that we can relax in the trust that he has situations in hand, that his perceptions are guaranteed to outstrip our own. Perhaps, hints Davenport's observation, he is too reassuring, too predictive. All films relentlessly move onward, but in films starring Eastwood, a curious stability and stasis override the motor device of the plot, as though he has always been here, waiting and guarding, and will always be outside the sepulcher. The events of the story are mere blips.

The Weapon Gaze

One fastidious recursion into the Eastwood gaze and its implications can be found in the opening sequence of *High Plains Drifter* (1973). The central figure here (Eastwood), familiarly unnamed, is riding his horse slowly into the town of Lago (that sits, unsurprisingly, at the edge of a large mirroring lake [*lago*]). As director, Eastwood calls smartly for cinematographer Bruce Surtees to have his camera not at ground level, typical for most shots in films of this genre, but at the rider's height, metaphorically "in a saddle" (which may be as high as two yards off the ground), thus offering one of the few visions available in the Hollywood Western of what the civic world looks like to those who ride through it. Over the title music, we hear the clip-clop tread as the character "dollies" first into the town precincts and then down the main street, inspecting the everyday activities taking place on both flanks. The camera shows, among other things, a man sitting lazily in the shade outside the sheriff's office, a woman in a clean white shirt (a madam?) standing on her balcony, a timid older lady standing outside the hotel, a worried-looking barber, four men outside a saloon suspiciously watching this watcher, and a driver whipping his horses to tug a freight wagon. But by cutting into, and back out of, close-ups of these characters—the sweaty sheriff and his fly swatter, the serious face of the woman with the broom, Eastwood squinting back from beneath the shading brim of his hat—the filmmaker simulates the interplay of intensified gazes, as in a chain of showdowns. The townsfolk read his—and he reads their—surfaces for clues to identity and signals of alignment in a world of display and detection.

To again follow Davenport's clue, in decoding an unfamiliar world, one may be informed but never *enough*. What one "learns" is always provisional, insufficient, riddling—reason, indeed, to keep looking for more, with an eye that is insatiable. A way of looking that preceded (and prepared) the omnivorous, deeply focused, performance-oriented gaze of this rider, developed, according to Michael Fried, in eighteenth-century Europe (the tradition from which the American Western took its models). Fried notes, "The constitution of a new sort of beholder—a new 'subject'—whose innermost nature would consist precisely in the conviction of his absence from the scene of representation." This subject would possess an elevated, withdrawn view, open to all things. "The constitution of this new sort of beholder," Fried continues,

> envisioned a narrowing, a heightening, and an abstracting of the functions traditionally associated with beholding: a narrowing in that an entire universe of sources of interest and delight was now conceived to be, if not irrelevant to the experiencing of pictures, at any rate secondary in importance to the crucial issue of theatricality; a heightening in that the concern with theatricality signaled the attainment of an unprecedented level of cognitive acuteness with regard to the detection of proscribed actions and effects; and an abstracting in that the activity of beholding was now imagined to have found its rightest occasion and most intense satisfaction in its engagement with the fully realized *tableau*.[6]

After a quick drink at the saloon, our man is in the barber shop, awaiting a shave and hot bath. As he unbuttons his coat, we see the barber in the extreme foreground anxiously stropping his razor on leather. Eastwood is in the chair, covered by the barber's sheet and lathered up. Now three provocateurs amble across the street, enter, and surround Eastwood as the barber tries to work. They toss taunts and barbs, then open insults. But as the first man tries to swing the barber's chair around, the silent customer fires at him from beneath the sheet. The bullet hits the man square between the eyes, which pop open as he falls. With two successive shots, terminating the remaining pair, we see the pointed gun—not Eastwood's face—a utensil now metonymizing its aiming user with his aiming gaze. A late nineteenth-century critique in *St. James's Gazette* of James Whistler's etchings of palaces—etchings made in the 1880s, around the time depicted in *Drifter*—apotheosizes and predicts this sort of visual secrecy, by which action is hidden under the cover of perception: "He has been content to show us what his eyes can see, and not what his hand can do."[7]

The weaponized gaze was a central feature of Eastwood's earliest performances. In fact, it helped solidify his reputation as a coldhearted, businesslike, razor-sharp advocate of "fairness and justice"—or at least the well-balanced quid pro quo. The finale of Sergio Leone's *The Good, the Bad, and the Ugly* (1966) is both seminal and archetypal in this respect. Blondie (Eastwood) has finally outsmarted Tuco (Eli Wallach) and intuited his intent of stealing the bags of gold they have long sought and now located in an abandoned graveyard plot. Standing Tuco upon the narrow lip of one of the stones, with his hands bound and a noose around his neck, Eastwood loads the gold into his saddlebags, mounts, and rides off. Through all of this, there proceeds a dramatic chain of intercut facial portraits: Tuco, Blondie, and back again, with the light keyed on Tuco's desperately bugged-out, cupidinous eyes and Blondie's trademark narrow, diagnostic slits. Blondie rides off to the far horizon, there aiming his rifle, squinting capably and knowingly into the sight, and firing a single shot that splits Tuco's rope. This entire rhythmically extended sequence works through a conversational interplay between the two personalities, each embodied on-screen by virtue of his gaze. One is hungrily perspiring, conniving, grossly immoral; the other, having already performed his work of detection, is coolly cautious, professional, superior: "I see you and raise the ante."

The Gaze Iconized

A critical moment of establishment and iconization shows San Francisco cop Harry Callahan (Eastwood) in *Sudden Impact* (1983) pointing his immense Smith & Wesson pistol into the face of a thief he has cornered in the Acorn Café. This desperado has Harry's favorite waitress by the neck and is pointing his gun to her head. We look into Eastwood's face as he aims at the man's face, his gun barrel protruding toward the camera's wide-angle lens: "Go ahead, make my day." We sense that blowing the man's brains out would bring Harry a distinct, if perverse, pleasure. His face shows a relentless, chiseled, ugly determination, the eyes in a squint so that the corners of the lids sag to import a curious sagacity. This moment, more optical than merely dramatic, converts "Make my day!" into a gloatingly reassured self-evaluation, a bold claim that Eastwood can see everything everywhere—and better than anyone else—unblinking. Harry's seeing displaces mental reflection because it *is* reflection itself. For him, to see is always already to know, think, judge, rationalize, understand.

There are certain performative advantages to the accentuation of the gaze. First, as psychoanalytic criticism would argue, a dominating quality is lent the gazer, whose attention—essentially aesthetic admiration—displaces the object gazed upon as disempowered artifact. John Berger notes how "for the Impressionists the visible no longer presented itself to man in order to be seen. On the contrary, the visible, in continual flux, became fugitive."[8] Here is an alignment between the controlling gaze and its ever-evasive object founded in aesthetic theory, while in detection and policing, surveillance has linked the state's power to examine and observe with a methodical system of cataloging and measurement. "The exercise of discipline," writes Foucault, "presupposes a mechanism that coerces by means of observation" as he proceeds to imagine "observatories" operating with "eyes that must see without being seen" and in which "using techniques of subjection and methods of exploitation, an obscure art of light and the visible was secretly preparing a new knowledge of man" wherein "all power would be exercised solely through exact observation; each gaze would form a part of the overall functioning of power."[9] But the power to observe is not enough. "The mere possession of a criminal's image could be useless, or at least unwieldy, [Alphonse] Bertillon maintained," explains Tom Gunning[10]; what was needed was a systematization of the visioning process, based on typification, labeling, measurement, comparison, and recording. The narrative plinth upon which Eastwood's characters stand invariably posits him accomplishing an act not merely of sight but of detection, a systematic but invisible package of calculations that form the observations he makes into a theory of human behavior: "Under the Bertillon system [of charting and cataloging] the photograph [read, Eastwood's photographic gaze] finds its place within a logic of analysis into paradigmatic components, which are separated from a specific singular body in order to be circulated, compared, and then combined in order to point the finger of guilt."[11]

As Berger suggests, the male gaze—Eastwood's—disempowers its object as well. "Men act and women appear," wrote Berger[12]; and "in a world ordered by sexual imbalance, pleasure in looking has been split between active/male and passive/female. In patriarchy, this feminization subjugates, organizes, shapes, and delimits."[13] In the scene from *Sudden Impact*, the waitress must become Harry's "male" ally as she is threatened by the thug's gun, since it is the criminal and his masculinity that must be diminished ("feminized") by Harry's focus and direct threat. We see the thug turn his head aside but keep an askance gaze on Harry, his eyes bulging open in fear and subjection. To the extent that the Eastwood character can be made dominant only by virtue of his ocularity, the audience perhaps feels empowered looking at him, and he need exert himself only minimally in action to support or reassert the augmentation of power that gazing has already provided him.

Further, the gaze is most clearly and emphatically seen in a facial close-up, the cinematic technique that frames and circulates the star persona most intensively. But the close-up in and of itself, absent the ocular expression, is itself reductive to the degree that it draws forward the surface of the face and the proportions of the facial organs in a "beautiful" construction. To emphasize in a close-up that as subject Eastwood is watching, taking the world in, noticing life, is to empower him as an active agent. The commercially useful image of the face that he derives can thus be achieved without resulting in the simplification of aestheticization. The gaze brings the observed being closer to the audience—in Kracauer's terms, "summon[s] physical existence"[14]—and thus embodies Eastwood's performance in a material ground that is unquestionably real.

By utilizing the gaze to establish characterological feeling and alignment, Eastwood is freed from having to use bodily gesture to the same purpose—and freed as well from speech (this way becoming an actor liberated from the script). The eyes enunciate by looking, through the squinting focality and the perduring nature of their openness, and the looking is tellingly (and wondrously) silent. One might note that in his moments of signally idiosyncratic diegetic looking, Eastwood joins the figures of silent film in a special way. Less what they saw than the intensity with which they saw it was the radiant point with Lillian Gish, Buster Keaton, and others. And so with Eastwood, who resembles such icons as Gary Cooper, Henry Fonda, Randolph Scott, and John Wayne in using the eyes expressively but carries the gaze distinctively further, both temporally on-screen and diegetically in terms of the way his eyework fashions the story.

Could it not be said, as well, that a staring, navigating, comprehending, assimilating, cataloging, dominating, ennobling, triumphing, and self-aggrandizing Eastwoodian eye artfully contradicts the revolutionary eye in the surrealist paradigm offered up by Bataille and Dalí—what Martin Jay calls "the most ignoble eye imaginable"?[15] That one was an eye that dared to descend, an eye for which swimming in the dirt elevated it into the light, an eye, in fact, that brought light to all that proper civilization had boldly secreted and banished—thus, an anti-Eastwoodian eye, as Eastwood is only a symbol of what he claims as the highest proprieties: just behavior, cleanliness, balance, sincerity, piety.

As to the explicit link between Eastwood's penetrating gaze and his characters' heroism—for he is always the hero of his films, to the extent that the films have a hero—even in this there is a conventionality and secular piety, a looking toward the vast garden of the untrammeled space of the West and a hope for purity. This, too, runs against the surrealist grain. Georges Bataille writes of the decortication of a bullfighter producing a female's orgasm[16]; does Eastwood's gaze on-screen ever lead a female character to such heights? "The pornographic imagination," writes Susan Sontag, "tends to make one person interchangeable with another and all people interchangeable with things"[17]; one might argue it carries us into the ethereal miasma where organic form becomes its constituency, where boundaries are eclipsed. Eastwood is against all this. His gaze is specific, pointed, defining. It measures space, estimates personalities, calculates probabilities, aligns motives, weighs outcomes, knows the territory.

Behind a Camera

It can be misleading to attempt an understanding of Eastwood unilaterally on the basis of his screen acting, since his directorial efforts, begun when he had become a notably bankable star, have progressively produced interesting films containing passages of significant philosophical allusion. And in him we may find a case where Richard Dyer's proclamation about Eastwood, Chaplin, Keaton, Lupino, and others, that "We have to make a theoretical distinction between their role as star and their other role in the production," is perhaps overdetermined.[18] Even his earliest directorial work uses ocularity to make suggestions about point of view, attitude, and philosophical approach. For example, Eastwood directed the suicide jumper sequence of *Dirty Harry* because Don Siegel shied away from it, as I was informed by Rubin.[19] As Harry ascends toward the jumper on the precipice, we see that he operates the manual controls of a cherry picker with his eyes trained down on the ground that is dropping away from him, not on the controls themselves. He is a camera in deep focus. Once he is up at the ledge, he scans the scene below, spending relatively little time looking at the threatening jumper who is right next to him. Even after knocking the man unconscious and "flying down" with the body in his grasp, he gazes beyond the present surround, into a broader, if slightly disorienting, perspective on the city as the topos of moral trouble. "That's why they call me 'Dirty' Harry, they always give me the dirty jobs," he tells his colleague: for "dirty job," read "scanning the faraway."

The centrality of ocularity is especially noteworthy in a number of Eastwood productions, including, for example, *Gran Torino* (2008), with its numerous optical confrontations, hoarsely whispered threats, pistol and rifle pointing, and squinting menace bringing it near the top of a list of Eastwood classics. Especially provocative here, beyond the moments of interracial inspection and sour-tongued meditation, is a new kind of showdown, this one mediated intensively by camera placement and lighting. Walt Kowalski (Eastwood) has been visited by Father Janovich (Christopher Carley) for a nocturnal consultation about evil. As they sit in the Kowalski living room, Eastwood arranges for the shot/reverse-shot construction outlaying their dialogue to be built from images lit with extreme contrast, so that one side of each character's face is in total darkness. Then with a slight repositioning, Father Janovich is in full profile and Walt partially lit in his armchair with an ocean of darkness around him. This darkness is not shadow, but an absolute lack of light, a quintessential nothingness. Eastwood's directorial point is made visually, not through talk: men live against an utter void, one that Walt can see quite plainly. No light (no sight), no form; no form, no life. "I work very closely with the DoP," Eastwood told Geoff Andrew,

> and I'll often say "That's too much light!" I just want a sketch, I don't want to see everything. The audience will make up what they see. In the old days they'd have special little lights on a character's eyes. But sometimes you don't want to see the eyes. It's a question of looking *in* at a movie, rather than have it look *out* at you: the audience has to come to a film, be part of it. It's like acting. I've seen a lot of actors throw themselves at the audience, whereas with others you have to go to them a little, put yourselves into them. That makes for a more thoughtful movie.[20]

What gains emphasis through this cinematographic/directorial trick in *Gran Torino* is Walt's extremity and clarity of viewpoint, his definitive intellectual posture regarding the imminence of death but more generally all matters of moral commitment. For him the world really is darkness and light, evil and goodness; there are moral imperatives. But also visible is the filmmaker's indebtedness to the camera as an articulator of a point of view. What we learn here about Walt and about moral life we learn most fully through the shaping of light in the scene. In the conversation itself, Janovich's platitudinous balm has been rinsed away by the gang threats to Walt's now-befriended Asian neighbors. Though neither he nor Walt knows what steps Walt will take to remedy the situation, they are in perfect agreement that the darkness must somehow, in reality, be banished, yet this very dark, too dark, quintessentially dark darkness merely sucks in and swallows light, negates light completely.

Watching the Screen

In *Changeling* (2008), we discover a remarkable directorial strategy involving not the filmmaker's, not the character's, but the audience's opticality, which reveals Eastwood's real majesty of staging for display as well as his keen attentiveness to the importance, for spectators as for filmmakers, of using the eyes. To make plain what Eastwood accomplishes here I must take a lengthy synoptic pass, but my intent is to try to replicate the structure of the film:

We are in the Lincoln Park section of Los Angeles in March of 1928. Christine Collins (Angelina Jolie), a supervisor at the Pacific Telephone Company, and her young son Walter (Gattlin Griffith) live in a cozy bungalow where we follow them as, in dappled shadows, they dance through their daily routine: Christine rousing Walter, measuring his height in a door frame, serving up his cereal, escorting him to school; roller-skating through her jabbering team of telephone operators; picking Walter up later on, walking with him in long shot while he confesses that he had a fistfight. As tightly bonded friends, these two do not need to pay rigorous attention to one another. Daily life is happening as always in a quiet, tree-lined, comfortably unpretentious neighborhood.

When Christine bends over Walter to ask about the fight, we note with some delicious clarity the period-style clothing the boy is wearing—wool cap, necktie, striped shirt, jacket. The conversation migrates to the boy's father, who left the family, and as they walk and converse about him, we look down upon Walter (from her point of view) and up to Christine (from his). Now it is evening, and she is holding his hand as he tips toward sleep. They hug in the shadow, and she carries him to his bedroom.

The next morning, an overcast sky. She takes a telephone call, finds that she has to go into work even though she promised to take Walter to the movies,

FIGURE 7.1 Angelina Jolie in her cloche hat and scarlet lipstick in *Changeling* (2008). Frame enlargement.

and leaves him sitting in a chair facing the radio. "I'll be home before it gets dark," says she. He assures her he's not afraid of anything. A long dolly shot of him waving from the window as (with our accompaniment) she walks away, the tidy house gliding behind her.

A busy day makes Christine miss her tram. A medium portrait shot of Jolie in her cloche hat and scarlet lipstick, walking wearily to her house, turning on the lights, calling Walter . . . opening the door to his room . . . finding the food she had prepared still in the refrigerator.

In her bedroom, in the sitting room, on the porch outside, no one. "Walter, it's time to come in, honey." Dusk, all the colors are muted. Two little girls roll up but haven't seen Walter. Ah, she thinks she sees him play-swordfighting on the sidewalk, but as she approaches, no, it's two other boys. Back home she phones the police. A cold voice at the other end of the line, querying her relation to the child, how long he's been gone. Has she checked around the neighborhood? Maybe he's lost track of time. "Our policy is that we don't dispatch on missing child cases for twenty-four hours."

Close shots of Christine distraught. Fade to morning, a police car pulling up. Two uniforms on the sidewalk as neighbors spy. Christine in shadow, her house lights turned out. Gently touching Walter's bedspread. Sitting with his teddy bear.

Move forward to DeKalb, Illinois, more than three months later, a young boy and man eating at a country lunch bar, the boy in shadow and the man a well-lit, rather hopeless type. He can't pay now but will run home to get his wallet, leaving his "son" as collateral. The day winds on without the man returning and finally the owner calls the police. We cut back to Christine at work. Captain J. J. Jones (Jeffrey Donovan), Lincoln Park Juvenile Division, enters the operator's room: "He's alive, Mrs. Collins. He was picked up two days ago by police in DeKalb, Illinois. He's unhurt." She breaks down in tears, embraces the other operators. Transition to Jones and Christine moving swiftly through a crowd of reporters and photographers at Union Station. "The important thing now is to reunite this little lady with her son." She is introduced to the police chief, who stands pompously in full dress uniform, ready to use Christine and Walter as promotions for his department's efficiency. The train pulls in behind him, brown passenger cars full of promise. She strides along the platform, breaks into a run. The camera zooms in on the child who stands on the before her, a slightly different woolen cap on his head now, a different bowtie and jacket. His little-boy gaze burns into her, the typical Eastwood gaze. But, "That's not my son!" she says.

This is twenty-two minutes into the film.

And as (Eastwood-style) we peer hard into the boyish face, as the kid rushes forward to throw his arms around Mom, we are suddenly positioned to realize what Eastwood has done to us with his long narrative unreeling, his unwinding and devious rope: we have no way to be certain whether Christine is right in denying this child or whether—having lost some delicate control of her mind, lost her picture of Walter in the profound anxiety of the past months while agonizing in his absence—she is making a mistake. Because *we cannot remember* what he looked like at the beginning of the film, having failed to look at him closely. Eyes had we, but we did not see.

The story presses onward, both the child and the mother urging their conflicting claims. But it is more and more difficult to achieve certainty. Christine, we may recall, has consistently been (a) perceptually handicapped, that cloche hat partly covering her eyes; or else (b) preoccupied and distracted at work with the carping demands of dozens of eager and confused telephone operators; or else (c) moving nervously around a largely unilluminated house; or else (d) chatting with Walter without really stopping to see what he looks like (as will happen with those whose bonds are tightest). Walter himself was only rarely seen face on, this by Eastwood's kenning design, and even when we did see the young face, it lacked telltale marks or features, sweet enough yet not really what one could call "personable"—not, for example, the intensively marked face of his mother. Further, the scenario jumped from one location to another, each a loving re-creation and rich entrancement to the eye. The same can be said for the actors' clothing, the dilute sense of color, the lulling music. *Everything in all directions . . . except that little boy's face.*

Can we claim, ever, to have taken a good look at Walter? Can we be absolutely certain that this child on the platform is *not* him, as Christine claims? Jolie's huge ocularity in *Changeling* (Eastwood emphasizes her big eyes) metonymizes—by simulating and referring back to—Eastwood's calculated ocularity as filmmaker and as performer himself. She observes by searching, thus looking to the immediate future (the space ahead of her as she moves) to predict and guarantee itself. But the failure to locate her son—hers and ours—conforms to a particular complication Eastwood had begun to explore with *Blood Work* (2002): that the world becomes increasingly complex and visually rich as we age. There is more to note, and notation is harder.

Tiring Eyes

With *Blood Work*, released when the filmmaker was seventy-two, we see the beginning of an exploration of his own process of aging, his own deterioration. Eastwood stars as Terry McCaleb, an aging detective and beneficiary of a heart transplant. He becomes involved with a complex and cruel crime, not disconnected from the death through which the substitute heart was provided for him. But regardless of the complication of the plot, what is fascinating to watch is Terry's slow movement, his notable shortness of breath, and his perceptual weakness, which finally leads to a disastrous situation involving the killer he has been seeking and a woman to whom he has become attached. Here Eastwood is manifestly no longer the hero of *Dirty Harry* or *The Good, the Bad, and the Ugly* and their sequels, no longer that sharply reflexed protagonist of *The Outlaw Josey Wales* (1976) or *Pale Rider* (1985). This is a man who struggles for success but can never be certain of achievement. When he looks forward, he sees only what is directly in front of his face.

Ironically, then, in a visit to Dr. Fox (Angelica Huston) for a routine examination, yet also extended throughout the film, Terry is an optically passive force, a figure quite explicitly to be looked at. Eastwood frames the beginning of the scene with a shot upward into the glaring medical lamp under which we will find him during Terry's endoscopy. A screen shows the medical probe jiggling near his heart, while he lies passively on the table. Dr. Fox, at this

FIGURE 7.2 Eastwood's scrutinizing "Dirty" Harry, gone from *Blood Work* (2002). Frame enlargement.

moment the Eastwood doppelgänger, is the one looking. As they converse about his medication, Terry's eyes are closed while she scans his face carefully. Even when he partially sits up to look into her face, Terry's is not a gaze, merely an awakeness to the moment. But in an ensuing shot, as he is wheeled down the corridor by an orderly, there is a pause as they pass the door of a young boy. From inside the kid's room, we look out at Terry on his stretcher, turning his head and optically sucking in everything he can see (while we cannot). In this swift look, the functional detective has returned, dogged if bedraggled, a pickup of sorts on the Henry James who recollected as the "germ" of one of his stories "a seed as minute and wind-blown as that casual hint . . . dropped unwittingly."[21]

For the most part in *Blood Work*, the character choreography shows how aging and physical injury or deterioration can disable the active gaze and thus how there is nothing natural or essentialist about Eastwood's recurring optical display of acuity, sensitivity, forward-lookingness, and calculated estimation: it is all an achievement, learned, honed, refined, and expanded according to occupational need. When time and entropy have at him, the Eastwood character is degraded into a shell passing in and out of self-consciousness, in and out of sleep.

By contrast, *American Sniper* (2014) is an unmistakable paean to youthfully sighted, targeting, prescient vision—a vision associated in this film with male militarism. In Chris Kyle (Bradley Cooper), we have not only a man whose character and identity direct him to an aggressive and precise way of looking but a human weapon, a kind of robotic presence, all of the energies and abilities of which have been focused on a single systematized principle of detecting, aiming, and extending the self brutally by means of the fired projectile. As a soldier, the sniper has the advantage of acting at a distance and is thus prepared and established to make contact with an enemy agent who does not sense his presence, notwithstanding an irony illuminated by Marvin Harris:

> When warfare was a prominent means of population control, and when the technology of warfare consisted primarily of primitive hand-held weapons, male chauvinist lifestyles were necessarily ascendant. Insofar as neither of these conditions is true of today's world, liberationists are correct in predicting the decline of male chauvinist lifestyles. . . . Let us hope that this occurs as a result of the elimination of the need for police or military personnel rather than as a result of perfecting battle tactics that don't depend on physical strength.[22]

The controlling male gaze is an anachronism, since the object of control, the "beautiful" focus, is in another space and since the kill betrays not a molding and reforming power but a judgment and a terminus. Yet the technology and tactic of *Sniper* go beyond distance-warfare, a mode we also see enacted in, say, *Syriana* (2006) when, from a closeted war room in Washington and through computer-enhanced communications technology, a drone strike is enabled halfway around the world. With Kyle, part of the equation is the shooter's physical emplacement secretly at the periphery of the scene, his ability to see with human eyes the character and action of the enemy he is about to slay. Thus is built a deeply rooted moral structure within and behind the act of looking. Far more relevantly than a declaration of power relations, this open engagement of the shooter's eye and the target's movement—reflexive—asks where the good is in looking, how right it can be to act upon what one (merely) sees. One is reminded, indeed, of Debord's assertion that "spectacle isn't a collection of images, but a social relation between people, mediated by images."[23] For a filmmaker, this is, of course, *the* pungent and overwhelming question.

Metaphysical Gaze

Clint Eastwood is fundamentally a transcendental filmmaker, whose work, in both performance and direction, moves beyond a depiction of our social predicament—seen in contemporary or allegorical, historical terms—and our confining personalities. More and more as he ages, he is interested in what lies outside of all this eyework, a ring of uncertainty that includes philosophical speculation, aesthetic astonishment, and religious doubt. Thus the importance of the confrontation with the priest and the eye contact with the Asians in *Gran Torino*. Thus in *Unforgiven* (1992), quite beyond a plot woven with tales of revenge and true justice, there is a visual concentration on the purposiveness in men's eyes: Morgan Freeman's doomed Ned Logan, Gene Hackman's malevolent Little Bill Daggett, and Eastwood's Bill Munny, all intent in their lives to serve different purposes but each coming alive through characteristic ways of looking. Indeed, as Munny finally confronts Daggett, central to his preoccupation is that Daggett should watch him at his gruesome and punitive gunwork in the same way that Logan had been given no choice but to watch Daggett at his. In this film, people see the violence being perpetrated upon them, and this metaphysical insight goes beyond the simpler question of balancing the equation of right and wrong, powerful and powerless, looker and subject of the eye. What we might call the "metaphysical gaze" is present in the development of Hoover's self-questioning and malicious bent for surveillance and examination in *J. Edgar* (2011) as well as throughout *Blood Work*, as Terry sees in every moment of exertion the possible limit of his life. We find it in *Mystic River* (2003), in the forlorn gaze of young Dave Boyle (Cameron Bowen), driven away from his home and friends, or in the helpless, Job-like gaze of Jimmy Markum (Sean Penn), crying to heaven when he learns that his daughter has been slain. The metaphysical gaze inhabits *Jersey Boys* (2014), too, within a strange transformation where the ocularization becomes orality: the four young male protagonists (now become the Four Seasons) repetitively avoid gazing at one another or at the people they talk to but instead morph into a virtually electric onstage mode with eyes deadened and focus lost, their mouths magically expressing observation of the circulating world.

Yet there is no work of Eastwood's—nor, perhaps, a work of any filmmaker now—more profoundly engaged with the conundrum of special vision and its questionable powers than *Hereafter* (2010), with its psychic, George (Matt Damon), able to see into the future or the past merely by touching someone's hand, and its tormented news reporter, Marie (Cécile de France), recapitulating the voyage of Lazarus as she succumbs to a tidal wave and is then reborn as someone who has seen the Other Side and cannot get the experience out of her mind. George is making a lot of money reading hands, but he feels he has come to the end of his tether, and although his cupidinous brother wants him to continue the business, George has been touched once too often by the horrors of other people's lives (a subtle homage to the angels' plight in Wenders's *Wings of Desire* [1987]). Sight having become, for him, a nightmare, the only route to salvation is to stop allowing people to touch him, in this particular case touch him literally, since it is through the contact of hands that his extraordinary vision is activated. (One may reflect how, with a handshake, Eastwood's creative vision is activated into a film project: the touch of hands brings about a vision.)

Marie, by contrast, has had an astounding, enriching, deeply enchanting vision of a domain more glorious than this one. Her problem is not finding a way to retreat into this other world but finding a way to sustain conviction in it, having seen "another possibility." She must finally leave her boyfriend, quit her job, and proceed into authorship, since only by writing the truth of what she's found can she make her way forward in life. That George should meet Marie is, of course, the viewer's fondest hope for him, a proper end to his envisioning, and like Claude Lelouch in *Toute une vie* (1974), Eastwood makes us linger until the film's very final moment to see played out the conjunction we have already imagined. As Douglas McFarland reminds us, "In the conclusion to her book, [Marie] admits that she will probably never know if her glimpse of the afterlife was genuine or merely a fantasy," and in the end, much the same can probably be said of George and his visions.[24] Yet more than either of them, Eastwood's concern is what the viewer can come to know by seeing: how all of us touch our way forward, toward an incalculable otherworldliness, one vision at a time. In the anticipation of visual pleasure that George and Marie guide us to experience lies the link between sight, transcendence, beauty, and the clear light of mortality.

Notes

1   Joan Didion, "In Hollywood," in *The White Album* (New York: Noonday Press, 1990), 162.
2   Amy Taubin, "Staying Power," *Clint Eastwood: Interviews, Revised and Updated*, ed. Robert E. Kapsis and Kathie Coblentz (Jackson: University Press of Mississippi, 2013), 193.
3   Bob Rubin, interview with author, July 4, 2015.
4   Sigmund Freud, "A Mythological Parallel to a Visual Obsession," in *On Creativity and the Unconscious: Papers on the Psychology of Art, Literature, Love, Religion*, ed. Benjamin Nelson (New York: Harper & Row, 1965), 42.
5   Guy Davenport, "Finding," in *The Geography of the Imagination* (San Francisco: North Point Press, 1981), 366.
6   Michael Fried, *Absorption and Theatricality: Painting and Beholder in the Age of Diderot* (Chicago: University of Chicago Press, 1988), 104, emphasis in original.
7   James Abbott McNeill Whistler, *The Gentle Art of Making Enemies* (New York: Dover, 1967), 103.
8   John Berger, *Ways of Seeing* (London: Penguin, 1972), 18.
9   Michel Foucault, "The Means of Correct Training," *Discipline and Punish* (New York: Pantheon, 1977), 170–171.
10 Tom Gunning, "Tracing the Individual Body: Photography, Detectives, and Early Cinema," in *Cinema and the Invention of Modern Life*, ed. Leo Charney and Vanessa Schwartz (Berkeley: University of California Press, 1995), 29.
11 Gunning, 32.
12 Berger, *Ways of Seeing*, 45.
13 Laura Mulvey, *Visual and Other Pleasures* (Bloomington: Indiana University Press, 1989).
14 Siegfried Kracauer, *Theory of Film: The Redemption of Physical Reality* (Chicago: University of Chicago Press, 1995), 231.
15 Martin Jay, *Downcast Eyes: The Denigration of Vision in Twentieth-Century French Thought* (Berkeley: University of California Press, 1994), 221.
16 Lord Auch (Georges Bataille), *Story of the Eye*, trans. Joachim Neugroschal, accessed July 7, 2015, http://supervert.com/elibrary/georges_bataille/story_of _the_eye.
17 Susan Sontag, "The Pornographic Imagination," in *Styles of Radical Will* (New York: Picador, 2002), 53.
18 Richard Dyer, *Stars*, new ed. (London: BFI, 1999), 154.
19 Rubin, interview with author.
20 Geoff Andrew, "The Quiet American," in *Clint Eastwood: Interviews*, 220.
21 Henry James, *The Art of the Novel: Critical Prefaces* (Chicago: University of Chicago Press, 1934; 2011), 119.

22 Marvin Harris, *Cows, Pigs, Wars, and Witches: The Riddles of Culture* (New York: Vintage, 1989), 106–107.

23 Guy Debord, *La Société du spectacle* (Paris: Éditions Champ Libre, 1983), 10, my translation.

24 Douglas McFarland, "Eastwood's Dream: The Philosophy of Absence in *Hereafter*," in *The Philosophy of Clint Eastwood*, ed. Richard T. McClelland and Brian B. Clayton (Lexington: University Press of Kentucky, 2014), 224.

8

"You Ain't Ugly like Me; It's Just That We Both Got Scars"

Women in Eastwood's Films

LUCY BOLTON

A stark dichotomy exists between Clint Eastwood's own conception of his attitude to women in his films and the more popular perception of his films as misogynist.[1] He has stated that he gives strong roles to women—indeed, stronger than his own roles—and has argued that this makes him a feminist.[2] On the other side, allegations of misogyny abound in relation to the way in which women are so frequently raped, assaulted, and disposed of in many of his films. As ex-partner Sondra Locke writes sarcastically in her tell-all autobiography, *The Good, the Bad, and the Very Ugly: A Hollywood Journey*, "The woman in *Misty* was a psychotic killer; in *Beguiled* all the females cut off Clint's leg, then murdered him with poisonous mushrooms; in *Two Mules [for Sister Sara]* the woman was a foul-mouthed person posing as a nun; in *The Gauntlet* I play a hooker who'd been raped in an unthinkable fashion; and in *Tightrope* almost every woman in it was a sadistic or masochistic hooker. That's a pretty good record for a feminist filmmaker."[3]

Appraising all of Eastwood's films, including those in which he has starred or directed, or fulfilled both these roles, reveals a more complex relationship with women than many scholars and viewers imagine. Here I want to bring some of these female characters to the foreground, while thinking about how the Eastwood persona relates to them, and consider how women have shaped his star image by reflecting, supporting, diverting, and occasionally exceeding his on-screen presence.

Only a few of Eastwood's films feature leading female characters. The vast majority are studies of masculinity, from excessively macho killers to emasculated victims.[4] Within his body of work stretching from 1964 to the present day, however, there are several unconventional and defiant female protagonists and other more minor but significant female characters. For a star whose persona is based so squarely on the figure of the male loner, it is surprising how many women feature in the motivations, journeys, and final outcomes of his many excursions into the flights, fancies, and perils of masculinity.

Genres, Classics, and Star Types

Eastwood is known primarily for his Western films, notably the Sergio Leone spaghetti Westerns, and for the *Dirty Harry* (1971) cycle, in which he inhabits the persona of the cynical lone avenger. Within these broad-brush types lurk variations and permutations that are interestingly related to women on-screen. For example, in the Leone Westerns, the female characters are barely developed beyond hostages, victims, and bystanders, but in Eastwood's own Westerns such as *The Outlaw Josey Wales* (1976) and *Unforgiven* (1992), women's relationships with the Eastwood character are a sustained element of the film's story. Similarly, although women are usually victims of killers and rapists in the *Dirty Harry* cop films, in subsequent Harry movies such as *The Enforcer* (1976), he is paired with a challenging female partner, and in the Eastwood-directed *Sudden Impact* (1983), it is a female avenger who is the perpetrator of the crimes. In films such as *Tightrope* (1984) and Eastwood's *Blood Work* (2002), the Eastwood character has to engage with women in various roles during the course of his investigations; as victims, yes, but also witnesses, fellow professionals, and superiors in the workplace. These women contribute to the development of the Eastwood characters in specific films and thereby also to his star persona.

Thinking in terms of character types is helpful for understanding the complexity of Eastwood's relationship to women in his films. In his Jungian analysis, "Outside the Walls: Men's Quest in the Films of Clint Eastwood," Al Collins describes the archetypes of masculinity as "Warrior," "Lover," "Magician," and "King."[5] Collins sees all these in the Eastwood persona, but I want to elaborate upon them. In relation to women, Eastwood plays four main roles: lecher, lover, father, and ally. These types are not always clearly demarcated, but rather they coalesce into the whole Eastwood persona. *Sudden Impact*, for example, features Eastwood as lover and ally; *True Crime* (1999) depicts

Eastwood as lecher and father; and *Unforgiven* portrays him as ally and father. The category of ally is particularly noteworthy in the Eastwood films and is the dynamic in play in my opening title quote from *Unforgiven*, taken from the conversation between wounded gunfighter William Munny (Eastwood) and facially scarred prostitute Delilah (Ann Levine).[6] Allegiances between Eastwood and a female character are not necessarily based on sexual attraction but upon his appreciation of the women's position as an outsider whose voice is not being heard.[7] This is not to say that Eastwood always treats women well—in *High Plains Drifter* (1973), he is callous and exploitative, and in *The Gauntlet* (1977), he is relentlessly patronizing—but it is a regular feature of the Eastwood character that he is singularly aligned with a female character in need. Paul Smith claims that these alliances, presented as being with women's voices and the strength of their femininity, are always finally negated in the narrative in that the women are recouped by patriarchal law, "their independence replaced by a traditional, disempowered status in relation(ship) with the male protagonist." Still, as Smith observes, "they leave their marks on the experience of the movie."[8]

There are plenty of Eastwood films where women barely speak, such as *Firefox* (1982), or where women are cut-out characters fulfilling the basic functions of girlfriend, secretary, and movie star, as in *White Hunter Black Heart* (1990). Also, plenty of "sexist arena" films exist, such as crime capers *The Rookie* (1990) or *City Heat* (1984) or action-adventure stories like *The Eiger Sanction* (1975), where women are decoration or function merely to demonstrate an aspect of Eastwood's character. For example, in *The Eiger Sanction*, rejecting the sexual proposition of his student (Candice Rialson) shows he is a man not easily tempted but slapping her backside shows in an overtly sexist way that he is not immune to her charms, as does his frantic effort to mount a rock face when trying to reach the young mountain guide George (Brenda Venus) who has just flashed her breasts at him as an enticement.

In this chapter, I will briefly develop Eastwood's four types of masculinity in relation to women, which I identified above, and then examine how these types enable the creation and development of some striking partnerships with women on-screen before concentrating on the women who stand out as individuals across Eastwood's sixty-year career.

The Lecher

Occasionally, Eastwood is an outright lech. The opening scene of *True Crime* is an excruciating picture of Eastwood as Steve Everett, an aging journalist, attempting to seduce Michelle Ziegler (Mary McCormack), a young female colleague. Ziegler is killed in a car accident on her way home, leaving Steve to take over her investigation of a troubling death row case. The film proceeds to present Steve as a serial seducer, who is sleeping with another colleague's wife, and as a negligent father as well as a faithless, heartless husband to a depressed wife at the end of her tether. His wife, Barbara (Diane Venora), finally throws him out, and the film ends with the pitiful image of the unchanged Steve, trying to pick up a young shop assistant (Lucy Liu). Although the main narrative has resolved neatly and the execution of a wrongly convicted man has been avoided due to Steve's efforts, the film ends with the pessimistic image of the unreformed lecherous Everett, now older and single, still a lascivious skirt chaser. Eastwood refuses to console us with the idea that this leopard might change his spots.

Another lech is the eponymous *Joe Kidd* (1972). Eastwood's Joe shamelessly makes a move on the girlfriend of the man trying to hire him, Frank Harlan (Robert Duvall), while Harlan is in the room next door. Joe receives a welcoming response to his intense advances, but his overwhelming behavior is too strong to be termed *seduction*. He is a force of sexual potency, not brooking resistance. Similarly, in *High Plains Drifter*, he rapes the peculiarly insulting Callie Travers (Marianna Hill) and assumes (wrongly) that Sarah Belding (Verna Bloom) is an inevitable conquest. In a film where the Drifter brings out the worst in nearly all the town's inhabitants, it is in the arena of sexual appetites that the women are targeted. In *Joe Kidd*, and *Coogan's Bluff* (1968), Eastwood's characters are aware of their sexual attractiveness, and they use it forcefully, "coolly laying any woman around."[9] Don Siegel says of him, "Clint is a tarnished super-hero, actually an anti-hero . . . He's not a white knight rescuing the girl; he seduces her."[10] This seduction, however, is sometimes closer to sexual assault. Embracing young Amy (Pamelyn Ferdin) in *The Beguiled* (1971) while claiming that at twelve years she is "old enough for kisses" is a signal of the sexual omnivore he will become in that film, and in *Coogan's Bluff*, the cowboy in the city happily sleeps with the killer's vulnerable girlfriend, Linny Raven (Tisha Sterling), and the police psychologist, Julie Roth (Susan Clark), in order to further his investigation.

This is a surprising twist on the popular Eastwood persona of "the Good," the independent male loner who is not particularly interested in women on-screen. In these "lecher" roles, Eastwood is a sexual force who overwhelms women, his "erotic allure used as lethally as a gun."[11] Here a surprising confluence occurs with reports of his offscreen fascination with women and his complicated love life. Although keeping a low profile in the media and maintaining a notoriously private life, his relationships with women are charted in several biographies, including *Sexual Cowboy* (1993), where Douglas Thompson talks about how Eastwood has always "brazenly pursued the ladies. And not just to flirt but in a serious way."[12] This element of sexual predator is not at the foreground of the Eastwood persona: his characters are more often shown as the erstwhile, potential, or temporary lover.

The Lover

In his first appearance in episode one of *Rawhide* (1959), "Incident of the Tumbleweed," where he is described as being "always first in the chow line," Eastwood is the member of the gang who is interested in the ladies, evident from his instant appreciation of voluptuous prisoner Dallas (Terry Moore). Eastwood's beautiful facial features, luscious hair, and tall, broad-shouldered body ensure he is often fetishized on-screen as the focus of female attention and set up as an unequivocal lust object for all. In *Hang 'Em High* (1968), having been nearly hanged and then later shot, Cooper's injured body is ripe for nursing by Rachel Warren (Inger Stevens). Although her caring is interpreted as "nagging" by Cooper, he is moved by her story of loss and assault, and they share a common desire for revenge: "We all have our ghosts, Marshall; you hunt your way, I hunt mine." Their kinship and intimacy lead them to become lovers, and the sheriff observes that they have "lit a fire" in each other, suggesting that they may go on to build a relationship.

No such future is envisaged by Dave, the philandering disc jockey in *Play Misty for Me* (1971), the first film Eastwood directed. Drawing on his sometime lecherous qualities, Eastwood plays Dave as a ladies man who is unable to resist the prospect of a single lady at the bar where he is drinking. As we later learn, however, he is the conned party: the woman, Evelyn (Jessica Walter), an obsessed fan, goes to his favorite bar to pick him up. He believes he is drawing her attention via a card trick, but in fact the pickup goes according to her plan, and the two spend the night together. Evelyn develops a suffocating, obsessive attitude toward Dave and envisages them together in a committed life of exclusive domesticity. Dave is actually in the process of trying to negotiate a relationship with his real love, Toby (Donna Mills), and so is not only unfaithful to her but also cowardly with Evelyn, who eventually becomes a homicidal banshee hiding in the shadows. Toby, meanwhile, is a glowing blonde angel, vulnerable and duped—by both Dave as her lover and Evelyn as her roommate. As a template for the "bitches from hell" films to come[13] and "grandmother of all *Fatal Attraction* films,"[14] Evelyn meets her end at the hands of the ultimately triumphant hero, leaving Dave and Toby to walk off together, turning their backs on his "little mistake." In this film, Eastwood's character is both a serious and a casual lover, displaying his perception of some women as disposable and others as a prospect for commitment.

Eastwood's role as the answer to a woman's prayer is figuratively realized as the Preacher in *Pale Rider* (1985), where young Megan (Sydney Penny) summons him as she prays over the grave of her murdered dog. Although Megan is romantically interested in the Preacher, it is her mother, Sarah (Carrie Snodgress), who takes him as her lover, despite being engaged to the loyal but insipid Hull Barret (Michael Moriarty). As she moves toward Preacher to kiss him, knowing he will leave the next day, she says, "This is just so I won't wonder for the rest of my life." Eastwood's character is an object of desire and a fantasy lover for both mother and daughter. As Paul Smith writes, "The girl's adoration of the gunfighter and the mother's explicit submission to him bespeak an ordering of things that [more] fully or extensively implicates the ideal masculinity of the protagonist."[15] This is founded on his physical prowess but also, more significantly, his role as their savior, riding in to rescue them from bullying, assault, and in Megan's case, rape. There are elements here of being an ally, which will be discussed further below, but also of an ideal lover who arrives, overwhelms, transforms, and leaves. There are elements here of being an ally, which will be discussed further below, but also of an ideal lover who arrives, overwhelms, transforms, and leaves.

This is how the Eastwood character of Kincaid could be seen in *The Bridges of Madison County* (1995). Robert Kincaid and Francesca (Meryl Streep) fall in love under laboratory conditions for an affair: she is an unappreciated wife and mother, left at home alone while her husband and children are away; he is an unattached and unfulfilled photographer passing through her town on an assignment. They develop a loving relationship, founded on respectful romancing and empathetic understanding of each other's lives, conveyed in the film's intimate evocation of their cherished time together. Francesca seriously considers leaving her marriage to pursue the romance with Robert but ultimately does not. They never see each other again, but their lives are forever changed by the encounter. It emerges that Robert held her in his heart and head for the rest of his life, dedicating his book to her and leaving her a box of precious belongings. Francesca's voice-over says that their meeting helped her stay in her marriage, and she nursed her husband until his death. The film suggests that the brief but intense relationship enabled them both to lead richer lives; perhaps they needed to experience this passion, knowing it would not last forever but emerging feeling more complete or fulfilled.

Robert Dolliver compares the connection between Kincaid and Francesca with Gail Sheehy's term, *pilot light lover*, referring to the beneficial aftereffects of a love affair on the middle-aged woman.[16] Sheehy discusses how this lover "reignites a midlife woman's capacity for love and sex."[17] There is also an element of this about Eastwood's persona in *Pale Rider*, but Dolliver is right to distinguish the role of Kincaid. *Bridges* shows Eastwood as his usual unattached self, ending the film as solitary as he begins it, but demonstrates that he has been transformed by the love affair. This is an instance of Eastwood being genuinely in love on-screen, as he is with Toby and Rachel, but here revealing intense vulnerability, emotionally and physically, and—perhaps uniquely—being rejected by the woman he loves.

In *Dirty Harry*, we meet widower Harry Callahan and see him at work in a realm where he is surrounded by female bodies (shot dead in a rooftop pool, baring breasts through a window, frolicking naked in an orgy or being lifted nude and dead from a hole in the ground) but has no relationships with actual, live women. In the sequel *Magnum Force* (1973), Harry's desirability to women becomes a significant feature of the film, whether as the object of an interrupted seduction by a friend's wife, Carol McCoy (Christine White), or lusted after by his young neighbor, Sunny (Adele Yoshioka), who asks, "What does a girl have to do to go to bed with you?" Harry replies nonchalantly, "Try knocking on the door," but things are not quite as casual as that quip suggests. Harry goes into his apartment, cracks open a beer and sits on the bed, then looks at the portrait of his late wife by his bedside with resignation. The permanent presence of his wife next to his bed demonstrates the loyalty that he still feels for her, even if it fails to impinge upon his present casual love life. As Tania Modleski points out, a number of dead wives haunt Eastwood's films, notably *The Outlaw Josey Wales*, *Absolute Power* (1997), *Unforgiven*, *Gran Torino* (2008), and *Trouble with the Curve* (2012).[18] This trope functions to establish the male loner as a man with a shared past but a present grounded in loss, which further highlights what is at stake for him in terms of what he has to lose, overcome, or live for. In *Unforgiven*, for example, he has to overcome the peaceful ethos of his late wife in order to carry out his vengeful tasks, and in *Gran Torino*, he is willing to lay down his life in pursuit of natural justice for his neighbors because he has nothing left to live for.

The Father

In *Tightrope*, Detective Wes Block is a single parent wrestling with his loneliness and sexual curiosity while trying to care for two young daughters. A loving but vulnerable father, he is in danger of switching roles with elder daughter, Amanda (played by real-life daughter Alison). Sensible but with concerned, wary eyes, Amanda cares for her father, finds him passed out clutching a photograph of her mother, and is embroiled in his work when the killer he is tracking breaks into their house and ties her up on the bed, gagged and possibly sexually assaulted. Block is tempted by the dark side of his investigation into sex crimes, but this is counterpointed by his respect and fascination for rape counselor Beryl Thibodeux (Geneviève Bujold). The possibility of a relationship with Beryl offers a positive future for Amanda and her sister, Penny (Jenny Beck), with a sympathetic and solid role model who will presumably enable their father to revert permanently to the straight and narrow.

In *True Crime*, Steve Everett forgets dates with his daughter and is generally a disinterested father. One reluctant trip to the zoo, which Steve is trying to cut short, is made sinister by the way it is shot off-kilter as he hurtles around

FIGURE 8.1 Eastwood as a reckless father playing "speed zoo" in *True Crime* (1999). Frame enlargement.

FIGURE 8.2 Kate is a disappointed, loving, and conflicted daughter in *Absolute Power* (1997). Frame enlargement.

the animal enclosures with his tiny daughter, Kate (played by a real-life daughter, Francesca), who is enjoying the helter-skelter element of it all until she is thrown out of her stroller and sustains a head injury.

Irresponsibility and absenteeism characterize his parenting of children, leading to the dysfunctional relationships with his adult daughters portrayed in *Absolute Power* and *Trouble with the Curve*. A widower in both films, the combination of his lifestyle and personality has led to his daughters feeling resentment and anger toward him. Father and daughter are able to communicate through the world of work, and this functions as a forum where emotional bitterness and frustration can be played out and tentatively resolved. In

Absolute Power, Luther Whitney is a jewel thief who has spent his life in and out of prison or on the run, meaning that his relationship with his daughter, Kate (Laura Linney), is characterized mainly by disappointment and memories of his absence.

As with Kate, Mickey (Amy Adams) and her father in *Trouble with the Curve* rekindle a deep-seated love and respect for each other when the daughter is called upon to help her father in need. Both films display an affinity and like-mindedness between fathers and daughters, evident not only in the daughter's devotion to her profession (as a lawyer in both cases) but also in the father's recognition of their individual qualities and strengths. This adds a further facet to the way Eastwood relates to the feminine in intimate relations on-screen without asserting patriarchal authority and conventionally coded fatherhood. This is not to assert that these representations of adult daughters are unproblematic—and indeed it is suggested that the absence of paternal love and support is an ongoing element of these dysfunctional relationships—but they are formed less on bonds of obligation and more on bonds of allegiance.

The Ally

Eastwood's characters are often aligned with women in his films through their similarly peripheral places in story worlds usually ordered along patriarchal lines. At times, Eastwood's character is deliberately enlisted to investigate, inquire, or seek vengeance on the part of women. In *Blood Work*, he is trying to solve the murder of Graciella's (Wanda De Jesus) sister; in *Pink Cadillac* (1989), he is the sympathetic bail bondsman, searching for the wrongly accused young mother on the run Lou Ann McGuinn (Bernadette Peters) and soon becoming her accomplice; and in *Unforgiven*, he is hired by a group of prostitutes aggrieved at the form of restitution meted out by Sheriff Little Bill Daggett (Gene Hackman) for the vicious slashing of Delilah's face because she laughed at a punter's "teensy little pecker." These contractual allegiances are foundational to the films' stories and set up equivalence between Eastwood and women. In these films, Eastwood functions as a helper and an avenger.

He is also a rescuer, in that he repeatedly saves women from assault and proceeds to be an ally, albeit one who may not be domesticated or assimilated into coupledom. Having saved Sue (Ahney Her) from assault once by local youths in *Gran Torino*, Walt and Sue strike up a friendship, and Sue explains the ways of Hmong culture to him. When Sue is raped by the gang and Walt sees her injuries, he is driven to avenge her and ensures that the gang is arrested for his murder.[19] As Megan's savior in *Pale Rider*, he has a knowing communion with her, shown in their shared looks and his arrival in her moment of need. He also appears to be the chosen ally of young Marlene (Alexa Kenin) in *Honkytonk*

Man (1982), who identifies Red as a fellow freedom-seeker, with a trajectory that does not involve the exploitation of her. Her gaucheness and vulnerability enable Eastwood's character to demonstrate that he possesses moral decency that might not otherwise be apparent, particularly in light of his taking young nephew Whit to a brothel so he might lose his virginity. In this world where women's bodies are commodities to be bought and sold or traded, Red is shown to be able to draw a line in a way that establishes the parameters of his moral code.

This streak of a specific kind of cinematic morality, interpreted in Eastwood films as evidence of decency, often manifests in the rescuing of women from sexual assault. In *The Outlaw Josey Wales*, he rescues Laura Lee (Sondra Locke) as she is being stripped and assaulted. Similarly in *Two Mules for Sister Sara* (1970), *Pale Rider*, and *Bronco Billy* (1980), the Eastwood character intervenes when a woman is about to be raped, establishing a tentative relationship with the assault victim, which can then develop into a further allegiance, as in *Josey Wales*, or possibly romance, as in *Two Mules*.

Arguably Eastwood's most overtly official ally is Inspector Kate Moore (Tyne Daly) in the third Dirty Harry film, *The Enforcer*. Despite unpromising beginnings when Harry shows himself to be a surly, challenging interviewer for new police inspectors, once Kate is assigned as Harry's new partner, they form a frank and mildly combative relationship. Harry patronizingly exposes Kate's inexperience and naïveté on the job, and Kate undermines his masculine confidence by teasing him about the phallic penetration powers of his gun. A simpatico partnership develops between them, including some sexual innuendo and flirtation, but by the end of the film, Kate appears to be a potential pal for Harry: there is respect and affection between them. Kate, however, is shot and killed by the terrorist and dies uttering the plaintive words that she "messed up." In Smith's words, Moore becomes a "generic sacrifice."[20] Harry is then left with all the more reason to catch and kill the criminal, and he ends the film as singular and isolated as he began it but also returning to stand over Moore's dead body, having had a glimpse of female friendship. This friendship functions to show that the Eastwood character may be short-tempered and not one to suffer fools gladly but that he is capable of seeing a woman on an equal footing—and not just as one of the prostitutes, victims, or go-go dancers that frequent the beat of Harry Callahan.

Out of all these films with significant and interesting women, one particular set of six films made between 1976 and 1983 is notable for its vibrant, challenging, and consistent female lead actress, who enables Eastwood to be both a lovelorn sap and a conquering hero: Sondra Locke.

The Locke Films

Small and slight, with huge eyes and a commanding voice, Sondra Locke was nominated for an Academy Award for best actress in a supporting role as Mick Kelly in *The Heart Is a Lonely Hunter* (1968). Her first appearance in an Eastwood film was in 1976, as Laura Lee in *Josey Wales*, where she is rescued by Josey and becomes part of his band of settlers and then his lover. They also became lovers offscreen and were in a relationship for some fourteen years, during which time Locke played the lead female role in *The Gauntlet*, *Every Which Way but Loose* (1978), *Bronco Billy*, *Any Which Way You Can* (1980) and *Sudden Impact*. In these films, the diminutive, vibrant Locke shows she can overpower the rangy, languid, Eastwood through vocal resonance, verbal dexterity, and sheer force of personality. In *The Gauntlet*, Locke plays intelligent and eloquent prostitute Gus Mally, who survived a sexual assault by a senior police officer and is now a witness in need of protection by second-rate cop Ben Shockley. Ben is a drinker in search of a big case, set up to fail by his superiors, who intend to see Mally killed. Mally impresses Shockley with her fearless attitude and intelligent insight, and the two together manage to see her arrive safely at the courthouse in order to give evidence, having run "the gauntlet" of the police force with all their armory.

The film becomes more focused on action than sexual politics, and the ending is a prolonged and farfetched set piece, but one scene is remarkable for the power of Locke's dialogue and delivery. Mally is in the back seat of a cop car and Shockley in the passenger seat. Through a line of prurient questioning that becomes increasingly personal and sexualized, the cop that is driving reveals a licentious interest in her trade secrets. Shockley is uncomfortable and tries to shut him up. Mally, by contrast, is not uncomfortable in the least and proceeds to entrap and then destroy the cop's lewd, easy confidence. Having listed all the ways in which cops act dirty, she says that the only difference between a cop and hooker is that when she finishes work she can take a long hot bath and she's clean as the day she was born. Mally observes, "Oh, I know you don't like women like me—we're a bit aggressive, you're frightened—but that's only because you got filth in your brain, and the only way you'll ever clean it out is to put a bullet through it." Shockley is amused by Mally's outspokenness and the two become united in their aim to survive the corrupt policemen who are after them.

Locke's character in *Every Which Way but Loose*, Lynn Halsey-Taylor, is a country and Western performer with a sweet way of singing "what's a girl to do" and a forthright sexual confidence that knocks Philo Beddoe sideways. A far less nuanced role is given to Locke when she reprises Lynn Halsey-Taylor in the sequel, *Any Which Way You Can*. Here, unconvincingly, Lynn has seen the error of her ways and is now happy to take up a romance with Philo. This film

FIGURE 8.3 The straight-talking Mally in *The Gauntlet* (1977). Frame enlargement.

offers Locke little in the way of character development and is perhaps most notable for a love scene during which Philo swings from the chandelier aping his orangutan pal. Reduced to playing "the girl," Locke's role is that of benign onlooker, at one point kidnapped in order to persuade Philo to take part in a fight.

Bronco Billy is a *Taming of the Shrew* story, with Locke's snooty society heiress, Antoinette Lily, being brought down to earth by Eastwood's idealistic circus cowboy. Locke's parodic performance in this film draws upon classic femme fatales such as Phyllis Dietrichson (Barbara Stanwyck) in *Double Indemnity* (1944). Her character is stripped of her fine clothes, money, and resources and forced to work for Bronco Billy by circumstances, so she is duly "tamed." In the world of this film, however, her journey is from a life of soulless mercenary misery, where marriage is a matter of fulfilling the conditions to inherit under a will, to a community of idealist joy-givers who look after and forgive each other and make do on very little money. This is a morality tale, with a light touch and comedic performances, that allows Eastwood and Locke to subtly exaggerate their character traits in complementary ways.

Locke's next and final on-screen collaboration with Eastwood more than compensates for the passivity of Lynn's second outing. In the fourth Dirty Harry film, *Sudden Impact*, Locke plays vigilante killer Jennifer Spencer, whose project is to hunt down the men—and woman—who raped her and her sister, and to dispatch them in a suitably genitocentric style. With her sister, Elizabeth (Lisa Britt), in a vegetative state following the rapes, Jennifer becomes a ruthless killer, as well as a painter who expresses her torment and fury on her canvases. Again, she approaches Eastwood's character with sexual assertiveness, saying, "Do you wanna be alone tonight Callahan? Neither do I." Encompassing elements of the lover and the ally, here Harry understands Jennifer's motivation and her desire for vengeance, which fits with his conception of natural justice, enabling him to cover up her role in the killings.

Although Sondra Locke occupies a uniquely strong place in the Eastwood oeuvre, there are other women who give as good as they get, if not far more on occasion.

More than a Match

In the Eastwood one-off musical *Paint Your Wagon* (1969), Pardner is embroiled in a three-way marriage with Elizabeth (Jean Seberg) and Ben Rumson (Lee Marvin). Pardner strolls through the wood singing "I Talk to the Trees" in a softly crooning vocal and is smitten with Elizabeth's beauty and strength. Elizabeth loves both Ben and Pardner and is clear that she is very happy with being married to two men. She is keen to continue this relationship even after the men decide it is no longer feasible to share, as Pardner wants her to be in a committed relationship exclusively with him. Another woman who looks tiny next to Eastwood but whose on-screen dynamism dominates their scenes together, in which he tends to stare at her mutely with besotted eyes, Seberg's performance is natural and physically confident, perfectly suited to the role of this unconventional woman who wants two husbands.

Eastwood has said that the role of Sara in *Two Mules for Sister Sara* was the best part, "something I'm quite sure that Shirley (MacLaine) noticed."[21] The film begins looking very much what we might expect from Clint Eastwood: a lone cowboy, Hogan, rescuing a near-naked woman, Sara, from sexual assault by three men. The film then takes the first of several surprise turns when the woman emerges in a nun's habit and prays over the grave of her attackers. Hogan is attracted to Sara and wastes no opportunity to make it clear to her how much he wishes she were not a nun so that he might act on his desires. Further intrigue ensues when Sara reveals she is fighting for the Juarista Mexicans and they find themselves in various gun battles. The relationship is far from asexual on Hogan's side, as his eyes run over her sleeping body. Sara is increasingly surprising, as she drags on a cigar, swigs liquor from a bottle, and starts to use crude language. Her biggest surprise however is when she reveals that she is in fact a prostitute, working at "the best whorehouse in town." Reclining in a bathtub full of suds, with a cigar in her mouth, she tells Hogan to wait, but he is so overcome with lust that he cannot even wait to undress himself before he climbs into the bath on top of her. The film's final scene is an amusing reinscription of the film's images of Sara in her nun's habit following Hogan on a mule, as she now trails him wearing a bright scarlet outfit adorned with black lace and fripperies, burdened with hat boxes and a parasol.

Sara is one of the few women to remain involved with Eastwood at the end of the film, let alone to literally ride off into the sunset with him.

One year after *Two Mules*, Eastwood appeared as John McBurney in *The Beguiled*. In some ways, Eastwood is lecher, lover, father, and ally in this film, plus many more character types besides. As an injured Union soldier found by a girl in the woods and cared for in a Confederate girls' boarding school, McBurney becomes enamored of his own erotic power over the women. He lies about his past, revealed by footage of his memory of events shown while he tells the women of far more heroic or praiseworthy deeds, and he cunningly responds to each girl and woman in the way guaranteed to affect them most. As Headmistress Martha (Geraldine Page) observes, "The corporal seems to be having an effect on all of us." He overestimates his omnipotence, however, and when he chooses to go to the bedroom of pupil Carol (Jo Ann Harris) rather than headmistress Martha, he finds himself at their mercy.

Distraught at his betrayal of what she believed was their love, young teacher Edwina (Elizabeth Hartman) flies into a rage and hurls him down the stairs, breaking his leg. Surveying the injury, Martha deems the only prudent course of action to be amputation, and she carries this out in a slow, tense sequence around McBurney's strapped-down body. Close-ups focus on the women's faces as they realize the impact and severity of what she is doing.

Upon waking, and being told that his leg has been surgically removed, McBurney accuses Martha of doing it out of sexual jealousy. As McBurney recovers physically, he begins to attempt to exploit the guilt of the women by sexual threats. When drunk, he hurls Amy's pet turtle at the wall and kills it,

FIGURE 8.4 Seduced by and seducing Carol in *The Beguiled* (1971). Frame enlargement.

which proves to be his ultimate undoing. Devastated by the betrayal of their friendship and the murder of her pet, Amy collects poisonous mushrooms from the forest and the women feed these to McBurney at dinner, thereby killing him and avenging all the wrongs he committed. Burying him in the gardens, the girls show little sadness, believing Martha when she says his heart must have given out after all. The menace and vitriol that McBurney exacerbated seem to be replaced by pathological coolness and acquiescence. In this film, Eastwood's easy charm, beautiful face, and fetishized body are undercut and destroyed by angry women in a Southern gothic nightmare of sexual castration. This is not the usual Eastwood fare. Herring writes, "All of the women are hungry for power; all act as sexual aggressors. And they refuse to be victimized sexually or psychologically."[22] In *The Beguiled*, "the sexually arrogant man suffers. The women get off scot free."[23]

Combining elements of ally and father, *Million Dollar Baby* (2004) tells a devastating story about the relationship between elderly boxing coach Frankie Dunn and committed amateur fighter Maggie Fitzgerald (Hilary Swank). Again a single man, estranged from his daughter, Eastwood's character is burdened by guilt over many things he has done wrong. After a good deal of pressure from Maggie, Frankie agrees to become her coach, and this brings fresh purpose to both their lives. As Amy Taubin writes, Swank's "eager, bright spirit is a great foil for Eastwood, and together, they create a complicated map of loyalty, trust, and love."[24] Maggie's boxing career progresses well until an illegal punch from a dirty opponent causes her head to smash against a stool in the ring and break her neck, rendering her a quadriplegic. When her visiting money-hungry family are revealed to be only after the proceeds of her will, and bed sores lead to the amputation of her leg, Maggie decides she has had the best her life will give her and asks Frankie to help her die. Frankie refuses and so Maggie tries to take matters into her own hands and bites off her tongue in an unsuccessful attempt to bleed to death.

The horror of seeing Maggie in this state moves Frankie to accede to her wishes, and he kills her one night with a lethal overdose of adrenalin. As she dies, he reveals the meaning of his nickname for her to be Gaelic for "my darling, and my blood." This disturbing and traumatic film may in part resemble other boxing rags-to-riches stories, in the mold of *Somebody Up There Likes Me* (Robert Wise, 1956), or *Rocky* (John G. Avildsen, 1976), and it may call to mind montages of feminine determination in the gym such as those from *Girlfight* (Karyn Kusama, 2000). *Million Dollar Baby*, however, is one of those Eastwood films that takes his roles in relation to women—here ally and father—and combines them in a story that is ultimately about his battle for redemption rather than her fight to become a boxer. In the film's final voice-over, revealed to be Scrap (Morgan Freeman) reading a letter to Frankie's estranged daughter, a cinematic ideal of justice is invoked: the depth of love

Frankie is capable of feeling for a daughter figure who is not even his blood asks us to consider just how bad a father could he have been to his real blood daughter? In light of this, the film ends with its focus on the effects of Maggie's journey on Frankie, and despite Hilary Swank's Academy Award–winning performance as Maggie and the actor's physical and emotional bravery on-screen, Eastwood's star persona as a woman's ally against the world of public opinion—legal, societal, familial, or medical—is consolidated as heroic and self-sacrificing.

A second tier of strong women in Eastwood's films play mainly supporting roles but do so with particular individuality. Secret Service officer Lilly Raines (Rene Russo) in *In the Line of Fire* (1993) is a fellow professional—albeit younger, fitter, and more in favor with their superiors—who spars with Frank Horrigan about his age and his sexist attitudes. A similar battle between long-in-the-tooth old-timer Chief Red Garnet and criminologist Sally Gerber (Laura Dern) takes place over the course of *A Perfect World* (1993). In *The Eiger Sanction*, *The Enforcer*, *In the Line of Fire*, *True Crime*, and *Blood Work*, Eastwood's characters wrestle openly with the politics of sexual difference in the workplace, depicting the sexism rife in the institutions and offices of America across the decades. In this way, Eastwood's films quite deliberately engage with femininity and women's experiences in society, as well as the examinations of masculinity with which he is so indelibly associated. This is also true of the films that he has directed but in which he does not appear. There are films in which women play wives and girlfriends in tales about groups of men, such as *Mystic River* (2003): notable here is the pivotal role of Celeste Boyle (Marcia Gay Harden) in reporting to Jimmy Markum (Sean Penn) her suspicion that her husband, Dave (Tim Robbins), killed Markum's daughter. *American Sniper* (2014), a film that could have been solely a psychological profile of Navy SEAL sniper Chris Kyle (Bradley Cooper), instead becomes more a story of a couple, from their meeting through marriage, children, and Kyle's return from war, with his wife Taya (Sienna Miller) as his constant confidante, partner, friend, and lover.

It is in *Changeling* (2008), however, that Eastwood tackles a woman's story entirely from her point of view. Based on real-life events in California in the 1920s, *Changeling* tells the story of Christine Collins (Angelina Jolie) and her battle to find her missing son and then to prove that the boy produced triumphantly by the police is an imposter. Christine, accused of being an unfit mother by police and press because she rejects the boy, is incarcerated in a mental asylum and threatened with electric shock therapy. Her real son is never found, and although a man is convicted of his murder, along with the murder of several other boys, doubt hangs over the veracity of his confession. Christine Collins remains hopeful that her son might still be alive, and the final shot of Jolie's striking face illuminated with this glimmer of possibility is a heartbreaking moment of emotional intensity. Collins battles the police, the courts, the doctors, and the media, as well as the man who stole her son and the man who left her to raise the boy on her own. This is a single woman's story, and Jolie is a female star of a magnitude, both on- and offscreen, to play a role that echoes the many lone avenger roles played by Eastwood across his career. Without a partner, either at the beginning or at the end of the film, Collins pursues the path of righting her loss, a journey Eastwood has enacted numerous times.

Conclusion

As a feminist, one way to approach women in the films of Clint Eastwood is to identify who the women are, afford them the dignity of an identity, acknowledge the actor's performance, and, as Modleski does, lament their loss where there may be no markers of it in the film.[25] In this chapter, I have named them and begun to explain them, and, in so doing, demonstrated that the majority of Eastwood's films rely on the contribution of women. Often the characters are victims of sexual assault, and usually they are in need of his assistance. Sometimes women support his star persona, but occasionally Eastwood steps back, and then they dominate. Eastwood may sometimes play a husband, but never a good one, and his relationships with his cinematic daughters are dysfunctional and damaged. The romantic relationships between Eastwood and women in his films are all about snippets of connection. Eastwood is a dream lover, and that's why *Bridges* works so well: he is a fantasy of a partner, a romantic, attentive lover who sees Francesca as a person with a history (he has visited her hometown, Bari), not simply a functionary of domesticity. In this way, Kincaid is a perfect fit for Clint Eastwood, since his suitability for the role of long-term lover is not tested—for Francesca or any of us. Perhaps we—and Eastwood—know as well as Francesca does that her daily life with Kincaid could not live up to those four magical days, and she would be better to remember him at his temporary best.

Notes

1   As Paul Smith notes, Pauline Kael, Judith Crist, and other critics have long been antagonistic to the gender politics of Eastwood's films. Paul Smith, *Clint Eastwood: A Cultural Production*, 2nd ed. (Minneapolis: University of Minnesota Press, 1993), 113.
2   Douglas Thompson, *Clint Eastwood: Sexual Cowboy* (London: Time Warner Paperbacks, 1993), 70; Peter Biskind, "Any Which Way He Can," in *Clint Eastwood: Interviews, Revised and Updated*, ed. Robert E. Kapsis and Kathie Coblentz (Jackson: University Press of Mississippi, 2013), 152.

3 Sondra Locke, *The Good, the Bad, and the Very Ugly: A Hollywood Journey* (New York: William Morrow, 1997), 350.

4 Peter Lehman writes that Eastwood "has been one of the major stars to shape and embody masculinity in cinema since the mid-1960s." Peter Lehman, "In an Imperfect World, Men with Small Penises are Unforgiven: The Representation of the Penis/Phallus in American Films of the 1990s," *Men and Masculinities* 1, no. 2 (1998): 129.

5 Al Collins, "Outside the Walls: Men's Quest in the Films of Clint Eastwood," *San Francisco Jung Institute Library Journal* 23, no. 4 (2004): 70.

6 Lehman explains the differences in the loss of power resulting from these facial disfigurements: Delilah has suffered irreparable loss; Munny has emerged as a powerful figure and a survivor. Lehman, "In an Imperfect World," 130.

7 For a consideration of how this dynamic results in the assertion of white patriarchal power, see Mary Evans, "The Love of a Good Woman: Morality v. Law in Clint Eastwood's *Unforgiven*," *Women and Cultural Review* 4, no. 3 (1993): 313–316.

8 Smith, *Clint Eastwood*, 168.

9 David Thomson, "The Beguiler," in *Movies of the Seventies*, ed. Ann Lloyd (London: Orbis, 1984), 176.

10 Quoted in John C. Tibbets, "Clint Eastwood and the Machinery of Violence," *Literature/Film Quarterly* 21, no. 1 (1993): 12.

11 Kathleen Murphy, "*The Good, the Bad and the Ugly*: Clint Eastwood as Romantic Hero," *Film Comment* 32, no. 3 (1996): 18.

12 Thompson, *Clint Eastwood*, 31.

13 Deborah Jermyn, "Rereading the Bitches from Hell," *Screen* 37, no. 3 (1996): 251.

14 Gail Jardine, "Clint: Cultural Critic, Cowboy of Cathartic Change," *Art Journal* 53, no. 3 (1994): 74.

15 Smith here is comparing *Pale Rider* with *Shane* and noting in particular the effect of substituting a young girl for the young boy in the Alan Ladd film. Smith, *Clint Eastwood*, 50. See also Henry Sheehan, "Scraps of Hope: Clint Eastwood and the Western," *Film Comment* 28, no. 5 (1992): 26.

16 Robert H. Dolliver, "Late Life New Romance in the Movies," *LLI Review* (Fall 2008): 23.

17 Gail Sheehy, *Sex and the Seasoned Woman: Pursuing the Passionate Life* (New York: Random House, 2006), 125.

18 Tania Modleski, "Clint Eastwood and Male Weepies," *American Literary History* 22, no. 1 (2010): 149.

19 For a fuller analysis of the gender dynamics of *Gran Torino*, see Modleski's analysis of the privileged place accorded to white male suffering. Modleski, 136–158.

20 Smith, *Clint Eastwood*, 126.

21 Richard Schickel, *Clint: A Retrospective* (New York: Sterling, 2010), 79.

22 Gina Herring, "The Beguiled: Misogynist Myth or Feminist Fable?," *Literature/Film Quarterly* 26, no. 3 (1998): 218.

23 Herring, 219.

24 Amy Taubin, "Staying Power," in *Clint Eastwood: Interviews*, 194.

25 Modleski, "Male Weepies," 145.

9

"I Know I'm as Blind as a Slab of Concrete, but I'm Not Helpless"

● ●

The Aging Action Hero

DAVID DESSER

There is something quite poignant when we go to the movies and there on the screen, in that movie from forty years ago, is the *star*, glowing with youth, with health, with that certain *photogenie* that made us sigh then and makes us sigh again but for different reasons. We have a very different reaction when we see James Dean in his classics of the 1950s than when we see, say, Marlon Brando from the same period. We may mourn for the young man who never aged beyond twenty-four, but we titter or are embarrassed when we see the bloated Brando of his later years. Greta Garbo understood this well; she did not simply retire when she was thirty-six, but famously wanted to be alone, remembered for her astonishing appeal, not the withering away of her famed looks.

Clint Eastwood's career is unprecedented in so many ways: his combination of superstar actor and superstar director; his duration as a leading man across six decades; and his longevity as an action-hero for over fifty years. Hollywood's prior action heroes did not have such protracted screen lives: Douglas Fairbanks made his final action film when he was still under forty, Errol Flynn was under fifty, and John Wayne was sixty-nine.[1] Unlike his action predecessors, Eastwood, at age eighty-five, has already enjoyed a long, healthy film life, including being the oldest person ever to win an Oscar for Best Director. Yet Eastwood has hardly ignored the vicissitudes that aging brings. While the likes of Arnold Schwarzenegger and Sylvester Stallone have, in recent years, paid lip service to their aging bodies, their films have attempted to disavow what is clearly the case. Not so with Eastwood. As early as *Heartbreak Ridge* (1986) Eastwood began to work out on film just what being an aging action hero means in a Hollywood slavishly devoted to youth and beauty. Not that Eastwood has been immune to disavowing what can be plainly seen: like many other older Hollywood men, he sometimes has required a younger woman to confirm his virility and validate his masculinity.

Unlike other actors, however, Eastwood has also proven willing to sacrifice romance and even sex for an exploration of the inevitable shifts of the aging male body. For virtually all commentators on Eastwood's late career, aging is intimately bound up with masculinity. Drucilla Cornell's *Clint Eastwood and Issues of American Masculinity* (2009), for example, traces its meaning and significance across the corpus of his work as she moves beyond the "action-film" mentality into broader issues of ethics and politics.[2] Walter Metz's "The Old Man and the C" imagines a "crisis" in masculinity that Eastwood's later films take up in "ambiguous ways."[3] Here, as with Cornell, Metz defines masculinity as what the aging male body can and cannot do. Eastwood's films, however, often separate the issues of "aging" from the issues of "masculinity," examining the diminution of certain abilities but not branding it as a crisis in masculinity.

What is also notable is the degree to which Eastwood-as-aging-star is subject to intensely intertextual readings. Metz continually compares Eastwood's actions and the shift in his abilities to his younger self, comparing the old(er) Eastwood to the Man with No Name and Dirty Harry. Has any other actor ever been so consistently scrutinized from the point of view of his own image? Part of this results from Eastwood's sheer longevity, but it also has to do with the fact that the entirety of Eastwood's lengthy career is now readily available on home video and streaming services. Intertextuality, of course, is at the heart of auteur criticism in terms of a director's repeating, insistent concerns— some of which may change or shift over time. But it is far rarer to see this concept applied to an actor in terms of his physicality.[4] Metz claims that "Eastwood is using himself . . . to explore the meanings of the aging male body in our image-obsessed culture."[5] Indeed, in many of his later films, Eastwood deliberately presents the body for viewing and asks it to be read against both the norm of Hollywood's youth obsession and our own cinephiliac image of Eastwood as a handsome, hard-body hero.

In what follows I will suggest the ways in which Eastwood, as he ages, both disavows and perceptibly acknowledges his body's alterations and increasing limitations. He completed his last action film when he was seventy-eight and his last starring role when he was a healthy and ripe eighty-two. He continues to direct and work on new projects, but his body has, at least thus far, stayed behind the camera at this late age. Although chronology is not always the best way to appreciate a director's or actor's achievements, it is precisely chronology—time and age—that is of concern here. As such, the best place to begin is with the film where Eastwood's character overtly contemplates retirement, getting older, and settling down.

"Are You Freeze-Dried or Doing Hard Time?": *Heartbreak Ridge* (1986)

Tough-talking, cigar-chomping, authority-hating marine gunnery sergeant Tom Highway sounds like the perfect role for Clint Eastwood. Perhaps it was, but in 1986, Eastwood was fifty-six years old and already at the age when one tends to start receiving AARP's membership solicitation letters. Still, he produced the kind of film for which he was already well known while playing a variation on his staple character. Yet the film is very cognizant of its star's age and highlights this through a story about the generation gap: the tale of a decorated Korean War veteran facing retirement from the only adult life he's ever known and dealing with cultural changes in the perennial battle of the sexes. Eastwood claims that "*Heartbreak Ridge* is my ultimate statement about macho. [My character] is super macho, and he's full of shit—just completely ignorant."[6] Maybe so, but he wins both battles he faces, the war in Grenada and the clash between the sexes, the latter embodied by Marsha Mason, twelve years younger than Eastwood. Mason plays his ex-wife, Aggie, whom he is trying to win back by using advice proffered in new age–type women's magazines. Although he actually changes very little, Aggie, both amused by and appreciative of his efforts, accepts him. Yet he does adjust his approach in one way—a willingness to listen to and appreciate what it is that she wants, which turns out to be what he now wants too.

Eastwood himself may think that his Sergeant "Gunny" Highway is something of a spoof or exaggeration of the macho man, but he nevertheless redeems him by demonstrating the validity of his macho attitude in the training of misfit marine recruits—a typical combat film trope—and leads the platoon into battle in the Grenadian jungle. While many critics appreciated Eastwood's attempt to portray the 1980s "New Man," Paul Smith rightly understands that it is "Highway's bringing of his company to the point of old-fashioned military readiness [that] is the crux of the film."[7] Eastwood, who served in the army during the Korean War–era though he did not see combat, employed his memories of basic training at Fort Ord to create images of the grueling morning runs, forbidding obstacle courses, and complex war-game maneuvers. I am, however, much less interested in the film's ideology of war and its reflection of the Reagan era's "remasculinization of America" as in Susan Jefford's famous, if somewhat hyperbolic, reading of Hollywood's 1970s films.[8] What interests me here is the way in which Eastwood appears unconcerned with showing his age or casting himself among a group of young actors.

In what I have called above the "generation gap," Mario Van Peebles, twenty-seven years Eastwood's junior (at twenty-nine he was himself already somewhat long in the tooth to play a raw recruit), represents the younger recruits as "Stich"—their leader and Gunny's nemesis. On the one hand, it is typical of Eastwood to go with a racially blind casting. Van Peebles is African American, but his race never becomes an issue in the film. On the other hand, as an African American, he represents the emerging youth culture of the time—hip-hop and rap music emanate from his radio in the barracks—a product of black urban youth, marking Eastwood's first significant engagement with black culture.[9] Frequently taunted by Van Peebles's Stich, Eastwood's Gunny wins the new recruits over not by being their friend but by demonstrating the value of his knowledge, expertise, and physical prowess. He can run longer, shoot more accurately, and fight more skillfully than any man on the base (perhaps somewhat unlikely given the superb physical shape of the frequently shirtless Van Peebles). And his way of doing things—the older generation as compared to the feckless youngsters—bears fruit with the combat on Grenada. Victory in Grenada translates to Gunny's graciousness in retirement and more receptive and easygoing attitude with Aggie. Aging gracefully indeed. *Heartbreak Ridge* deals with growing older, on the one hand, to disavow it, yet, on the other, to acknowledge it fully.

"I Don't Miss It All That Much": *Unforgiven* (1992)

By 1992, it had been seven years since Eastwood had appeared in a Western (*Pale Rider*), which was nine years on from his previous one, *High Plains Drifter*—a sure indication that the genre was pretty much played out. Although he had appeared in seven Westerns in the previous sixteen years (not counting the Musical *Paint Your Wagon* or the Gothic *The Beguiled*), over this same period, he appeared in more films that were not Westerns. *Unforgiven* would be the last Western that the then sixty-two-year-old Eastwood would either direct or star in. There is something undeniably elegiac about *Unforgiven*: a summing up of the mythos he created; an examination, though not a repudiation, of the legacy he left on the genre and maybe on American culture. As he aptly said, "I'm not sure this will be my last western, but if it is, it'll be the perfect one."[10]

For many critics, this Oscar winner for Best Picture has a seriousness and moral reflexiveness about it, managing to encompass a complex meditation on the "consequential nature of murder."[11] Yet it is difficult to support this claim unconditionally, for the film "suffers from being unable to criticize convincingly the very violence that it itself is involved in and that it does not shrink from re-representing."[12] However, as with my look at *Heartbreak Ridge*, I am not so much interested in the film's ideological contradictions as in the nature of Eastwood's portrayal of aging. Cullen sees one of the themes of *Unforgiven* as revolving around "a man's growing awareness of his vulnerability," while Sally Chivers describes Eastwood's Bill Munny as "an aging cowboy figure" who "represents the fading of a sense of justice wherein real men are free to fight for what is right, even if it is an outdated and paternalistic set of morals."[13]

In a poignant scene between Bill Munny and the mutilated prostitute Delilah (Anna Levine), she discloses that his partners have been getting "free ones" from the whores, and their interaction reveals Eastwood's asexual characterization of William Munny. She asks if he, too, would like a free one. When he turns down her offer, she says that she doesn't mean with her, but with one of the other women. He says, "I meant I didn't want a free one with Alice or Silky. Because of my wife back home. I reckon if I was to want a free one, it would be with you." Delilah, who imagines that no man could find her attractive because of the disfiguring facial scar, gratefully accepts Munny's comment as a compliment. The audience knows well that Munny's wife is dead, yet in a certain way, she is back home, buried on the family farm. So perhaps he means his wife's memory. His wife had him mend his killin' ways, which he has forsaken to earn enough money to support his children. So the comment contains some inherent ambiguity. Earlier in the film, a discussion between Munny and Ned Logan (Morgan Freeman) leads to talk of masturbation. When Logan asks, "So you just use your hand?," Munny's answer is more significant than most critics have noted: "I don't miss it all that much."[14]

The elegiac sense of loss is an integral part of how Eastwood understands what it means to get old. As Matthew Carter notes, *Unforgiven* is ultimately mythic, not historical. For Carter, this mythologization takes the form of a style consisting of glorious sunsets and characters silhouetted against stunning landscapes (shot in Wyoming and Alberta) that contrast with the more restricted and corrupt space of the town of Big Whiskey. This visual style must also be seen intertextually as recalling the work of John Ford, particularly, as Carter notes, *She Wore a Yellow Ribbon* (1949) and its Academy Award–winning color cinematography.[15] Ford's film is similarly about aging, in this case, through the highly sentimental treatment of a long-serving cavalry officer's retirement. Eastwood goes so far as to dedicate the film to his late mentors Sergio Leone (died 1989) and Don Siegel (died 1991), as both an acknowledgment of their importance to him as an actor and director and a sad farewell to men who meant so much to him personally. With aging inevitably comes loss.

Early in the movie, Munny displays few shooting skills, but as it progresses Eastwood's character regains the legendary gunslinger prowess of his cinema predecessors. He kills all of Sheriff Little Bill's henchmen and Little Bill (Gene Hackman) himself with Ned Logan's Spencer rifle in tribute to the man the brutal sheriff whipped to death (an obvious allusion to slavery). As he leaves Big Whiskey he resembles an avenging angel resurrected once more, as in *High Plains Drifter*. Indeed, he threatens to return if they don't take care of Ned's body and leave the women alone: "You better bury Ned right! . . . Better not cut up nor otherwise harm no whores . . . or I'll come back and kill every one of you sons of bitches." The violence at the climax is undeniably intense but also satisfying in that it rids the town of the sadistic Little Bill. In this case, the aging cowboy—who, according to the Schofield Kid, "sure as hell don't look like no mean-assed son-of-a-bitch cold-blooded goddamned killer"—hasn't lost a step, but he has lost a friend.

As with *Heartbreak Ridge*, *Unforgiven* represents, denies, and finally reaffirms the power of its aging hero. It begins by depicting Munny knee-deep in mud and barely able to corral sick pigs, much to the uncomfortable embarrassment of his children and the derision of the Schofield Kid (Jamiz Woolvett). He can neither shoot very well nor mount his horse very gracefully, two hallowed tropes of the classic sagebrush cowboy. It ends with an orgy of violence that stamps him as a far more lethal threat than any of the more famous killers—the source of mythic dime-store novels of the Old West—he encounters. Wedged between these dichotomous moments, Munny brusquely philosophizes on aging, violence, and their toll on a man's life. When, for example, the Schofield Kid kills a man for the first time, Munny tells him: "It's a hell of a thing, killing a man. Takes away all he's got and all he's ever gonna have." "Yeah," responds the Kid, "Well, I guess they had it coming," to which Munny adds mordantly, "We all got it coming, Kid." Such conversations are rare within the Western genre, and they reflect Eastwood's growing concern not only with morality but with his encroaching mortality as well.

"I Don't Know How to Break It to You, Frank, but You're an Old Man": *Space Cowboys* (2000)

In 2000, when Eastwood produced, directed, and starred in *Space Cowboys*, he was seventy years old. Costar Donald Sutherland was sixty-five; Tommy Lee Jones was by far the youngest of the cast, some sixteen years younger than Eastwood; and James Garner was the oldest cast member, two years Eastwood's senior. The film turns on the ability of these old(er) men to go through rigorous astronaut training and make the dangerous flight into space and back. It is also something of a "geezer revenge" movie: as in *Unforgiven*, the older characters initially function as figures of fun to the younger generation but ultimately prove to be far better astronauts than their youthful competitors. Their ability to succeed despite the ravages of old age permits the film to build "a narrative structure in which aging masculinity is redeemed."[16]

"It's ridiculous when you won't play your own age,"[17] Eastwood declared some eight years after the box-office success of this film, which humorously depicts both the physical decline that inevitably accompanies aging and how younger people insist that this decline is more severe and debilitating than it actually is. Whereas Eastwood attempted to disavow the effects of aging on his fifty-six-year-old body in *Heartbreak Ridge*, in *Space Cowboys*, he emphatically demonstrates that he is hardly ready for the comfortable rocking chair on the porch. All the stars play men whose glory days, when they were hotshot pilots in the air force's nascent astronaut training program, are forty years behind them. Best buddies back in the day, they went their separate ways thereafter. When a Russian satellite, whose computer codes are based on designs Frank (Eastwood) developed years earlier, threatens to crash into the Earth, NASA enlists his aid to fix it, but he agrees with the caveat that his old Team Daedalus go into space themselves to do the job.

Eastwood demonstrates the men's virility in realistic ways. "Hawk" Hawkins (Jones) is a stunt pilot providing cheap thrills for tourists; Jerry O'Neill (Sutherland) is married to a much younger woman, whom Frank initially mistakes for his daughter, and tests roller coasters he has designed; Tank Sullivan (Garner) has become a preacher; Frank is having sex with his wife (played by a charming Barbara Babcock, a mere seven years Clint's junior) in their garage when interrupted by the arrival of NASA's emissaries. Hawk falls in love with Marcia Gay Harden's Sara Holland, a female astronaut keeping the four veterans on point. Jerry, a charming lech, is also plagued with poor vision and must memorize the eye chart in order to pass his physical. Tank's few extra pounds also threaten his failing of the physical exam. The four men cheat and cajole their way into space and complete the mission successfully but at a high price—the death of Hawk. Yet their sadness is tempered by the fact that Hawk was dying of cancer and thereby willing to sacrifice himself for the sake of the mission and his old friends.

The damages that aging inflicts on the male body are not ignored in *Space Cowboys*, but more important (as in several of his late movies), Eastwood's characters inevitably accomplish their goals despite their various disabilities. Often, their antagonists are younger men who deride their older counterparts, only to discover that age gives as well as takes away: what is lost in physical prowess is gained in intelligence, discipline, and pride. It is all too easy to take the gift of a young body for granted, to view wrinkles and sagging muscles as signs of weakness rather than a different kind of strength, and Eastwood's younger figures commit this error in film after film, only to witness the older men's triumph over them.

"I'm a Retired FBI Man, Not a Psychic": *Blood Work* (2002)

A Clint Eastwood character with the heart of a woman—literally—seems like a farfetched SNL sketch. That scenario, however, is operative in *Blood Work*, where retired FBI profiler Terry McCaleb has received the heart of the murdered Gloria Rivers and is hired by her sister, Graciela (Wanda De Jesus), to find her killer. "At this particular stage in my maturity, I felt that it was time to take on some roles that maybe had a different obstacle than I would, say if I was a young man in my thirties or forties doing this kind of job," said Eastwood.[18] And in taking on this role, Eastwood has never before (and rarely since) presented his own body as so vulnerable and weak, even "feminizing" his actions: he frequently looks in the mirror at himself; he is physically assaulted by a larger man; he requires help in most physical activities, such as driving. Yet he still solves the case, engages in a climactic duel, and gets the girl.

Eastwood adapted *Blood Work* from best-selling author Michael Connelly's novel of the same name, and the changes from page to screen are tremendously significant. To start with, protagonist Terry McCaleb is forty-three in Connelly's thriller; Eastwood was seventy-two at the time of the film's release. The novel's Terry had a congenital heart condition, which led to his heart attack and transplant. The film's first scene implies that Terry's heart attack occurs because of his advanced age as he attempts to pursue the killer on foot. Graciela's age is not mentioned in the novel, but one presumes it is comparable to Terry's. Not so in the film. Wanda de Jesus was forty-four, an age difference of twenty-eight years between her and Eastwood. Her character is also a waitress instead of an ER nurse, an alteration that shifts her class status. Change the killer to Buddy, Terry's wacky next-door neighbor played by Jeff Daniels, and the film version becomes "a color-by-the-numbers film." Yet it also manages to be "remarkably engaging in its acknowledgment of Eastwood's age" and should be seen, in a certain way, as answering the question, "What is Dirty Harry . . . aged to the point that his coronary disease precluded his behaving like a Neanderthal?"[19] Metz insists that Terry's feeble actions are a reflection of Eastwood's fading masculinity and claims that "for all its attempts to make a mature movie about the aging of the action star's body, *Blood Work* ultimately sinks back into generic formula, one in which Clint Eastwood tracks down punks and disposes of them."[20] One is not sure what Metz means. No punks inhabit the film, and Eastwood does not, in fact, himself dispose of anyone. Besides, it is hard to criticize a man who has worked in generic formulas most of his career for working in generic formula.

Certainly, Eastwood's Terry McCaleb is far different than any incarnation of Dirty Harry. Given his heart transplant, McCaleb is leery of physical exertion, and the menacing Bolitov (Igor Jijikine) easily manhandles him. Thrown on a couch, he practically cowers as the Russian suspect searches him rather than vice versa. One only has to think back sixteen years to *Heartbreak Ridge*, where Eastwood's Gunny routinely and easily beat up men thirty pounds heavier than him—or, for that matter, thirty years younger—to recognize the stark difference. As for his feminization: "Before they sleep together, we see McCaleb examining his deeply scarred body in the mirror, doubting his own attractiveness and desirability. This kind of self-critical gaze is associated more with women than with men. Nothing here resonates with the perfect, phallic male body—and McCaleb's body is not wholly masculine any longer, because it now contains a woman's heart."[21] But it isn't just the jagged scar across his chest that has changed Eastwood's physicality. At his age, he no longer has that hard body of *Every Which Way but Loose*; the pecs sag a little, the stomach has just a hint of flab. Of course he is still in good shape . . . for his age. Yet as Dennis Bingham has humorously noted, Eastwood has reached a point where *Sudden Impact*'s "Go ahead. Make my day" has turned into "I've got to go home and take my pills."[22]

"Tough Ain't Enough": *Million Dollar Baby* (2004)

By the year 2004, neither Eastwood nor anybody else would dream of putting him in a boxing film where he did the fighting without being arrested for elder abuse. Somewhat surprisingly, however, the lead fighter in *Million Dollar Baby* is a woman. Just as Eastwood was hardly in the habit of casting women in a lead role, so, too, his character, former cut man and trainer Frankie Dunn, insists he would never train a woman. Eastwood takes advantage of the fact that Hilary Swank, as Maggie Fitzgerald, is both conventionally beautiful and also somewhat "masculine." (Her first academy award for Best Actress came with the role of Brandon Teena, a female-to-male character in the powerful

FIGURE 9.1 Self-scrutinizing, something new to the Eastwood persona, in *Blood Work* (2002). Frame enlargement.

transgender drama, *Boys Don't Cry* [1999]). And although women's professional boxing had its moment in the sun, Eastwood isn't interested in gender parity between male and female fighters; he is interested in myth, religion, and redemption. Boxing is a metaphor, as Eddie "Scrap-Iron" Dupris (Morgan Freeman) tell us: "If there's magic in boxing, it's the magic of fighting battles beyond endurance, beyond cracked ribs, ruptured kidneys and detached retinas. It's the magic of risking everything for a dream that nobody sees but you." Clearly Maggie is fighting such a battle: she wants to start training at thirty-two (actress Hilary Swank was thirty at the time), an age when most boxers have retired. But Frankie has a dream too. He has long wanted to manage a contender, but a kind of moral rectitude prevents him from allowing his fighters to go for the big one. Years ago, Scraps was blinded in one eye in a fight, and Frankie never forgave himself. He only reluctantly lets Maggie fight for the championship even after she keeps winning. Finally, he agrees to the bout, but a sucker punch lays Maggie out and she hits her head on the corner stool as she falls, breaking her neck. In a very controversial plot turn, Frankie euthanizes Maggie after she begs him to do so following a leg amputation and paralysis.

For Jim Cullen, the climactic assisted suicide is a function of Eastwood hanging "on to vestiges of his receding masculine virility."[23] Maybe. But Metz's reading of the scene seems more convincing: "Frankie's redemption lies in his being there as a father for Maggie in her time of suffering." He goes on to say that Maggie's desire to be euthanized derives from her having been inaugurated into the "masculine ideals of potency" that is the way of the boxer.[24] But Maggie has been "inaugurated" into those ideals long before that: she is the one who comes to Frankie for training in the first place. She already wants to box; she knows the *why*; she just wants to know *how*. Frankie obviously treats Maggie as a daughter and assists her when she asks to end her life because it will no longer contain the youth, energy, and cheering crowds. To understand the poignancy of this moment, recall an earlier conversation when Maggie asks Frankie, "You're going to leave me again," to which he replies, "Never."[25]

The relationship between Frankie and Maggie is utterly devoid of sexual attraction. The forty-four-year age difference certainly has something to do with that, but more to the point, this is a daughter-substitute for Frankie.

Frankie is long estranged from his own daughter, Katie, never seen or heard in the film. Frankie has tried over the years to reach out to her via letters that, sadly, always come back marked "Return to Sender." Scrap's voice-over attempts to explain to her "what kind of man your father really was." Frankie's estrangement from his daughter is never explicated, though Frankie feels strongly that it was his fault. And maybe it was. But the point of this transgression imbues the film with the weight of the past upon the characters.[26] It is here, then, that the film intersects with Eastwood and the issue of aging. For such a powerful film to have any weight, any gravitas, necessitates a lifetime of

FIGURE 9.2 The glasses, the completely gray hair, and the daughter-substitute in *Million Dollar Baby* (2004). Frame enlargement.

experience behind it—in the characters and in the director. The process of aging forces us to look back over our lifetimes, to recognize our shortcomings and sins, and to seek redemption wherever we can find it. More crucially, *Million Dollar Baby* asks viewers, and no doubt Eastwood himself, to contemplate what makes life worth living and what, if missing, would justify a person ending it—questions that might well be on the mind of an aging man, even a superstar.

"I'll Blow a Hole in Your Face Then Go Inside and Sleep like a Baby": *Gran Torino* (2008)

Biographer Marc Eliot writes that Eastwood was attracted to the figure of Walt Kowalski because in him he "found yet another reluctant, one-last-time character who is not afraid to use force against those he feels are his enemies and to defend those he thinks are his friends." Walt is more aged and cynical than Eastwood's earlier screen heroes, while the man himself, as Eliot points out, also shows the effects of aging. Where Clint was once six feet four, he was now down to six foot one due to chronic back problems.[27] Perhaps it was this latter fact, combined with the character's death at the end of the film, that gave rise to persistent rumors that *Gran Torino* would mark Eastwood's final screen appearance. It would be four years until Eastwood's next screen appearance and that one would, as of this writing, be his last as an actor.

The plot of *Gran Torino* is reminiscent of many of Eastwood's movies, the most obvious parallel being *Unforgiven*. Both movies begin with the death of the Eastwood character's wife and end with a confrontation with evil of over-whelming odds, although Munny's wife has passed a while ago whereas *Gran Torino* opens with Kowalski's spouse's funeral service. Nevertheless, the basic point is that neither man has a live woman influencing him. Further, Walt is a recognizable Eastwood type—irascible, full of bile and powerlessly rail-ing against a changed world. But while Walt's politics may be retrograde, the film juxtaposes the funeral of Walt's wife with the celebration of a baby's birth next door among the Hmong, as if to say that Walt represents death, the past, and the Hmong life, the future. Walt is the past in many ways. The one white person left in a neighborhood whose ethnic character has radically changed, he holds on to his 1972 Gran Torino, a Ford car that he helped produce on the line in Detroit, while his children drive not only SUVs but Toyotas at that. Walt seems to be an unabashed racist, but he has gotten to the point where he hates everyone, including his children, grandchildren, and his parish priest.

Walt willingly goes to his death at the climax of *Gran Torino*. Rather than confronting the gang with guns blazing in the kind of apocalyptic ending seen in so many of Eastwood's films, he simply lights up a cigarette and then dies in a hail of gunfire from the cowardly gang. Many good reasons exist for such a sacrificial death, both at the level of plot and metatextually. At the plot level, he leaves it to the community to testify against the gang for their kill-ing of him, thus demonstrating both the propriety of the law and the bringing together of the community. Not since *The Beguiled* in 1971 has an Eastwood character been killed or otherwise died, so Eastwood put to rest his taciturn macho image, at least on-screen. It is likely, then, that *Gran Torino* marks the finale of Eastwood as on-screen action hero, putting an end to his fifty years of heroic bloodshed. He would let others take the role of action hero for a new generation—Dwayne Johnson, Vin Diesel, Mark Wahlberg—while he him-self would act in only one more picture. In his review of *Gran Torino*, Patrick Goldstein exclaimed, "At 78, when most filmmakers have lost their fastball, been put out to pasture or are racking up posthumous awards, Clint isn't just still making great movies, he's still a big-enough movie star to open them all by himself too."[28] Whether or not Eastwood took this review to heart, a few years later, he used the metaphor of baseball to talk about the vicissitudes of old age and the attempt to repair a father-daughter relationship.

"Get Out of Here before I Have a Heart Attack Trying to Kill Ya": *Trouble with the Curve* (2012)

As a baseball expression, "trouble with the curve" refers to a batter who cannot hit a curve ball and typically marks the difference between a player who can make it to the majors and one doomed to a life in the minors. Gus, Eastwood's

FIGURE 9.3 The Eastwood squint is more to help him see than to instill dread or fear in *Trouble with the Curve* (2012). Frame enlargement.

aging baseball scout, notices that a batter whom his team wants to sign cannot hit a curve ball, something that has gone unnoticed up to that time. His team, however, no longer trusts him—they favor computer-generated statistics and probabilities; he favors good old-fashioned knowledge and instinct. "A computer can't look a kid in the eye after he's gone 0–4 and see if he will be able to come back the next day," he claims. Yet Gus's vision is literally declining, and he is clearly aging. Eastwood insists both that Gus is right about his baseball savvy and that his days as a scout are coming to an end. He rejects the idea that the team needs "new blood, young new blood," thus highlighting the young versus old duality that structures the film.

In the film's first scene, Gus demonstrates signs of decrepitude. His urine stream is uneven—he stands over the commode and tries to coax it out of him; he bangs his shin on the coffee table and in a pique kicks it across the room; at the ballpark we see a POV shot where the umpire is out of focus and Gus must put on a pair of glasses. Yet while the umpire comes into focus, the pitcher goes out. He has lost depth of field. He leaves with a disparaging comment about the pitcher and claims that his daughter can throw better than that. The film continues to insist on Gus's declining abilities: we learn that Gus is the only scout who doesn't use a computer; we see him struggle to get his muscle car out of his one-car garage; he must use a magnifying glass to read the newspaper. He gives a fifty-dollar bill to a delivery boy, instead of a twenty. Finally, a visit to an optometrist reveals that he has macular degeneration, possibly glaucoma: most commonly a function of aging—the most frequent version of the disease is indeed called "age-related macular degeneration" (AMD). Naturally, the gruff Gus rejects a suggested visit to a specialist. All these ailments put him in a foul mood and when a friend at a bar offers a friendly game of cards, Gus angrily rejects him. When then asked, "What crawled up your ass?" Gus replies, "Old age." Later he will claim, "I know I'm as blind as a slab of concrete, but I'm not helpless. I'll put a bullet in my head when that happens."

The mention of his daughter leads to a direct cut to Mickey (Amy Adams) in her office, where we see that she is a driven lawyer up for partner at a high-powered firm. This cut, from ballpark to law firm, marks yet another Eastwood film with a father-child conflict, specifically, indeed, a father-daughter gap. This is revealed clearly in the film's third scene, when a dinner, eaten at a counter in a diner, abruptly ends with Mickey walking away following a series of obviously sexist remarks from her clueless pop. Yet she still wants to connect with him. When she learns that all she need do is win a big case (of which she is confident she will) and she'll make partner, she immediately calls her father. Yet Gus, asleep in an armchair at home, is angered at being awakened by a phone call, not knowing it's his daughter (no caller ID for him, of course). Mickey sadly hangs up the phone without saying a word.

A general auteur analysis of Eastwood's career up to this point would highlight the manner in which alienation on the part of a father from his child(ren) would mark a recurrent motif, especially in his later films.[29] Frankie's complete alienation from his daughter marks a structuring absence in the plot of *Million Dollar Baby*, whose narration by Scrap is addressed to her. Frankie's willingness to train Maggie is partially some kind of attempt to redeem that relationship; in *Gran Torino* Walt has no use for his children, their spouses, or his grandchildren, symbolized by the fact that Walt built Ford cars, while his son works in sales for Toyota. As far back as 1984's *Tightrope* (Richard Tuggle), Eastwood toyed with the father-daughter motif, even casting his own daughter, Alison, as his on-screen child. He is clearly a father figure to the new recruits of *Heartbreak Ridge*, where the generational struggle is forefront. That the father-daughter relationship occupies his psyche most, however, may be seen in the shift from a young boy to a teenage girl in the transformation of *Shane* (1953) into *Pale Rider* (1985). Gus is, then, one of a long line of fathers with ambivalent relationships with their daughters. In *Trouble with the Curve*, for example, he gives his daughter an androgynous name and drags her around to numerous amateur ballparks and their attendant barroom dives when she is young.

Mickey, as even a casual fan knows, is a classic baseball name: for example, Mickey Mantle, whose picture is one of a handful of famous ball players hanging on Gus's living room wall. Mickey is well into her thirties (thirty-three in the film; star Amy Adams was thirty-eight at the time) and single. She does, however, have a boyfriend who tries to convince her at dinner one evening that they are perfect together. Yet at that very moment Mickey overhears guys talking about a ball game where a pitcher threw a no-hitter. She interrupts their conversation to have that confirmed and then demonstrates her superior knowledge of the pitcher: one guy says he was blowing guys away, but Mickey says he's a crafty sinkerball pitcher who makes his living on the corners. This serves three functions. The first is that Mickey knows the game well, the second is that she is willing to interrupt her boyfriend's attempts to demonstrate their perfect compatibility, and the third is to foreshadow her eventual transformation from lawyer to baseball scout.

The film becomes a dual-focus narrative with the introduction of Johnny (Justin Timberlake), a former prospect whom Gus signed a few years back, but who ruined his arm and is now a scout. Of course, in his gruff manner, Gus says to Johnny, "You don't know anything about scouting," but Johnny doesn't take offense. We might expect Gus to mentor Johnny in the fine art of scouting, but in fact, Johnny is immediately attracted to Mickey and the film thereafter focuses on their romance. But it doesn't lose sight of Gus, who will actually mentor Mickey in scouting while the younger stars take on the romantic angle. Perhaps no Eastwood film in which he stars has so easily abandoned its focus on the superstar himself. *Trouble with the Curve*, if it proves to be Eastwood's last screen appearance, allows him to show his age but, yet again, triumph over his younger rivals, in this case the obnoxious Phillip Sanderson (Matthew Lillard), who lacks any respect for Gus's accumulated years of baseball scouting experience. Gus's passing on of his extensive knowledge and love of baseball to his daughter represents a recognition of the changing gender roles in contemporary times. No longer is "America's pastime" the domain of solely of white men, but knowledgeable women who love the game can become part of it as well. As in *Heartbreak Ridge*, his first film to think about aging and to try to come to terms with the new battle of the sexes not by fighting but by compromising and listening, here in what might be his last film, he recognizes that aging does not necessarily mean a loss of masculinity, just an acceptance of what women want too. People can change as they age and can do so gracefully and graciously.

Notes

1 It is important to point out that Walter Metz gives John Wayne's age, incorrectly, as seventy-nine when he made *The Shootist* (Don Siegel, 1976). He was sixty-nine. Metz has written provocatively on Eastwood and aging, so it is important to acknowledge just how much longer a career he has had than his forebears in action-film superstardom. Walter Metz, "The Old Man and the C: Masculinity and Age in the Films of Clint Eastwood," in *Clint Eastwood, Actor and Director: New Perspectives*, ed. Leonard Engel (Salt Lake City: University of Utah Press, 2007), 210.
2 Drucilla Cornell, *Clint Eastwood and Issues of American Masculinity* (New York: Fordham University Press, 2009).
3 Metz, "Old Man and the C," 204.
4 This is not to say that no actor has ever been read intertextually. But in such cases the director is given credit for utilizing an actor's persona against itself—for instance, Alfred Hitchcock's use of Jimmy Stewart in *Vertigo* (1958) or Cary Grant in *North by Northwest* (1959). The notion of an actor "playing against type" also requires an intertextual dimension. Dennis Bingham was among the first to

examine Eastwood's career from the point of view of how he played off his early persona to develop his later one, but his major point, as the title of his book indicates, is gender, not aging per se. See Dennis Bingham, *Acting Male: Masculinities in the Films of James Stewart, Jack Nicholson, and Clint Eastwood* (New Brunswick, N.J.: Rutgers University Press, 1994).

5 Metz, "Old Man and the C," 212.

6 Richard Schickel, *Clint Eastwood: A Biography* (New York: Alfred A. Knopf, 1996), 421.

7 Paul Smith, *Clint Eastwood: A Cultural Production* (Minneapolis: University of Minnesota Press, 1993), 199.

8 Susan Jeffords, *The Remasculinization of America: Gender and the Vietnam War* (Bloomington: Indiana University Press, 1989). See also Smith, *Clint Eastwood*, 190.

9 I take it as neither a surprise nor a coincidence that this film marks Eastwood's first engagement, however tangential, with black culture and that his next directorial effort would be *Bird* (1988), not only a film whose central character is African American but a film about jazz, a musical form dear to Eastwood personally but also one antecedent to the kind of black music (and much of youth music) then becoming dominant, rap and hip-hop—the kind of music Eastwood, most likely, knows little about.

10 Smith, *Clint Eastwood*, 264.

11 Smith, 266–267.

12 Smith, 267.

13 Jim Cullen, *Sensing the Past: Hollywood Stars and Historical Vision* (New York: Oxford University Press, 2013), 48; Sally Chivers, *The Silvering Screen: Old Age and Disability in the Cinema* (Toronto: University of Toronto Press, 2011), 112.

14 See Chivers, 113; Cullen, 47.

15 Matthew Carter, *Myth of the Western: New Perspectives on Hollywood's Frontier Narrative* (Edinburgh: Edinburgh University Press, 2015), 128.

16 Metz, "Old Man and the C," 214.

17 Bruce Headlam, "Interview with Clint Eastwood," *New York Times*, December 14, 2008, L1; quoted in Chivers, *The Silvering Screen*, 119.

18 Gershon Reiter, *The Shadow Self in Film: Projecting the Unconscious Other* (Jefferson, N.C.: McFarland, 2014), 98.

19 Metz, "Old Man and the C," 205.

20 Metz, 210.

21 Cornell, *Clint Eastwood and Masculinity*, 63.

22 Dennis Bingham, "Clint Eastwood," in *Men and Masculinities: A Social, Cultural and Historical Encyclopedia*, ed. Michael S. Kimmel and Amy B. Aronson (Santa Barbara, Calif.: ABC-CLIO, 2003).

23 Cullen, *Sensing the Past*, 49.

24 Metz, "Old Man and the C," 216.

25 See also John Gourlie, "*Million Dollar Baby*: The Deep Heart's Core," in *Clint Eastwood, Actor and Director*, 244.

26 Gourlie, 244.

27 Marc Eliot, *American Rebel: The Life of Clint Eastwood* (New York: Crown, 2009), 329.

28 Patrick Goldstein, "Clint Eastwood's 'Gran Torino' Is Hollywood's Coolest Car," review of *Gran Torino*, directed by Clint Eastwood, *LA Times*, January 12, 2009, quoted in Chivers, *The Silvering Screen*, 119.

29 I am well aware, of course, that Eastwood did not direct *Trouble with the Curve*.
That credit belongs to Robert Lorenz. And although I will not go so far as to
claim that Eastwood really directed the film, it is also not coincidental—and is
completely typical of Eastwood—that Lorenz had a long history with Clint. He was
the second assistant director on *The Bridges of Madison County* (1995) and became
first assistant director on eight of Eastwood's films, beginning with *Absolute Power*
in 1997. He has fourteen producing credits; thirteen of them are Eastwood films.
Trouble with the Curve was his first (and so far only) directing credit.

10

"Seems like We Can't Trust the White Man"

• •

The Theater of Race

ALEXANDRA KELLER

Clint Eastwood's relation to race is, as the saying goes, a mass of contradictions. In a moment in which Donald Trump was able to run as highly racially divisive a presidential campaign as the United States has ever seen, it is hard to let those contradictions lie. Academics would often prefer that significant directors have a coherent vision of race (or gender, or class, or any other aspect of identity) to go with the putative visual signature, consistent thematic preoccupations, and triumph over constraints that define someone like Eastwood as an auteur. (I say this even of those of us who understand the limitations of auteurist methods and rely on them nevertheless to produce meanings, however contingent, over a range of films.) Some might prefer that vision to be coherent and abhorrent than to be inconsistent and tap into the best, worst, and everything in between of white America's morphing relation to people of color and the symbolic representation of race in Hollywood, which remains fundamentally a signification system by, for, and about white folks. Clint Eastwood's career as a director is so long, so dogged, and so unconcerned with playing Hollywood's game that his films seem neither strictly symptomatic of white U.S. conservatism or liberalism nor simply random cinematic utterances.

This is partly because Eastwood's multiple assertions, through his films and his political behavior outside of them, correlate with such a wide range of (largely white) American sentiments about race. It is hard to square Eastwood's frequent collaborations with Morgan Freeman—who narrated Hillary Rodham Clinton's introductory video at the Democratic National Convention in Philadelphia in 2016[1]—with his assertions that same summer that he'd be comfortable with a Donald Trump presidency and that the Republican candidate's rhetoric did not rise to the level of racism, or his performance at the 2012 Republican National Convention in which he performed with an empty chair representing President Barack Obama.[2] If it's possible to produce a spectrum of political behavior from conservative to liberal and for that to mean something in relation to race in America, Eastwood's career suggests the difficulty of mapping cinematic production point for point onto politics. *The Outlaw Josey Wales* (1976), a bicentennial Western, established a template for an Eastwoodian take on race in the United States that is altered little in a range of films in which race is a central preoccupation of the narrative (including *Bird* [1988], *White Hunter Black Heart* [1990], *Unforgiven* [1992], *Gran Torino* [2008], and *Invictus* [2009]).

Attention to race in Eastwood's films proceeds from the position of a white male heterosexual who is relentlessly focused on individuals at the expense of an equal interrogation of the systems in which they live. This stems from one of the most powerfully expressed political beliefs that intersects in Eastwood's films *and* his public speech: that people succeed in producing both themselves and community in spite of governments, not because of them. And his definition of community, which is often racially and ethnically diverse, arrives at inclusion through exclusion. The exclusionary inclusion of community nevertheless typically cannot come into being qua community without the leadership of a White Savior (usually played by Eastwood), occasionally collaborating with an Exceptional Negro, if not quite a Magical Negro.[3] There is a profound disconnect between the way most of his films emphasize the importance of words, rhetoric, and discourse in constructing racial parity and inclusion and the way Eastwood himself speaks as a public figure. Racial naming and name-calling are central to so many of his films. For Eastwood, it appears that exclusionary speech becomes inclusionary if it's mutual and pervasive enough. Often, characters enter into the discourse of ethnic and racial name-calling as a sign they have transcended race and ethnicity and, especially if you're male, it's an indication of an accession to a kind of postracialism.

When I was asked to write an essay on Clint Eastwood and race for this volume, Trump was a scary joke of a Republican presidential candidate in the academic echo chamber in which, and through which, so many of us habitually understood our world. By the time I finished it, Trump was the president-elect of the United States.[4] The most manifest shift in behavior in the United States immediately after the election turned on race and ethnicity. I live and teach in Northampton, Massachusetts, a place that boasts—probably statistically slightly wrongly—that it is the bluest town in the bluest state. Even so, any number of students of color here quickly experienced harassment by white men as they walk through the streets downtown. One Chinese student reported that her Uber driver told her that all Americans should have guns so they could kill people like her. Confederate flags popped up in places they'd never been before, as did swastika and N-word graffiti. These incidents were repeated across the country.[5]

Eastwood himself seemed to welcome the Trump presidency. He tweeted, "Thank you America, I don't have long left to live but now I know the last few years will be great, I can't thank you enough #PresidentTrump." Except that he didn't. Eastwood's daughter, Morgan Eastwood, tweet-shouted back, "STOP POSING AS MY DAD EVERYONE KNOWS HE WOULD NOT KNOW HOW TO USE SOCIAL MEDIA."[6] The issue here is not that Eastwood wouldn't praise Trump, but that it couldn't have been her father, because, unlike Trump, he can't operate Twitter. If the platform was not believable, the sentiment certainly was. Eastwood's backing of Trump was a more passive one than his endorsements of both John McCain and Mitt Romney, for whom his support was more full throated and empty chaired, but it seemed to solicit enough criticism that it needed defending. In an interview in *Esquire* in August 2016, he explained,

> [Trump]'s onto something, because secretly everybody's getting tired of political correctness, kissing up. That's the kiss-ass generation we're in right now. We're really in a pussy generation. Everybody's walking on eggshells. We see people accusing people of being racist and all kinds of stuff. When I grew up, those things weren't called racist. . . . You know, he's a racist now because he's talked about this judge. And yeah, it's a dumb thing to say. I mean, to predicate your opinion on the fact that the guy was born to Mexican parents or something. He's said a lot of dumb things. So have all of them. Both sides. But everybody—the press and everybody's going, "Oh, well, that's racist," and they're making a big hoodoo out of it. Just fucking get over it. It's a sad time in history.[7]

Before the majority of U.S. voters cast their ballots for Clinton, Eastwood had squarely stepped into a firestorm about race, as he made clear he'd vote for anyone who wasn't going to carry on the legacy of Barack Obama.[8] On CNN, *New York Times* columnist Charles Blow pushed back on Eastwood's assertion that Trump's outspokenness didn't amount to racism: "It is fascinating to me and in fact supremely insulting when people who were never subjects of the bitterness and pain and subjugation of racism tell people who were that you

should just get over it."[9] *Slate* staff writer Christina Cauterucci called Eastwood a "grizzled bigot."[10] Elsewhere, however, the estimation was more mod-
erate. More specifically, what wanted defending were Eastwood's positions on
race in the United States *as expressed in his films*. Critic Lewis Beale enumer-
ated a long list of cinematic moments over decades that seemed symptomatic
of Eastwood's open-mindedness, his insistence on a constructive approach to
race and race relations. His rhetorical questions included the following:

> Does a racist make a film like "Gran Torino," in which a grumpy old rac-
> ist learns compassion for others when a Hmong family moves in next
> door?
> Does a racist make a film like "Bird," the story of black jazz musician Char-
> lie Parker?
> Does a racist appear in a film in which his lover is a black woman, as
> McGee was in "The Eiger Sanction?"
> Does a racist consistently appear along with, or cast black performers in
> key roles in his films (Morgan Freeman in "Unforgiven" and "Million
> Dollar Baby," Isaiah Washington and Lisa Gay Hamilton in "True
> Crime")?
> Does a racist become a lifelong lover of blues and jazz, and make a 2003
> documentary called "Piano Blues," that features performers like Ray
> Charles, Pinetop Perkins, Big Joe Turner and Oscar Peterson?

Beale lamented that Eastwood's relation to Trump's rhetoric had made him
something of a joke. But he concluded, "His current antics do not negate the
years when he was one of the few white filmmakers in Hollywood who showed
some sensitivity toward minority performers and their stories."[11]

One treads carefully into the comments section after such opinion pieces,
but it does reflect the slipperiness of conversations about race, in which even
that word doesn't mean the same thing to everyone. One commentator wrote,
"It's possible that Clint Eastwood has become old and bigoted. It is also possible that a man with a lifelong track record of inclusion and tolerance sees
things about the new left that are not inclusive or tolerant."[12] Another commentator took the rhetorical cast of Beale's questions away, cautioning that
"yes, a racist can appear in a film with minorities. Yes, a racist can marry
a minority. Yes, a racist can make a film about minorities. Obviously, Lewis
Beale doesn't have a clear idea of what racism is."[13] What also slips, here, and all
through the comments—more than a thousand in number—is whether anyone is talking about Eastwood himself or his films.

That slipperiness is a good place to start talking about *The Outlaw Josey
Wales*, a model for much of what was to come, and a film in which Eastwood as

Wales seems to slip in and out of social categories with surprising ease. No one ever mistakes him for anything but a white man, but *discursively* he opposes himself to that category in important ways. Put succinctly, for Eastwood, it would seem that whiteness is only truly whiteness when it comes with a range of enfranchisements including economic means and governmental power. The film's title situates it clearly as one of the counter-Westerns so prevalent in the 1970s. Eastwood plays an outlaw, but he is the hero of the film. Where a film like *Bonnie and Clyde* (1967) turns the tables by making criminals sympathetic, *Josey Wales* suggests a world so hopelessly damaged and upside down (the Vietnam War had just ended) that the only way to be a hero—or even a decent human being—is to act outside the law. The film bears this out as men in uniforms or in official government capacities perpetrate most of the violence visited on innocent people. Like Martin Scorsese's *Taxi Driver* and Robert Altman's *Buffalo Bill and the Indians, or Sitting Bull's History Lesson*, which both came out that same year, *Josey Wales* became part of a cinematic bicentennial portrait of the United States, and however it reflected and refracted the American individual, it offered few compliments to U.S. bureaucracy. If America's commemorative coins, tall ships, and fireworks glorified two hundred years of democracy, the most important American films of that year suggested something far darker. And Eastwood knew this should include a revision of what Western heroism means. "I do all the stuff Wayne would never do," he said pointedly in a *Variety* interview circa the film's release.[14]

In the context of the mid-1970s, it may seem anomalous for the Union to be the source of repression and the film's primary villain (as the surrendered rebels take their oath to the Union, an unseen Gatling gun shoots them in the back). But Wales's vendetta is personal—he never fought for the South, and his racial politics don't match the Confederacy's. Early on, he describes to his ragtag compatriots the safety they will find with "the Nations," groups of Native Americans he declines to name, though later he quickly recognizes a Cherokee when he sees one. And it is the Blue Coats, not the Southern rebels, who make and break Native treaties. In Eastwood's hands, this becomes a broader indictment of big government, which marginalizes its own citizens based not just on race (Lone Watie) but also on class (Wales). Not only is *Josey Wales* a post-Vietnam Western; it's a particularly 1970s-specific subgenre of survivalist Western (e.g., *Man in the Wilderness* starring Richard Harris and the Robert Redford vehicle *Jeremiah Johnson* [both 1972]). In these films, the hero's cunning is as important as his bravery, and the individual is far superior to the bureaucratic institution—a favorite theme of Eastwood's.

Wales's first meeting with Lone Watie (Chief Dan George) involves each trying to ambush the other. Wales silently walks up behind Watie, gun raised. Watie begins one of his monologues about how the White Man lied, broke treaties, and decimated families on the Trail of Tears—not unusual in a 1970s Western. Most interesting is the exchange between him and Wales that concludes it—by which point Wales has put down his firearm.

> WATIE: And now the White Man is sneaking up on me . . . again.
> WALES: Seems like we can't trust the White Man.
> WATIE: You bet we can't.

On the one hand, this is comic irony. On the other, Eastwood seems to suggest that any white man so disenfranchised from his prerogative to disenfranchise others is not, in fact, a white man. And for Eastwood disenfranchisement is what governments do, not people. *Lone* and *the Outlaw*—like terms—are equals because neither any longer has land or family. Later, Watie will say to Josey of another character, "You're the only kin she had," to which Wales responds, "We are at that." This discursive inclusion, expanding the pronouns from "you" to "we" allows Eastwood to suggest something Westerns will largely stay away from until John Sayles's contemporary Western *Lone Star* (1995): that aspects of disenfranchisement shared by the underserved far outweigh whatever differences mark them racially, and that to insist otherwise is one of the more insidious rhetorical maneuvers employed by dominant culture. It is a view fully fleshed out by Walter Mosley in *Workin' on the Chain Gang: Shaking Off the Dead Hand of History*, in which he compellingly argues that what disenfranchises blacks and whites (and all others) produces common experiences that exceed racial division—or would, if largely corporate interests didn't work so hard to continue to divide us by racial and ethnic lines precisely to avert the mobilization of the 47 percent, or the 99 percent, for their own interests. As Mosley elaborates,

> The dogma of racism attempts to deny any solidarity that may exist
> between the races. . . . [But] even if blacks and whites do not see—or do not
> want to admit—the similarities of their situations, those parallels still exist.
>   Class has a prominent role in the lives of *all* Americans. Poor medical care,
> job insecurity, the bane of old age, lack of proper education, and that nagging
> sense of mistrust of a society in which you are a productive member who does
> not seem to share in the fruit of that production—these issues pervade every
> cultural group, creed, race and religion.[15]

Mosley described this situation at the dawn of the twenty-first century, before 9/11, before the global financial crisis, before the United States elected its first black president to two terms. But it resonates with the divide-and-conquer strategy of Trump's campaign, which was acquitted at all times via rhetoric—*language*—rather than appeals to facts or arguments of any

FIGURE 10.1 "Seems like we can't trust the White Man." Eastwood and Chief Dan George in *The Outlaw Josey Wales* (1976). Frame enlargement.

substantive kind. What Trump called various groups of Americans, or implied they were, was central to reorganizing the political map of the country—Mexicans were criminals, blacks were desperate ghetto dwellers, women begged for sexual assault by a famous man with larger than average hands, poorly educated white men were champing at the bit to reassume their rightful place as the dominant group. And this returns us to some important ways that Eastwood produces language for making comprehensive racial maps in his movies. No matter the screenwriter, what people call each other in Eastwood movies, ethnically and racially speaking, what they are allowed to call one another, is centrally important. For Eastwood, the achieving of America is often signaled by the moment when a racial invective is flung, the receiver disavows offense, and returns service, also without offense.

In *Josey Wales*, cultures are defined by relative power, by centrality and marginality—the only paradigm in which it would be possible for both Wales and Watie not to trust the White Man. Late in the film on the eve of a major battle, Granny (Paula Trueman, a white woman) says to Watie, "We're sure gonna show them redskins somethin' tomorrow. No offense meant." Watie replies, "None taken." Later, as the same two characters fight against a common enemy—not the redskins to whom Granny referred but instead a white adversary, Watie says to Granny, "Now we're really going to show these palefaces something. No offense." To which she replies cheerfully, "None taken." In these circuits, Eastwood understands the interlocutors to have come to a point of common cause and purpose—and even common transracial identity.

Paul Smith suggests that *Josey Wales* is "concerned with the restitution of community values after their disruption by war," a resonant attempt at *e pluribus unum*.[16] Ultimately, Wales himself reluctantly founds the Western version of a traveling United Nations: his burgeoning traveling community includes Cherokee, Navajo via Cheyenne, Mexican, Northerner, and Southerner. At one point, Wales walks into a sparsely populated bar, orders whiskey, and, when there isn't any, he walks out, returning from one of his wagons with a case of the stuff and handing it out to everyone inside. This is the most comically pronounced version of a trope of Eastwood films, Western and otherwise: the fantasy of the Great White Provider. Eastwood seldom harms people of color in his Westerns, and though Eastwood himself takes a grim view of the welfare state, his characters certainly never shy away from personally seeing to it that all the good and righteous have what they need.

The film then turns to the settlement of the community that Eastwood will return to repeatedly over his film career. Under Wales's watchful, protective eye, a utopian ranch commune comes to life. In successive shots, a white man, an older white northern woman, a younger Native American woman, two older men—Mexican and Native American—and even a mangy dog go about the business of restoring the ranch. That this group is harmonious indeed is suggested by the way in which each individual's appointed task—chopping wood, beating the dust from a rug, mending a fence—is done in rhythm, as if each chore is the response to another's call. It's a complicated structure: everyone is welcome, yet all of the characters Eastwood plays typically won't, don't, or can't live within the diverse communities he has enabled.

To assure the long-term safety of the commune, Wales rides out to see Comanche chief Ten Bears (Will Sampson), and what follows is the revisionist version of Ethan Edwards's (John Wayne) meeting with Scar (Henry Brandon) in John Ford's *The Searchers* (1956), in which Ford makes explicit that the two are entirely equals, both traumatized by family loss and both out for vengeance. The scene is not without stereotype—the soundtrack seems to come from a can marked "Indian Music." But given all that's transpired so far, it's possible that this is metastereotype. The conversation gets off to a good start, as Ten Bears says, "You are the Gray Rider who would not make peace with the Blue Coats. You may go in peace." The enemy of my enemy is my friend. But Wales wants a little more. He wants a treaty with Ten Bears the likes of which the U.S. government cannot possibly keep but which Wales intends to make good on: "Governments don't live together; people live together." He speaks in the cadence of the (Hollywood perception of) the Indian: "I came here today to tell you that my word of death is true. And that my word of life is then true." He also offers the Comanche cattle to butcher when they need food and promises that the sign of the Comanche will be on their lodge and on their cattle. If Ten Bears doesn't like this peace proposal, the alternative is war: "I'm saying men can live together without butcherin' one another."

Ten Bears is amenable, and no treaty will be signed, because where there is a signed treaty, there is the likelihood of betrayal. So the two men keep it personal—sealing it in a mixing of their blood. As the commune celebrates their agreement with the Comanche, Wales observes from the other side of the fence, remaining at the periphery of both the shot and the group. The celebration is shown in extreme long shot, suggesting a certain finality, though in the end, Wales leaves the ranch, as is typical of almost every protagonist Eastwood plays in films he directs.

This very scene of parlay with Ten Bears was what Clint Eastwood had intended to show at the Republican National Convention in Tampa, Florida, in August 2012. Eastwood had volunteered to stump for Mitt Romney previously and had been very well received. Top campaign aide Stuart Stevens invited him to the convention for a repeat—a slot of four and a half minutes. Eastwood was scheduled to speak on the Wednesday that was canceled because of the hurricane. He arrived a day later with what Stevens called "a crazy thing he wanted to do which was to show this clip" from *Josey Wales*. That exchange crystallizes Eastwood's worldview, which has changed little in the forty years since he produced it. When Stevens vetoed the idea—"And, I was like, 'No, we're not going to do that'"—Eastwood, who doesn't like to use a teleprompter, was allowed to improvise, though the extemporaneous speech-cum-chair-prop extended over ten minutes.[17] You can't exactly yell, "cut," when Eastwood has yelled, "action." He ended his performance with a call-and-response: "Go ahead," he said, and the delegates shouted in conclusion, "Make my day!"

Eastwood both starred in and directed the performance and, as he does in the movies, told his supporting players what to do and say, putting words in the imaginary Obama's mouth that even Eastwood couldn't say on live TV. As Eastwood explained,

> [The empty chair] was silly at the time, but I was standing backstage and I'm hearing everybody say the same thing: "Oh, [Romney]'s a great guy." Great, he's a great guy. I've got to say something more. And so I'm listening to an old Neil Diamond thing and he's going, "And no one heard at all / Not even the chair." And I'm thinking, that's *Obama*. He doesn't go to work. He doesn't go down to Congress and make a deal. What the hell's he doing sitting in the White House? If I were in that job, I'd get down there and make a deal. Sure, Congress are lazy bastards, but so what? You're the top guy. You're the president of the company. It's your responsibility to make sure everybody does well. It's the same with every company in this country, whether it's a two-man company or a two-hundred-man company. . . . And that's the pussy generation—nobody wants to work.[18]

In 2012, Eastwood performed an imaginary version of President Obama telling Romney to fuck himself. In 2016, he called him a "pussy." If there is a fine line between misogynist and racist speech and plain disrespect, Eastwood

FIGURE 10.2 Eastwood's "conversation" with the imagined President Obama replaced his original plan to screen a clip from *The Outlaw Josey Wales*. Frame enlargement.

was riding it hard. Indeed, if inclusion through exclusion is the central opera-tion through which diverse communities are brought into being in Eastwood films, the monologue disguised as a conversation between a present white man and an absent black one precluded that possibility altogether. I have yet to say that *Josey Wales*, in many ways evidently a very progressive Western—set in and after the Civil War, with its multiracial, multiethnic communal ranch as its successful final locus—is utterly devoid of African Americans. In order to produce utopia, the pesky traumas of history need to be swept under someone else's carpet. They resurface elsewhere in Eastwood's own work, but they are certainly not here. Somehow it seems fitting that this glaring absence of black-ness in a Civil War Western has such an intimate connection to Eastwood's positing of the invisible Obama at the Republican National Convention in Tampa, Florida, 2012.

That, at these two moments, Eastwood either erased black presence or pro-duced it as "visibly invisible" should not suggest that at other moments black-ness isn't front and center in his films. There is a tight trajectory from *Bird* to *White Hunter Black Heart* to *Unforgiven* in which the complexities of race as lived in the Reagan Era seem to want airing. All three are period pieces of one kind or another, but all seem intently focused on thinking through aspects of life in a racialized United States. To return to Mosley's formulation of current race relations, in which a visible difference camouflages something far more binding, he suggests that "black American history is often presented in con-tradistinction to general (white) American history, [but] . . . the black Ameri-can experience *is* the history of America."[19] To expand on what Mosley means when he suggests that black history *is* American history, black citizens tend to understand what that means—white and black people inhabit the same coun-try in different ways because the legacy of slavery continues to have profound and unequal effects on us all. White people can disavow that in daily life if we choose to. We can pretend that slavery never happened. And Eastwood seems to go that way when he thinks about history as a series of segmented moments that can be uncoupled from each other like toy trains.

Elsewhere, however, Eastwood produces very clear maps of the instability of racial categories. In *Bird*, Eastwood's biopic of Charlie "Bird" Parker (Forest Whitaker), Eastwood takes on one of two titanic figures of blackness about whom he has made films, the other being Nelson Mandela in *Invictus*.[20] It is among the least melodramatic or formulaic of Eastwood's films, more impres-sionistic and invested in narrative montage than any of his others, and though this can be seen as an analog to Bebop, it isn't mimicking the structures of Jazz that Parker helped innovate.[21] The film moves fluidly around in time and contemplates Parker not only as a musical genius and a drug addict but also as someone who understood his own blackness in particular ways, though perhaps it is more accurate to say that Eastwood sees Parker's blackness in particular ways that are simultaneously fixed and mutable. About halfway through the film Eastwood pairs two moments, neither typically significant in the way that biopics usually prioritize, to occasion deliberate thinking about race in 1988. Red Rodney (Michael Zelniker), a Jewish American trumpet player, asks Bird and the rest of his combo (all African Americans) if they would play with him at a gig that weekend. They agree—the pay is decent. The audience is supposed to be tickled when we suddenly find ourselves at an Orthodox Jewish wedding and the quartet is playing klezmer music as the bride and groom are lifted up in chairs, as is traditional. Everyone's having a good time, and no one seems fussed that the musicians are largely not white. Suddenly Bird breaks out of klezmer and into bebop for the final few measures of the song. At first, the Jewish patriarch seems unpleased but a few bars later seems utterly comfortable with this blending of the two modes, as does everyone else at the party. Applause erupts. One can see this as an easy moment of music transcending cultural boundaries, but it's far more than that and deeply important to the racial politics and presumptions of the film.

Immediately after this scene, Parker hires Red Rodney to tour with his band in the Deep South. It is 1949 and segregated, so Rodney simply can't be a white trumpeter in a black Jazz quintet: he becomes "Albino Red." *Bird* suggests that both African Americans and Jews exist in an alterity that is often largely discursive. This seems the inverse of Eastwood's more habitual maneuver, which hinges on inclusion being about the ability to call each other slurs and take no offense. Merely calling Red Rodney "Albino Red" moves him from Jewishness to blackness and that moves Parker's whole quintet to relative safety below the Mason-Dixon Line. It would seem that for the cinematic Eastwood, naming, mapping names onto actual bodies, and the mobility of those bodies, both socially and geographically, are linked strategies. One may question whether Parker's mutable blackness has to do with his status as an Exceptional Negro or not. Certainly by Tampa 2012, Obama didn't merit that designation.

Eastwood followed *Bird* with what is arguably an even more experimental film—certainly at the level of performance. *White Hunter Black Heart* is a retelling of the production of *The African Queen* (1951). Eastwood as John Wilson is John Huston, Marissa Berenson as Kay Gibson is Katharine Hepburn, and one can match up the dramatis personae quite openly down the line in Peter Viertel's screenplay based on his roman à clef of 1953 about his experience as a scriptwriter on *The African Queen*. As Dennis Bingham has suggested, Eastwood's desire to do this project as star-director pushed him out of the realm of naturalized acting that bound him to other iconic male stars such as John Wayne and Humphrey Bogart who also merely seemed to be themselves on-screen and into the realm of acting with a capital *A*.[22] Jonathan Rosenbaum has offered that Eastwood might have been instinctively reaching for something quite Brechtian in this project. Rather than performing

Huston, Eastwood seems to be conducting "a detailed running commentary on Huston."[23] This approach to acting is important to the film's racial politics. Eastwood's knowing deconstruction of his own star persona also enables the film's contemplation of how race, gender, and class are mobilized within both the entertainment industry and (in a very connected way) colonial (and neo-colonial) contexts. And Eastwood resists any notion that someone enlightened on matters of race and colonialism would necessarily be enlightened on any other matters of identity.

Not only is Eastwood's own performance of Wilson/Huston one conducted at the meta level; the film pushes alienation and reflexivity even further. As soon as the cast is assembled in London, they meet at a supper club at which the entertainment includes a burlesque reenactment of *King Kong*, complete with a black drummer dressed in stereotypical tribal costume (no more or less removed from its source text than the movie we're watching is removed from *The African Queen*). The end of the routine sees a stunned faux–Fay Wray staring vacantly into the eyes of the gorilla that has stripped her. The drummer plays us to a map of the world and, *Casablanca* style, a red line shows us the cast and crew's progress via plane to the shores of Lake Victoria. After laying out a string of impersonations of Hollywood royalty, we're treated to an impersonation of Uganda—in 1951, still a British colony—with the requisite British agent (Alun Armstrong) who treats black Ugandans and gazelles as objects equally in the way of his car. The first twenty minutes of screen time in Uganda is a nearly relentless production of British colonial racism against Wilson's enlightened American sense of racial equality. By 1990, post–World War II British colonials were as easy a target as Nazis, and these are not nuanced performances. But Eastwood treads a fine line between excusing American racism and drilling down on it. As Rosenbaum describes the climax of the first part of the film, *White Hunter Black Heart*'s "centerpiece,"

> set on the patio of an African hotel restaurant, involves Wilson responding with emotional violence to anti-Semitic remarks from his female companion (Mel Martin) and then with physical violence to the white hotel manager's abuse of an African waiter. . . . And what is remarkable about them is the highly complex and conflicted sense of moral priorities that they reveal; in one fell swoop, Wilson's apparent hatred of racism, his virulent misogyny and sadism, his gallows humor, and his appetite for gratuitous violence are all exposed, and the viewer is left to pick up and sort out all the pieces.[24]

Is Wilson's enlightenment meant to make a white American audience feel better, or is it designed to point (via Wilson's comments about lynching, for instance) to the unfinished project of racial equality inside the United States' borders? Bingham concludes that Eastwood's direction and performance produces an essay on masculine masquerade, and because he's playing John Huston, it's "a masquerade of a masquerade."[25] In this layered masquerade, Eastwood seems to produce a discursive sense of whiteness that poses American racism as continuous with colonial racism.

Right before the fistfight that Rosenbaum describes, Wilson says to his Jewish screenwriter, Peter Verrill (Jeff Fahey), "We fought the preliminary for the Kikes, now we're going to fight the main event for the niggers." He looks directly at both a Jew and a black man as he speaks each slur. Like his production of inclusion in *The Outlaw Josey Wales*, these slurs are designed to fold the Other in the protective embrace of the White Savior. Though Wilson loses the fight, he does so on the right side, and this is indivisible from claiming a masculinity that goes with his seeming racial enlightenment. Using history as a theme park, Eastwood lays claim to a responsible ethic vis-à-vis racism but does it in the past, where the white knight can play savior for (most of) a two-hour movie—a far cry from changing reality.

The film's tone changes markedly between the first half with its more orderly, historically informed racial politics and the second half when Wilson meets Kivu (Boy Mathias Chuma), his expert local hunting guide, and the racial politics become more psychological. Wilson seems to need no translation with Kivu much of the time. They simply understand each other, which is to say that Wilson projects whatever he likes onto the chief hunter. That Kivu understands Wilson is merely to say that as unusual as Wilson might be to us, he's a category Kivu has seen before. In the end, Wilson's obsession with committing the legal sin of shooting an elephant costs Kivu his life. The last shot of *White Hunter Black Heart* is Wilson calling "action" on scene one, take one of *The African Trader*—then cut to black. It is as Brechtian an ending as Eastwood has ever produced, reflexive, alienating, and demanding of the audience that it find meaning in the film without definite closure.

Without *Bird* and *White Hunter Black Heart* before it, one might read *Unforgiven* with less resonant racial politics. Eastwood's last Western, to him an antiviolence and elegiac film, netted his first Oscars (for directing and best picture) and also marked the start of a partnership with Morgan Freeman that has lasted over three of Eastwood's directorial efforts. Freeman plays Ned Logan, the best friend and working partner of Will Munny (Eastwood). The two aging bounty hunters set off for Big Whiskey, Wyoming, to avenge the knifing of a prostitute, who is so badly maimed she can't work anymore, and claim the reward. They run afoul of the corrupt sheriff, Little Bill Daggett (Gene Hackman), who eventually kills Ned and on whom Munny releases the real vengeance of the film. We first see Logan as Munny picks him up off his idyllic farm and takes him away from his wife, Sally Two Trees (Cherrilene Cardinal). For a moment the frame is the very picture of racially mixed utopia—the next generation of Josey Wales's ranch, as a white man, a black

FIGURE 10.3 In *White Hunter Black Heart* (1990), Eastwood's strategies of alienation open up a conversation about race without conclusion. Frame enlargement.

man, and a Native American woman all coexist happily. But Sally eyes Munny with a squint as resonant as Clint's own, and while Ned is thrilled to see his old buddy, she knows his appearance doesn't bode well. For Native American women in Westerns, the appearance of a white man seldom does, and just because he has not come to rape and kill her doesn't mean he is not the agent of treaty breaking. Ultimately, he will be responsible for shattering her life.

Unforgiven is not merely a critique of violence in contemporary cinema and past Westerns, including those Eastwood himself made. Eastwood is also deliberately commenting on contemporary racialized police brutality—what he termed *overkill*—and specifically had the Rodney King beating in mind when he made *Unforgiven*. As he said, "I felt it was very timely to do a film where violence not only can be painful, it's also not without consequences for the perpetrators of the violence as well as the victims."[26] If Will is beaten by the police, it's his African American friend and partner who pays the ultimate price at the hands of a corrupt law. When Little Bill collars Ned, he acts out a violence that is entirely racially marked. Ned is tied by his wrists to the prison bars, and Little Bill whips him mercilessly. This not only is a clear evocation of slavery but also renders Ned, with his arms outstretched, as a Christ figure, which in most Eastwood films is what is implied about Eastwood's character rather than anyone else's. Ned only gives up false names—including his own, as "Ned Roundtree."[27]

Munny's vengeance of Ned's death brings him in line with all the other Western heroes Eastwood has directed himself to be. In *High Plains Drifter* (1973), Eastwood's Stranger empowers a Native American family, among others; Josey Wales founds a utopian ranch commune; and in *Pale Rider* (1983) Eastwood's Preacher galvanizes a small mining community. Not only are these men out for revenge, but they also become champions of the underserved and disenfranchised. (In this case, Munny kills Little Bill with Ned's own Spencer rifle.) Munny's final admonishment is to give Ned a proper burial, and to stop abusing the prostitutes, "or I'll come back and kill every one of you sons of bitches," which he is seen to say on horseback, with a large American flag waving behind him.

There is, then, a surprisingly straight line between *The Outlaw Josey Wales* and *Gran Torino*. Both produce a White Savior who is central to producing community at his own expense, and both rely heavily on racial epithets (and Eastwood's character spitting) to produce that community. Returning to Eastwood's suggestion that "when I grew up, those things weren't called racist," brings us back to at least these two films, in which who calls whom what, racially and ethnically, and on what grounds is of great importance. As Richard Dyer begins in his essential book, *White*, "Racial imagery is central to the organisation of the modern world."[28] Whiteness is something to which a nonwhite immigrant may accede, discursively at least, and this is at the center of *Gran Torino*. Widower Walt Kowalski (Eastwood) is exactly the grizzled bigot *Slate* describes Eastwood to be. Over the course of the film, he goes from intensely disliking and misunderstanding his Hmong neighbors to becoming their salvation, giving his life to keep them safe and ensure their freedom to pursue the American Dream.[29]

Eastwood patterns the film's narrative on *Bird*—two pairs of moments of racial calling out happen sequentially, inversions of each other, the first repeating with variation later in the film. Walt goes to his barber, where their mutual affection expresses itself as its opposite. Walt's been going to Martin (John Carroll Lynch) for years but insists he's lousy. He accuses "dago" Martin of overcharging him: "What are you, half-Jew or something?" Martin replies, "It's been ten bucks for the last five years, you hard-nosed Polack son of a bitch." The men call each other ethnic slurs, including each other in their exclusionary speech. This scene is followed immediately with one in which Walt's young Hmong neighbor, Sue (Ahney Her), walks down the street with her Irish American boyfriend, Trey (Scott Eastwood), and runs into a group of African American men on their corner. More racial slurs and sexual harassment ensue. The boyfriend tries to smooth things over using "bro" talk, including himself in the men's blackness, if only discursively. The men want none of it and continue. Rather than returning the slurs, Sue inserts metacommentary: "Oh great, another asshole with a fetish for Asian girls, that gets *so* old." One of the men asks her name. Sue responds, "My name? Take your crude overly envious come-on to every girl who walks past and cram it. *That's* my name." When he threatens her with physical violence she says, "What? You're going to hit me now? That'd complete the picture." Walt, driving back from the barbershop, observes all this from his truck. At the point where words become action, he swings in to help Sue out. Walt calls the black men "spooks"; they call him "honky." He pulls out an imaginary pistol and pretends to shoot each of the men. The men call him "crazy," at which point he produces an actual sidearm. Finally, Sue's boyfriend emerges from the sidelines and hails Walt: "Way to go, old man." Walt's reply: "Shut up, pussy. What's all that bro shit anyway? Want to be Superspade or something? These guys don't want to be your bro, and I don't blame them. Get your ofay Paddy ass on down the road." After Walt drives away with Sue, one of the men says, "I shoulda kicked that nigger's ass." The slurs go round and round but the inclusion of Walt as a "nigger" comes from two things: his mobilization of "ofay" to other Sue's white boyfriend and his ability to produce a kind of masculinity that the corner men find admirable.

Later in the film, when Walt has taken on Sue's brother, Thao (Bee Vang), as a surrogate son, he takes him to the barbershop, where Walt instructs him, "This is the way guys talk. Just listen to how Martin and I batter it back and forth." Martin peruses a girlie magazine when they come in. "Perfect," he says, "a Polack *and* a Chink." The conversation goes on unabated, with slurs

FIGURE 10.4 Eastwood in *Gran Torino* (2008): Walt Kowalski's performative violence is imbricated with his use of racialized language. Frame enlargement.

piling up.[30] Walt instructs Thao to reenter the shop and talk to Martin "like a man." Thao has seemingly just learned what that means, so he arrives with, "'Sup, you old Italian prick." Martin seems incensed and goes at Thao with his shotgun. In the end, that's a joke too, but Walt and Martin, who have the luxury of whiteness (and their immigrant status far in the rearview mirror), impress upon Thao that in spite of what they've just taught him, *he* can't use it. Instead he can talk about cars, girls, and his job. Take two: "Excuse me, sir, I need a haircut, if you ain't too busy, you old Italian son of a bitch prick barber." Now Martin's laughter is a little more inclusionary. Armed with a new, manlier haircut, Thao goes with Walt to secure a construction job with Kowalski's old "drunken Irish goon" friend Tim Kennedy, who's glad to see his "old, dumb Polack" pal. Thao thanks "Mr. Kennedy," who assures him that, between men, "Tim" will be fine. Kennedy asks Thao's name, who gives him "Tom." His assimilation continues. Having taken on an "American" name, he will also, in the end, inherit Walt's prize possession, his Gran Torino, which will put him in the enviable position of having masculinity and literal mobility come together in a way that speaks the class mobility his family seeks, one that the film suggests involves becoming *less* Asian, more the "model minority" whose nonwhiteness is forgiven through high participation and achievement.

Between the release of *Bird* and *White Hunter Black Heart*, Spike Lee released *Do the Right Thing* (1989), a film that was centrally about race relations, racially biased access to opportunity, and violence against black citizens. Even then Lee and Eastwood were foils in an ongoing conversation about who was allowed to make what films that included and excluded black subjects, and that feud has sustained over the years. As Eastwood recounted, "He was complaining when I did *Bird*. . . . Why would a white guy be doing that? I was the only guy who made it, that's why. He could have gone ahead and made it. Instead he was making something else. . . . A guy like him should shut his face."[31] Lee's transformational film makes clear the stakes of exclusionary inclusion that language produces in Eastwood's films by mobilizing ethnic slurs in a decidedly different way. The moment starts with a very intimate scene in which pizza delivery man Mookie draws out of his white racist coworker Pino that he believes high-achieving black stars like Eddie Murphy, Magic Johnson, and Prince are "more than black." The tone of the film, and its particular deployments of lighting and mise-en-scène, deliberately call back to the gritty realism of American film of the 1970s, and the performance style would have been right at home in a Scorsese film of that period. The last few lines of the scene devolve into telling off each other's cultural heroes, after which, in cinematic whiplash, Lee cuts to the famous "ethnic slur scene" in which characters in the film are ripped out of the diegesis and scream racial epithets straight into the camera—and therefore at the audience. Spatiotemporal continuity is thrown over in favor of a more Brechtian reflexivity. The point, of course, is to include a viewer in the spiky embrace of a demeaning name. No matter who you are, ethnically, you must, for as long as the scene lasts, be hailed as a dago, a spic, a slant-eye, a spade, a Jew asshole. The inclusion here is a destructive one, reminding us that Eastwood's capacity to produce exclusionary inclusion comes primarily from a place of white privilege. The "utopian" view of equal opportunity name-calling remains an ahistorical white fantasy, with only white authors such as Eastwood able to write it.

Notes

1 Eastwood cast Freeman as his best friend, Ned Logan, in the Oscar-winning *Unforgiven*; as Eddie "Scrap-Iron" Dupris in *Million Dollar Baby*; and as Nelson Mandela in *Invictus*. Freeman also narrated the PBS series *American Masters* episode *Clint Eastwood: Out of the Shadows* (2000).

2 Eastwood has held elected office. He was mayor of Carmel, California (1986–1988), after running on a platform of deregulation.

3 See, for instance, Cerise L. Glenn and Landra J. Cunningham, "The Power of Black Magic: The Magical Negro and White Salvation in Film," *Journal of Black Studies* 40, no. 2 (Nov. 2009): 135–152. The Exceptional Negro hews more to the notion understood by some white people, as expressed by Spike Lee in *Do the Right Thing* (1989) during an exchange between Mookie (Spike Lee) and his racist coworker Pino (John Turturro) in which Mookie gets Pino to admit that most of his musical, athletic, and other cultural heroes are African American. Pino's defense is that they aren't just black; they're "more than black." In *Invictus* the formulation is slightly altered: the Exceptional Negro needs the help of a white man (Springbok rugby star Francois Pienaar [Matt Damon]) to smooth the transition to post-apartheid life in South Africa.

4 That there are endless breakdowns of the electorate to explain where the electoral college votes came from hardly pierces the fog of disbelief. There has been a certain amount of predictable finger-pointing at the mainstream media, the weakness of the Hillary Clinton candidacy, the error of the neoliberal Davos class in not including the working and no-longer-working classes in the recovery (to say nothing of what caused the global financial crisis in the first place). See Naomi Klein, "It Was the Democrats Embrace of Neoliberalism That Won It for Trump," *Guardian*, November 9, 2016, accessed November 10, 2016, https://www.theguardian.com/commentisfree/2016/nov/09/rise-of-the-davos-class-sealed-americas-fate.

5 Holly Yan, Ralph Ellis, and Kayla Rodgers, "Reports of Racist Graffiti, Hate Crimes Post-Election," CNN.com, November 13, 2016, accessed November 13, 2016, http://www.cnn.com/2016/11/10/us/post-election-hate-crimes-and-fears-trnd/.

6 Chris Perez, "'Clint Eastwood' Twitter Account Suspended after Praising Trump," *New York Post*, November 10, 2016, accessed November 13, 2016, http://nypost.com/2016/11/10/clint-eastwoods-twitter-account-suspended-after-praising-trump/, all caps in original tweet.

7 Michael Hainey, "Double Trouble: Clint and Scott Eastwood: No Holds Barred in Their First Interview Together," *Esquire*, August 3, 2016, accessed November 13, 2016, http://www.esquire.com/entertainment/a46893/double-trouble-clint-and-scott-eastwood/.

8   Hainey.

9   Charles Blow on *CNN Tonight*, CNN, August 4, 2016, accessed November 13, 2016, https://mediamatters.org/video/2016/08/04/ny-times-columnist-charles-blow-reacts-clint-eastwood-s-racist-defense-trump/212203.

10   Christina Cauterucci, "Why Is Esquire Giving a Platform to Grizzled Bigot Clint Eastwood?," *Slate* August 4, 2016, accessed November 7, 2016, http://www.slate.com/blogs/xx_factor/2016/08/04/why_is_esquire_giving_a_platform_to_grizzled_bigot_clint_eastwood.html.

11   Lewis Beale, "Is It Fair to Slam Clint Eastwood over Trump Support?," CNN.com, August 7, 2016, accessed November 8, 2016, http://www.cnn.com/2016/08/07/opinions/is-it-fair-to-slam-clint-eastwood-over-trump-support/index.html. For another unpacking of Eastwood as what Paul Smith termed a *cultural production*, see Brogan Morris, "Clint Eastwood Is More than Another Stupid Bigot—It's Sad and Scary That He's Endorsing Trump," *Paste Magazine*, August 16, 2016, accessed November 8, 2016, https://www.pastemagazine.com/articles/2016/08/clint-eastwood-is-more-than-another-stupid-bigotit.html.

12   redcan, August 7, 2016, comment on Beale, "Is It Fair?"

13   Kris Amos, August 23, 2016, comment on Beale, "Is It Fair?"

14   "Portrait of a Mean B.O. Winner," *Variety*, September 15, 1976, Margaret Herrick Academy of Motion Picture Arts and Sciences Library archive. Eastwood did not intend to direct *The Outlaw Josey Wales*, but the tumultuous conditions wrought by its coscreenwriter Philip Kaufman—whom Eastwood himself had chosen to direct the picture—made it so. This upheaval was just one more bump in a very unusual road that led to the Western's making, and for all the turmoil, *The Outlaw Josey Wales* remains one of the best reviewed films Eastwood has directed.

      Forrest Carter, from whose little-known novel the film was adapted, was not at all what he seemed to be. His *The Outlaw Josey Wales* tells the story of the destruction of Wales's family by Union soldiers in Missouri, Wales's flight from them, his collection of a multicultural band of misfits, and his eventual treaty with a Comanche chief and settlement into a new life on a ranch in Comanche territory in Texas. But Carter's real first name was discovered to be Asa—the same Asa Carter who had written some of George Wallace's most rabidly segregationist speeches, including "segregation now, segregation tomorrow, segregation forever," and who had been, hardly surprisingly, a member of the Ku Klux Klan. That a rabid racist (who claimed to be part Cherokee) was responsible for writing a picaresque tale about a wronged Southerner who triumphs over Northerners even though they have triumphed over the South is not surprising. That this same Southerner would also have such an inclusive view of America might be.

      Different as they are, such incommensurabilities intersect with Eastwood's own. Kaufman saw improvisation as central to the production; Eastwood saw it as a waste of time. Ultimately, since Eastwood's relationship with Warner Brothers was far stronger than Kaufman's, and since he had put up the money for the rights to the story, Kaufman was let go, and Eastwood took the helm. It was Eastwood who expanded Chief Dan George's role as Lone Watie and, impressed by what he'd done in Arthur Penn's *Little Big Man* (1970) opposite Dustin Hoffman, allowed him, ironically vis-à-vis Kaufman's firing, to improvise long monologues. After Kaufman's firing, the Director's Guild of America implemented the "Eastwood Rule," which prevents a producer from firing the director and replacing that director with him or herself.

15 Walter Mosley, *Workin' on the Chain Gang: Shaking Off the Dead Hand of History* (New York: Ballantine Books, 2000), 10–11.

16 Paul Smith, *Clint Eastwood: A Cultural Production* (Minneapolis: University of Minnesota Press, 1993), 42–43.

17 *Candidate Confessional: Stories of Those Who Ran and Lost*, episode 3, "Mitt Romney's Top Aide on the White House Run." Stuart Stevens, interview by Sam Stein and Jason Cherkis, *Huffington Post* Podcast, January 24, 2016.

18 Michael Hainey, "Clint and Scott Eastwood: No Holds Barred in Their First Interview Together," *Esquire*, August 3, 2016, accessed November 13, 2016, http://www .esquire.com/entertainment/a46893/double-trouble-clint-and-scott-eastwood/.

19 Mosley, *Workin' on the Chain Gang*, 46–47.

20 Freeman's performance of Mandela is not only the Exceptional Negro but the perfect human being, with foibles delicately placed like flowers on a birthday cake. *Invictus* verges on "forgiveness porn." Mandela is more than black, as per *Do the Right Thing*, but is also almost more than human.

21 It is worth clarifying that to describe Eastwood's films as melodramatic and formulaic is not to denigrate them. Eastwood is a master of male melodrama, and his capacity to use a formula (generic or otherwise) to produce effective narratives is QED.

22 Dennis Bingham, *Acting Male: Masculinities in the Films of James Stewart, Jack Nicholson, and Clint Eastwood* (New Brunswick, N.J.: Rutgers University Press, 1994), 219–230.

23 Jonathan Rosenbaum, "Lout of Africa [*White Hunter Black Heart*]," joinathan rosenbaum.net, September 27, 1990, accessed February 25, 2018, http://www .jonathanrosenbaum.net/1990/09/lout-in-africa/.

24 Rosenbaum, "Lout of Africa." Or as Bingham has it, Eastwood is "managing to strike blows for racial tolerance and misogyny at the same time." Bingham, *Acting Male*, 224.

25 Bingham, 226.

26 Quoted in Joseph McBride, "Straight Shooting: Eastwood Looks West to Honor Mentor's Legacy," *Variety*, August 6, 1992, 23.

27 Just as Will previously gave his name to Daggett as Will Hendershot, using the last name of a dead man, so Ned's self-renaming is deliberate, and evokes not only the name of the man that John McCabe (Warren Beatty) supposedly killed in *McCabe and Mrs. Miller* but also the name of Richard Roundtree, the blaxploitation star of *Shaft* (1971). It also reconnects him to his wife, Sally Two Trees.

28 Richard Dyer, *White* (London: Routledge, 1997), 1.

29 This dream is a highly individuated one that relies on the Hmong American Dream mapping onto previous immigrants' assimilation into whiteness, a category that once upon a time, Italians, Irish and Eastern European Jews, for instance, didn't occupy. Kowalski dislikes all institutions: the government, the church, and even his own family, who are a comically execrable bunch—the grandchildren at Walt's wife's funeral attached to digital devices with earbuds that read like umbilical cords, their parents befuddled by their own father's curmudgeonly ways and his resistance to being shunted off to a retirement community. The priest who worries over Walt after his wife dies is a decent guy in spite of his priestliness. (The military fares better, but only because the character himself is a Korean War veteran. Eastwood himself has publicly opposed every war since that one, but he supports soldiers and

the mythos of soldiering, as *American Sniper* makes clear.) It's also the case that the Hmong family saves him—or at least his eternal soul.

30 Martin calls Thao a "Chink" and a "Nip," but never does he settle on Thao's Hmong identity, with or without a slur.

31 Quoted in Jeff Dawson, "Dirty Harry Comes Clean," *Guardian*, June 5, 2008, accessed November 10, 2016, https://www.theguardian.com/film/2008/jun/06/1.

11

Play Music for Me

● ● ● ● ● ● ● ● ● ● ● ● ● ● ● ● ● ● ● ●

The Film Scores

CHARITY LOFTHOUSE

For Clint Eastwood, long before the movies, there was the piano: "If I've had any regret in life, it was not paying more attention to it and not practice, practice, practice."[1] A jazz enthusiast from an early age, Eastwood formed perhaps his most important musical relationship with his piano, which offered him a means to cope with a peripatetic childhood and a way to relate to girls, to friends, and to the world: "You could channel yourself into an instrument . . . it was almost like a wall you could hide behind."[2] Spanning from plans for a college major in music to his film about jazz legend Charlie Parker and from commercial honkytonk recordings to a live performance at Carnegie Hall, music has arguably held at least as strong a place in Eastwood's life as his films.

If music was a wall Eastwood could hide behind, it was also a means to express himself artistically, as a performer and composer. He not only remains an enthusiastic pianist but has also amassed a sizable—yet largely overlooked—body of work as a film-score composer, creating the soundtracks to eight films since 2003's *Mystic River* as well as more than two dozen other solo and collaborative songwriting and musical performance credits. Indeed, musical support for his filmic ideas seems never to be far from his mind: "To and from work, I play music in the car; and then sometimes I'll play music that I want to use in the picture. Or I'll get an inspiration about something and I'll sit down and make up something and then I'll put it in the picture as a mock-up score or something."[3] Rather than pursue these artistic loves as separate enterprises, Eastwood has managed to fuse them throughout his long career.

Eastwood's strong interest in music notwithstanding, critics do not always seem to know quite how to confront and assess his film scores. Several of his soundtracks have won Golden Globe and Grammy awards and accumulated numerous other awards and nominations.[4] Even still, reviews tend to gloss over the scores in comparison to the cinematography, directing, and acting.[5] When the music is not ignored completely, reception tends to fall into two camps: praise for the music's "elegiac" and "hauntingly minimalist" qualities, as well as his emotionally direct themes, and complaints about the simplistic, limited, and repetitive nature of the musical content and the cues across his films as a whole.[6] The latter take is perhaps acknowledged most directly by William Weir in a 2011 article titled, "Clint Eastwood Is a Great Director. Is He a Good Composer?" Though the article more broadly takes up the perceived mediocrity of director/composers in comparison to the professional composers with whom they collaborated, the verdicts on Eastwood's scores from film scholars quoted in the article were decidedly unenthusiastic.[7]

Despite Eastwood's lengthy and lauded career and his deep involvement with music, close readings of his film scores are in extremely short supply, thus limiting the potential ability to respond more specifically to Weir's question, "Is he any good?" To address this gap, this chapter first goes directly to the musical notes themselves: in-depth analyses focusing on his award-winning and nominated scores (*Mystic River*, *Million Dollar Baby*, and *Grace Is Gone*) illustrate specific aspects of how Eastwood's scores are put together as well as his general turn toward the musical language of the intimate and personal. These range from his depiction of emotion and tragic reality through leitmotifs in *Million Dollar Baby* and timbre and instrumentation in *Mystic River* to the relationship between melody and phrase construction in helping knit a family back together in *Grace Is Gone*. These analyses position Eastwood's film scores in relationship to historical and stylistic precedents, each film's narrative, and the resulting emotional effect of his compositional style, made all the more poignant by the sparing use of musical cues. I conclude with an exploration of broader questions regarding his reception and compositional "professionalism" and process, examining the complicated characterization of Eastwood's film-scoring activities as more "amateur" than his filmmaking. Contrasting descriptions of Eastwood's soundtracks with his more respected filmmaking reputation, I contend that such consideration of his film scores stems in part from gendered comparisons between his masculine on-screen persona and the soundtracks from his iconic pre-2000 films and the intimate, emotional, and self-described "slow" sound language of his own compositions.

Once upon a Time in the Ring: Leitmotifs and Musical Allusions in *Million Dollar Baby*

Just under seven minutes into 2007's *Million Dollar Baby*, former boxer Eddie "Scrap" Dupris (Morgan Freeman) completes a voice-over introduction to Frankie Dunn (Eastwood) with the following: "Some people would say the most important thing a boxer can have is heart; Frankie would say, 'Show me a man who's nothing but heart and I'll show you a man who's waiting for a beating.'" Struggling with the juxtaposition of heart and fist proves to be a tragic undertaking for Frankie that unfolds from ministrations as a cut man at the film's opening to his final interaction with Maggie Fitzgerald (Hilary Swank), the woman he trains and comes to love like a daughter despite his rule that he "doesn't train girls."

Recognized with a Golden Globe Award for Best Original Score and a Grammy for Best Score Soundtrack for Visual Media, *Million Dollar Baby* is the fifth film soundtrack for which Eastwood composed music and the second of his own films that he scored himself. This soundtrack is also the first to display many of the general features Eastwood went on to employ in his subsequent movie scores: sparseness of texture, small instrument groups, alternation of piano, string, and guitar cues featuring the main theme(s), and the use of particular instruments or leitmotifs to represent the main characters. In addition to these more general techniques, this soundtrack draws on classic Hollywood practices and alludes to particular soundtracks to subtly highlight the film's larger themes (good and evil, familial ties and estrangement, life and death, hope and tragedy, prosperity and poverty) in a manner heard in the soundtracks of other Western-themed films.

Eastwood provides Frankie and Maggie each with a distinctive musical idea, or leitmotif, early on. These leitmotifs are similar to each other in shape, texture, and thematic design, yet clearly differentiated in instrumentation and melodic shape. Such similarities and differences reflect the shifting nature of the evolving relationship between them, as well as providing a musical embodiment of Frankie and Maggie's shared drive and love of boxing. They also poignantly amplify their loneliness, gambles with lethal risk, and intertwined yet ultimately divergent fates. Frankie's theme opens the film, a sparse guitar melody that comes to be associated with his emotional life. The theme is in some ways a duet, with pairs of notes simultaneously moving through a lilting stepwise rise and fall with the interval of a sixth between them (see fig. 11.1).[8] This cue accompanies the opening studio logos and credits, as well as Scrap's initial voice-over, stopping abruptly with the start of the first fight. At once spare and gentle, the theme connects the viewer not to Frankie the boxer, but to Frankie the man, offering passage through his tough exterior into the tender moments when Frankie is abandoned professionally (by his best

FIGURE 11.1 Frankie's theme, *Million Dollar Baby* (2007).

fighter) and personally (when his letters to his estranged daughter are returned unopened). Maggie's theme emerges several minutes after she appears, once she is ensconced at the gym and as she practices her hitting technique after Scrap takes her under his wing. Rather than the lilting arch of Frankie's theme, Maggie's theme starts high and gently descends, tumbling down over and over in alternating rise-and-fall motions outlining successive third intervals in the melody (see fig. 11.2).

From this moment of tentative hope offered by Scrap, Maggie's and Frankie's destinies become musically and emotionally linked: Maggie's third-saturated piano leitmotif may be heard as a flipped-over version of Frankie's guitar sixths (see fig. 11.3). Maggie's intervals are a reflection of Frankie's, as each views the other as a mirror for the possibility of achieving ambition and redemption, respectively. After appearing initially in a solo piano version, string accompaniment then joins in and provides harmonic support for Maggie's theme in the form of parallel sixths over an unmoving bass line. Frankie's sparse opening sixth intervals are transformed as they join in Maggie's theme: now stately string harmonies, the sixths prove sturdy enough to support Maggie's falling melodic line. As Maggie stubbornly practices without his permission, Frankie comes to see in her the determination, drive, loneliness, and loss that he harbors in his own inner life.

Their leitmotifs continue to intermingle throughout the film, most touchingly when Frankie finally agrees to train Maggie. Among the longest musical cues in the film, this two-minute montage features Frankie's theme first, with a noticeable new spring in its step: the theme is faster, features a wider

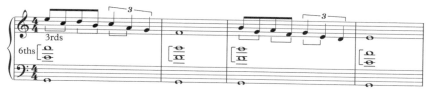

FIGURE 11.2 Maggie's theme, *Million Dollar Baby*

FIGURE 11.3 Inversional ("flipped-over")
relationship between third (featured in
Maggie's theme) and sixth (featured in
Frankie's theme) intervals

range of notes, and includes embellishments in the style of blues improvisation. After several repetitions of Frankie's "jazzed-up" theme, Maggie's melody
appears, played by the guitar, Frankie's instrument. His theme and her theme
are now directly combined and infused with the jazz-inflected atmosphere of
the music heard in the film's diegetic cues (most often presented in Frankie's
boxing club, the Hit Pit, and adding a nostalgic, old-fashioned ambience) to
create something greater than the empty third- and sixth-focused spaces of
each leitmotif on its own.

In addition to its connections to Frankie's theme, Maggie's leitmotif also
includes an additional reference: in a nod to iconic film composer Ennio Morricone, Maggie's theme bears extremely strong resemblance to Jill McBain's
theme from Morricone's score to Sergio Leone's 1968 Western *Once upon
a Time in the West* (see fig. 11.4). Common traits between the two themes
include beginning and ending on scale-degree 3 (shown with the symbol ^
below; scale degree indicates a particular note's position in the key or scale); a
two-part layout of the phrase with the halfway point punctuated by an ascend-
ing leap; the same or similar harmonies in the same order, changing at the same
rate (once per measure); and a strong emphasis on third intervals (see fig. 11.5).

This musical connection to Jill McBain highlights the many similarities
between these tales of women fighting against all odds: In each film, these
respective leitmotifs represent strong women overcoming disadvantaged
Southern backgrounds and leaving everything they know behind to venture
into a Western frontier that doesn't welcome them with open arms. Jill McBain
is a former prostitute who loses her family to murderous outlaws and fights
for the only thing she has left: her land and the hope of prosperity it represents. Maggie Fitzgerald, as we are told by Scrap, "grew up knowing one thing:
she was trash," loses her family to death, poverty, and betrayal, and fights
for the only thing she has left: a boxing career and the hope of prosperity it
represents. Musical and narrative elements of *Million Dollar Baby*, including

FIGURE 11.4 Jill McBain's theme, *Once upon a Time in the West* (1968)

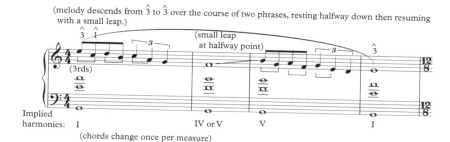

FIGURE 11.5 Comparison of Maggie's (top) and Jill's (bottom) themes

the sparse use of music cues, the cutting off of the music at the opening fight scene, the leitmotific approach to instrumentation and themes, and the over-arching plot and use of language (Maggie's accent and calling Frankie "boss") are all reminiscent of Leone's tale of family tragedy, isolation, and sheer determination in the face of evil.

If Frankie's and Maggie's themes represent father-daughter connection and collective achievement of a championship dream, their themes are liquidated along with their dreams at the film's climactic fight and subsequent heartbreak. At the moment Maggie reaches the biggest fight of her career, her solo piano and soft strings are replaced with diegetic pipers and music suitable for the grand entrance of a fighter who's finally made it. This musical supplanting of the previous leitmotifs not only lends a kind of grand artifice to the fight and a new (contender) identity for Maggie but also portends the event that will prematurely end her career and ultimately her life. The piano and low strings that accompany the arrival of her opponent, Billy the Blue Bear, eliminate both the victorious pipes and the lyrical consonant thirds and sixths in favor of menacing atonality along with dissonant, angular, fragmented melodies reaching both high and low in the strings. The soaring heights of the pipes are echoed by the anguished pleas of violins, grieving for the life and dreams lost in an unjust instant.

As Maggie learns of her prognosis and her condition deteriorates, the music shifts, alternating between moments of relative musical modernism and lush, almost romantic symphonic strings. Maggie's soft piano instrumentation and leitmotif makes one final appearance while Frankie tenderly washes Maggie's paralyzed body in a hospital bed. Noticing the bedsores, he once again performs as the cut man and father figure, getting her ready for a fight he knows she can't win. This is the last time they enact this ritual before Maggie's return to the rehab center where her life ends at his hand. In contrast to this tender moment, Frankie's theme never returns while Maggie is alive—his heart is as broken as hers.

Maggie comes to find life in her condition unbearable; the musical cue "Maggie's Plea" begins as she asks Frankie to do her the same favor her father had done for their ailing dog, Axel, years earlier: end her life. This cue, composed of stark open fourths and fifths, not only contrasts with the earlier, complementary leitmotifs but also evokes connection to a tragic death scene from a Western of a different kind: the euthanizing of Curly's dog as scored by Aaron Copland in the 1939 film version of John Steinbeck's *Of Mice and Men*. The fatal, tragic California of Steinbeck is now the emotional and physical landscape in which Frankie and Maggie are living: yet another dream is crushed, another partnership destroyed, and another tragedy plucked from the hope of prosperity the Golden State seemingly promised to Lennie and George and to Frankie and Maggie.[9] Less a direct quote than a musical allusion, the music from the Copland and Eastwood cues share sparse textures, tonally ambiguous and widely spaced chords, a small group of instruments spread over a wide pitch range, and angular, gestural melodies focused on lilting, two-note sighing figures. As Copland's music tenderly yet starkly depicts Curly simultaneously facing the anguish of life without his trusted and beloved companion even as he knows the dog is beyond hope, Eastwood's draws on a similar stark musical language to accompany Maggie's plea that Frankie put her down like a dog too lame to walk.

It is not until after Maggie's death—and after Scrap reveals in a voice-over that Frankie never returned home, prompting him to write Frankie's estranged daughter about "what kind of man your father was"—that Frankie's or Maggie's leitmotifs return. At the film's final scene, Frankie is shown at Ira's

Roadside Restaurant and a jazzy piano intro brings back Frankie's leitmotif, now performed by the piano, Maggie's instrument. As the camera shows us Frankie's location, a place wherein he earlier exclaimed, "Now I can die and go to Heaven," his sixths have been inverted to her thirds, turning his melody upside down, as his life finally seems right side up. Conversely, her piano is given the rising and falling arch of his leitmotif. It is a novel fusion of their music, a new, transformed permutation of their combined leitmotifs and a reflection of the appropriation of her theme by his instrument during that first night at the Hit Pit. This is, in sum, a new life for their combined leitmotifs, an infusion of hope appearing for the first time in the film's final seconds.

Mediating (and Mediatizing) Emotions: Diegetic Music and Subjectivities in *Mystic River*

One can perhaps imagine no greater terrors than those seen in Eastwood's 2003 film, *Mystic River*. At its opening, there is the senseless and seemingly random kidnapping and victimization of an innocent child, Dave Boyle (played as an adult by Tim Robbins), at the hands of two nameless pedophiles. Next is the equally senseless (and equally random) killing of Katie Markum (Emmy Rossum), the daughter of Dave's childhood friend Jimmy Markum (Sean Penn), just hours before she had planned to escape her own childhood and begin a new life as an adult in Las Vegas. And finally, there is the intertwining of Dave and Jimmy's fates as Jimmy fights back against the randomness of his trauma by wrongly blaming and executing Dave for Katie's murder. Like its eponymous body of water, the film's misery seems to flow from an origin, Dave's traumatization, and to progress incessantly to the friends, wives, and children of Dave, Jimmy, and Sean Devine (Kevin Bacon) despite their efforts to leave the pain behind.

The first of Eastwood's films that he scored in full, its soundtrack is notable for the lush orchestral timbre (recorded by the Boston Symphony Orchestra) and its evocative, heartfelt, and lyrical main theme.[10] Although this theme makes up the majority of the film's musical cues, Eastwood contrasts it with the interspersing of various diegetic cues, and their effects play an important role in bringing to life the complex emotional journey from trauma to recovery to revenge. Far from straightforward, *Mystic River*'s intertwining tragedies are embodied in the shape and flow of the main theme as an unpredictable, intersecting, ebbing, and flowing of fate, as well as in the on-screen depiction of the diegetic cues as both outside of the characters' control and intruding into their emotional and mental beings. The back-and-forth between the Greek-chorus-like underscore and intruding diegetic cues serves a particular role in shaping viewers' subjective experiences by facilitating migration between emotional states framed by Arnie Cox as "quasi-first-person" and "second-person" subjectivities, or feeling like a participant with the musical gestures and themes versus sensing the music as a sound object separate from the listener.[11] Eastwood accentuates this facilitation via the contrast between the underscore's corresponding to private, direct expressions of emotion by the main characters themselves and the diegetic music's public, mediated cues that emphasize a character's vulnerability to the imposition of the predatory music.

Examining this contrast in more detail starts with exploring the musical components of the main theme—a circuitous, repetitive, languid, and lyrical orchestral theme combined with slow-moving harmonies and smooth, overlapping transitions between intra- and interthematic repetitions. The film's opening and most oft-repeated cue is displayed in figure 11.6; the rich sounds of the orchestra bring to life a theme at once expansive and restrictive,

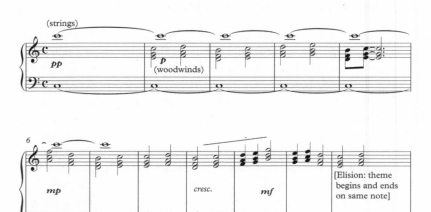

FIGURE 11.6 Transcription of the main theme, *Mystic River* (2003)

highlighting the wish to transcend the horrors of these childhood friends' lives while at the same time being doomed to repeat them. The sustained pedal tones in the high and low strings, holding steady at the extremes of the musical texture, maintain a strong sense of stasis that complements the constricted range and repetitive nature of the melody's opening phrase. The melody not only is circular and constricted within the phrase itself but also functions cyclically at the interphrase level: after reaching up for the G above its starting pitch in measure 10, the melody works its way back to its origins and the second phrase begins on the downbeat of measure 12 on the very same note, C, that both opens and closes the opening phrase.

The music strains against its limits by means of the space between its highest and lowest notes and via volume: the first of two wedge shapes between the notes of the melody and bass expands the sense of musical space in measures 9–10. This expansion is repeated and further highlighted during the clarinet solo in measures 14–17 through both increased volume and denser orchestral texture. This wedge is followed with another in measure 19, as a burst of volume features the whole orchestra's energizing presence. Each of these bursts is dramatically exhausted and ultimately discharged by means of silence, returning to the opening note and chord after each outburst and then beginning the cycle once again.

Finally, the phrase lengths themselves are somewhat erratic and unpredictable, due in part to the high degree of overlap. The opening phrase begins as what seems to be a common eight-measure unit; this expectation is thwarted on the downbeat of measure 8, where the phrase starts over a measure early. This repetition makes it only four measures before once again starting over at measure 12. The next phrase, measures 12–21, is also broken up irregularly by the silences into six- and four-measure subphrases, respectively. No phrase or subphrase is the same length as any other, breaking up the expectation of uniform periodicity typically experienced in similar musical themes and providing some sense of atemporal flow to complement the repetition of the melody.[12]

These factors set the stage for a high degree of identification from the viewer: physical and emotional empathy and a particularly strong quasi-first-person subjective positioning are evoked via three interrelated avenues: ease of mimetic participation, successful prediction, and a high perception of musical "liveness." The first of these, mimetic participation, may be traced to the constant efforts by individuals to make physical and emotional sense of sonic input through conscious and subconscious imitation. Every listening experience, from distant birds to a Beethoven symphony, involves conscious and unconscious attempts at comprehension. Most descriptions of film music as "empathetic" and "anempathetic" are engaging notions of mimetic participation and its effect on musical subjectivity; Cox sums up this process as a kind of exploring what it would feel like to "do" or "be" the sound one is hearing. A musical cue's encouragement or opacity regarding this predilection, what Cox calls its "mimetic invitation," is neither wholly "objective" nor "subjective" but some combination of what Cox calls the "acoustic fact" (pitch, duration, timbre, strength, and location) and a listener's receptivity to the impact of these acoustic phenomena.

The main theme from *Mystic River* can be said to extend a particularly clear mimetic invitation through its lyrical, highly singable melody that features smooth, stepwise motions, predictable rhythm, a restricted vocal range, a high degree of internal and large-scale repetition, a constant tendency to return to the note where it started, and clear reaching gestures (the wedges) that draw on one's tendency to follow along with and metaphorize musical motion in soundtracks (commonly referred to as "mickey-mousing") more generally.[13] In short, its design makes it especially inviting to "sing" along—consciously or subconsciously, vocally or just in our heads—and in doing so, we come to internalize the music as part of our emotional experience.

Second is the pleasure of successful prediction, a phenomenon integral to vicarious mimetic participation and to human experience in general.[14] Prediction in this case is positively coded not only in the short term but also for predicting the musical experience of the film as a whole. The main theme of *Mystic River* (and title sequences in general) creates successful rewards for prediction in two broad ways: in internal repetitions of a phrase or set of phrases within the experience of the cue itself and in recognizable recurrences of the cue throughout the entire film. In this case, the internal repetitions in *Mystic River*'s main theme and the theme's repetition throughout the film offer a cyclical confirmation, via successful prediction, of the characters' doomed fates.

Finally, due to several factors including its ubiquity and familiarity, invisibility, perceived acoustic and timbral purity, and conceptual role as a "neutral" presence held over from live theater, the underscore is perceived by the viewer as more "live," or the direct, unmediated, authentic product of human effort. Models of its location in a neutral position (the orchestra pit), though no longer a physical reality, are still prevalent in the modern viewer's psyche. This increases both its perception as emotionally live and "authentic" and the ease of vicarious participation that invokes Cox's first-person subjectivity most strongly. This "neutral" and "authentic" background, more than just emotional or semantic vestige, can be said to maintain what Sanden refers to as a high level of perceived "liveness of fidelity" and "corporeal liveness." The first involves a perceived absence of amplification, Auto-Tuning, artificial reverberation, and other alterations; this perception invokes a feeling of authenticity and fidelity stemming from the perceived lack of technological intervention in the musical events. Connected to the mimetic hypothesis, Sanden's "corporeal liveness" draws on the human propensity to understand music through embodied experience and also to perceive its converse, or "mediatized music's potential for eliminating all traces of bodies, at least from the process of musical *expression*."[15]

In contrast to the orchestral underscore's participatory and empathetic elements, the diegetic cues in *Mystic River* are mediated via public ritual and *mediatized music*, a term Sanden uses to connote a musical object that is the product of mass media or media technology. The striking dichotomy between public and private, diegetic and underscore, and second-person and quasi-first-person subjectivities is further accentuated by the mediation and mediatization of the diegetic cues, which emphasize artifice, mechanized or institutionalized production, and electrified timbres. The visuals reinforce this sense of remove by placing the characters and viewers in a vulnerable position vis-à-vis the music: the visual presence of a mediating device may serve to rein in the imagined, participatory body by presenting a heartless, mechanized producer. Collectively, these elements accentuate a second-person subjective experience that positions the characters and viewer as at the mercy of the inhuman, diegetic music-as-invading-object, presented as yet another victimizing force.

Two distinct forms of musical mediation flow through *Mystic River*: music that is represented as mediated via public ritual and music that is presented as mediated via its mechanized production. Examples of the latter include the handful of diegetic cues taking place in bars, with music produced through a jukebox or radio, and a scene early on in the film when Dave sees Katie enter the neighborhood bar with her friends and can't help but notice and comment on the girls' celebratory mood as they turn on the jukebox and dance on the bar. This human and musical intrusion on Dave's inner musings is out of his hands; the jukebox is too loud and its mechanized production out of his power to stop.

This cue offers several paradoxes: first, though the music is mediated and is represented as the result of a mechanized, bodiless process, it is both the recording of a human-produced performance and accompanied by the simultaneous intrusion of a "live" enactment featuring the girls singing and dancing on the bar. Moreover, this explicit mediatization of music is made possible through its display in the diegesis; in other words, it is recognized as "live" because of its visual placement in the character's universe, enabled through its mediatized production. This process is contrasted with the underscore, which may be viewed as less mediated—therefore more direct or "live" to the viewer—in part because of its very lack of visual representation. This lack of a visual source creates a concomitant heightening of the viewer's imagined orchestra, along with its participatory, "live," acoustic bodies.[16]

The other means of mediation, music mediated by ritual, includes two of the film's most poignant and complex scenes: the baptism of Jimmy's younger daughter, during which Katie is conspicuously absent, and the film's penulti-mate scene, a civic parade after Dave has gone missing and when Dave's wife, Celeste (Marcia Gay Harden), who suspects Jimmy had something to do with Dave's disappearance, lays eyes on Jimmy and seemingly confirms her deepest fears. If one takes McLuhan's adage that "the medium is the message" as a lens for these scenes, the medium of public ritual and mediatized music communi-cates both the firm boundaries of community life and the disconnect between the public facade of ritualized normalcy and the suffering of Celeste, her son, and the people whose lives are framed by these communal rituals.

While the parade scene at the film's end takes advantage of a blending of (or migration between) diegetic music and underscoring fairly common in film scores, the baptism cue sends a series of mixed messages both through the mediatizing ritual and through its use of timbre and instruments that evoke a blend of diegetic and nondiegetic elements.[17] As Jimmy waits for Katie's arrival at her younger sister's baptism, the opening shot of the scene, show-ing the church from outside, features a synthesizer playing the main theme. Unlike the acoustic timbre of the marching band and its migration to an equally acoustic sounding underscore, the synthesizer seemingly starts out as a quasi-diegetic stand-in for the sound of a pipe organ. As the children prog-ress down the church's center aisle toward their first communion, Eastwood intersperses the scene with the investigation of Katie's murder; the music thus serves as diegetic for one locale but not the other. The addition of orchestra and chorus drives the main theme toward its climactic outburst while shots of the procession provide a glimpse of the organ and choir loft in the back-ground, providing a potential visual source/correlate for the musical under-score's synthesized "organ" and choir.

The musical cue concludes with the main theme's climax, followed by silence that clears the rapturous texture of full orchestra and choir before a return to the solo synthesizer. Whereas the choir and "organ" suggest that the music may be live in the diegesis, the effect is more than a potential sleight-of-hand switch of synth and acoustic organ—the use of an identifiably electri-fied and mediated timbre as part of the underscore is noticeably incongruous among the "live" orchestra and choir and the only use of an electrified instru-ment in the film's underscore. Jimmy may be present in the ritual, but this media-tized timbral invasion into the sound world exposes that this ritual is no more protective than the parade; he is indeed in for a world of hurt.

Eastwood's use of this juxtaposition may find its roots in *Mystic River*, but is also used to very powerful effect in *Million Dollar Baby* and in East-wood's score to 2007's *Grace Is Gone*, taken up in more detail below. The use of diegetic popular music throughout *Grace Is Gone* emphasizes not only its mediation but also its mediatization: in one noteworthy example, Stanley

(John Cusack) approaches his daughters in an arcade and the viewer can see him visibly wince as he approaches their game of *Dance Dance Revolution*. The music is an assaulting force, emanating from a relentless and overbearing machine into his private (and at that point secret) grief and anxiety.

Perhaps the most compelling example of public, ritualized music takes place in Eastwood's 2011 film *J. Edgar*. This score as a whole features techniques similar to *Million Dollar Baby* and *Mystic River*, namely, the use of longer, somewhat irregular phrases, selective dissonance, mixtures of orchestra and solo piano, and the mediated presence of diegetic music. *J. Edgar*'s use of diegetic music largely serves as an indicator of time and place and is usually mediatized via radio or television. Among the film's only "live" diegetic cues, a jazz-club band is featured eighty minutes into the film, as J. Edgar Hoover (Leonardo DiCaprio) and his assistant and longtime companion, Clyde Tolson (Armie Hammer), decide to venture into public and dine out. Seated with Anita Colby, Ginger Rogers, and Ginger's mother, and repeatedly pressed about his relationship status, the warm, sensuous, and acoustic diegetic music once again comes to represent a public ritual—heterosexual courtship—and serves as an irresistible mimetic invitation to the women, who intend to dance "live" and vicariously fulfill the viewer's desire to do so.

Having sought to escape the bonds of their professional obligations and of heteronormative expectations, Edgar and Clyde have only become trapped once more, via the public ritual of dancing music. Here, the mediatized, highly participatory, and ultimately menacing music intrudes into their burgeoning and fragile ardor, and that kind of direct, subjective experience—dancing to music as part of a publicly mediated and ritualized courtship experience—is simply too much for Edgar to bear. The music at once shifts from the background to the foreground, becoming an oppressive, bullying object coming at him in the shape of domination and secrecy and bringing back his stutter. This music continues after the cut to Edgar talking with his mother about his refusal to "dance with women" and her veiled threat of disowning him if he reveals his homosexuality. Jazz won't return again until the ending credits, after J. Edgar has died and the viewer may give into its invitation to participate in that most human of experiences—quasi-first-person identification with the music—in his place.

Loose-Knit Themes and Unraveled Lives: Melodic Design and Musical Phrases in *Grace Is Gone*

While many have no trouble conjuring the emphatic, strident themes from the films Eastwood has starred in over the years, bringing to mind Eastwood's own film compositions is an altogether different experience. Rather than galloping-horse drums, iconic whistles, or twanging guitars, viewers are often greeted with lyrical piano, plaintive acoustic guitar, and gentle melodicism. Perhaps the most distinctive and pervasive trait of Eastwood's film scores is his predilection for heartfelt, slow, and reflective themes. *Grace Is Gone* (2007), the first (and so far only) film Eastwood scored but did not direct or produce, features song-like lyrical themes similar to those in *Mystic River* and *Million Dollar Baby*, culminating with a pop version of the film's main theme, "Grace," accompanying the end credits.[18] As the film traces the unraveling of a man after his wife's death and the subsequent reknitting of a family's new life without her, the music illustrates Eastwood's use of the "loose-knit" theme and what I call an "unraveled" phrase structure in creating melodies that reflect the film's emotional journey, one that is contemplative, intimate, and heartfelt.

The terms *tight-knit themes* and *loose-knit themes*, outlined in detail in William Caplin's 1998 book *Classical Form*, originated chiefly as a means to describe the differences between the tonal and melodic aspects of assertive primary themes and lyrical secondary themes in sonata and symphony movements, before being extended to broader uses. Tight-knit themes (or "theme zones") feature stability, confirmation and maintenance of the music's main key, conventional and symmetrical phrases, and firm conclusion. By contrast, loose-knit themes feature key instability or frequent key changes, unconventional phrase structures, asymmetrical phrases that feature extensions, expansions, or compressions, and lack of firm closure. In instrumental works such as symphonies or sonatas, the tight-knit characteristics are most commonly assigned to the opening, "masculine" theme at the work's beginning, while the contrasting, lyrical, subordinate, "feminine" theme features a more loose-knit design.[19]

In *Grace Is Gone*, the loose-knit theme traces the emotional journey of Stanley as he learns of his wife's death and tries to imagine his family's future without Grace. "Grace's Theme" is displayed in figure 11.7. The structure of the phrase, known in music-theoretical terms as a sentence, outlines a two-measure unit, labeled the basic idea, and its (typically varied) repetition; these two statements of the basic idea comprise the sentence's first half and launch the phrase. The second half of a sentence, coined the continuation, is occupied

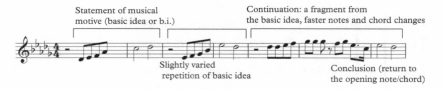

FIGURE 11.7 Transcription of the main theme, *Grace Is Gone* (2007)

with the task of fragmentation and liquidation en route to closure. In a typical continuation, a small portion of the basic idea is excerpted and repeated, while the chords change at quicker intervals, the rhythm speeds up, and the music accelerates toward the end of the phrase. This phrase type, with its relative potential for asymmetry (the *short, short, long* feeling of basic idea, basic idea, continuation) and feelings of speeding up and liquidation, is characterized by Caplin as relatively loose-knit in comparison to other kinds of phrase structures.[20] Sentences may be combined to form larger, more stable phrases and formal structures; such treatment commonly features a sentence with a less conclusive closing, followed by a repeat of the same sentence, which is then varied to produce a firm, conclusive closing. This dialectic (weak-strong, open-closed, question-answer) is a mainstay of both classical and popular music traditions.[21]

Grace's theme begins to unravel from the film's opening scene: as an answering machine message from Grace begins with, "Hi, it's Mom," an unaccompanied, lyrical piano theme presents one statement of Grace's theme with a conclusive ending, before repeating it with its various components out of order (the basic idea and its repetition are reversed, and part of the continuation is omitted). The theme concludes without a firm sense of closure and without a consistent tempo or any chordal support. By placing the most fully formed and most tight-knit version first, and the dismantled, unraveling repetition second, Eastwood cuts against the normative musical narrative of open-closed, question-answer typical of sentence pairings. This rearrangement and reversal thus becomes a form of undoing the normative musical structure, a technique I will refer to as "unraveling" the phrase. In this case, with the phrase's sense of direction and closure undone, the phrase dies off without any sense of conclusion or immediately recognizable inner structure.[22]

Unraveling the phrase at its expected ending becomes a stirring means of developing and transforming this simple melody, used throughout the film as a classic and somewhat predictable leitmotif. (In a manner similar to *Million Dollar Baby*, the solo piano becomes Grace's leitmotif, reappearing each time we hear her voice on the answering machine, while the guitar serves as Stanley's instrumental soul-searching identity: acoustic by day, jazz guitar by night.) The unraveling of Grace's theme is especially poignant as two uniformed visitors inform Stanley of Grace's death. After he is told that Grace is dead, a solitary horn takes Grace's theme, accompanied by an orchestra that oscillates between two obsessive, static chords and a piano soaring high above the texture, out of tempo with the rest of the instruments and with no clear sense of key. This rendering of the sentence comes completely unbound: as the end of the phrase is extended and recomposed to omit any sense of closure, the chords become trapped in a ruminating back and forth and an abrupt silence brings the cue to an almost violent dissolution. These techniques allow the theme to be at once consistent and ever-present while also dissolving into death and the grief that holds Stanley.

After a lengthy car trip during which Stanley keeps Grace's death from his two daughters, their arrival at the Enchanted Gardens theme park features the original full sentence in order, along with chordal support. This version of the theme mirrors the plot's turn toward truth: five repetitions of the theme's sentence phrase are sewn together to create a larger, more tightly knit ABABA song form. The A sections provide standard harmonic progressions and full sentences with strong closures, while the B sections supply a variation of the sentence that features an open-ended link back to the A sections, presenting a weak-strong paradigm. This knitting back together both foreshadows the song version at the film's end and corresponds to the end of Stanley's secret: as the phrases are knit back together into this standard ABABA structure, the family finds a way to go on and go home without Grace. The music ceases its anguished wandering and becomes more regular, more predictable, and less inconsolable.

Several of Eastwood's soundtracks feature loose-knit phrase constructions and similar explorations of liquidated or altered phrase endings, including *J. Edgar*, *Mystic River*, and, to some degree, *Million Dollar Baby*.[23] Eastwood seems to shift toward more tight-knit phrase structures and greater use of unaltered repetitions for both *Changeling* and *Hereafter*: each uses pairs of sentences at the film's opening to create a tighter and more stable combination rather than developing various transformations of a sentence phrase, then pairing it with a repetition. Eastwood's score for 2006's *Flags of Our Fathers* could even be considered an example of a theme too tightly knit: the main theme's lullaby-like structure features brief, two-note units repeated eight times during the theme's two phrases. This theme is both too internally repetitive and too limited from a tonal perspective for the kind of transformation or development heard in *Grace Is Gone*. Ultimately, Eastwood presents this repetitive cue in numerous scenes without any extension, transformation, introspection, or development. While this evokes a certain naïveté and innocence that highlights the soldiers' youth, this approach has also become a stand-in for all of Eastwood's scores, along with its correlating insult: "Too simple; too repetitive."[24]

"Is He Any Good?": Gendering Lyricism and Amateurism

The above analyses serve both to highlight the diversity of Eastwood's scores and to outline his compositional characteristics and techniques. Given these musical details and the awards he has received, the question "Is he any good?" becomes a more complex one for recognizing the relationship between his musical style and broader considerations of his professional status, age, gender, and on-screen persona.

Eastwood's musical style—emotional, lyrical, relaxed, and straightforward—could not contrast more with his on-screen characters. His musical sensibilities, allusions to *Once upon a Time in the West* and *Of Mice and Men* notwithstanding, present a vastly different effect than the strident, motive-driven, and tight-knit "masculine" themes of the professional composers who scored the vigilante films in which he acted. As a composite, films that highlight his masculinity so heavily through relative youth, violence, and aggressive, strident music are decidedly at odds with the mature Clint Eastwood as an aging, sentimental, dramatic actor and director as well as an amateur composer and musician with access to professional musical activities made possible mostly by his fame and talents as an actor and director.

Both lyricism and amateurism have a long history of being coded as culturally feminized forms of music and music-making. Musical lyricism may be positioned in response to "the music itself"; loose-knit themes have been associated with the feminine for two centuries, while emotionality and sentimentality are delegated to the realm of the feminine more generally.[25] Meanwhile, markers of musical modernism—compact, high-energy, atonal or quasi-tonal motives like those Morricone uses to such great effect—are considered the purview of educated, professional male composers.[26] Furthermore, listeners' mimetic responses to lyricism and lyrical music evoke less aggressive and fast-paced forms of physical participation. The emphasis on lyricism and acoustical "liveness" in Eastwood's scores not only grounds listeners in a quasi-first-person subjectivity, highly attuned to the affective nature of music but also implies the certain intimacy of "being there" that acoustic music affords through suggesting unaltered performance.

In terms of Eastwood's compositional amateurism, professional composition and music-making were the provenance of men until the twentieth century; whereas middle-class women were encouraged to become accomplished amateurs, access to professional musical exchanges was severely limited, and a woman's musical activities were largely expected to stop once she had attracted a suitably accomplished husband. Publishing under a male family member's name or with his permission was often the only access to professional activities for musically accomplished women. In some sense, this resembles how Eastwood's access to professional music circles emerged from his own sponsorship, derived from his hypermasculine persona and competence in the male-oriented and male-dominated realms of directing and producing.

Steven Spielberg has said of Eastwood's scores, "Clint even composes his own music. Thus, Clint not only expresses his point of view through the story he is telling and how he directs it. He is also making the effort and taking the time to sit down at the keyboard and tell us how he feels musically.

That is unique in our entire field, and probably in the entire Directors Guild of America."[27] Spielberg's framing of Eastwood's storytelling is striking in its depiction of Eastwood's filmmaking as expressing a masculine-coded, rational "point of view" in contrast with a description of Eastwood's music as a feminine-coded, emotional activity that tells us "how he feels musically." This characterization of Eastwood as creating direct emotional communication through music matches Eastwood's own sentimental attitude about his playing and his assessment of his own abilities as a self-described "slow" amateur musician.[28] These characterizations encapsulate the two sides of himself Eastwood presents in his films and scores: director/composer, head/heart, professional/amateur, masculine/feminine. The interactions of these two sides of Clint Eastwood create a body of work all the richer for the complexities.

Notes

1 Nick Tosches, "Do You Feel Lucky, Monk?," *Vanity Fair*, December 2008, accessed August 11, 2017, http://www.vanityfair.com/news/2008/12/eastwood200812.
2 Richard Schickel, *Clint Eastwood: A Biography* (New York: Knopf, 1996), 43.
3 Tosches, "Do You Feel Lucky?"
4 Eastwood's music has received a total of ten nominations for various music awards, including Golden Globe nominations for Best Original Score for *Million Dollar Baby* and *Changeling* and Best Original Song nominations for music from *Grace Is Gone* and *Gran Torino*. The score from *Million Dollar Baby* was also nominated for a Grammy Award and a San Diego Film Critics Society Award; *Changeling* was nominated for a Saturn Award for Best Music, and *Flags of Our Fathers* received a Satellite nomination for Best Original Score. *Grace Is Gone* won a Satellite Award for Best Original Song.
5 For example, reviews in the *Christian Science Monitor*, *San Francisco Chronicle*, *Variety*, and *Boston Globe* make little to no mention of the music in *Mystic River*, *Million Dollar Baby*, *Changeling*, or *J. Edgar*. *New York Times* calls the music in *Mystic River* "somber," *Million Dollar Baby* "gentle and unobtrusive," and *Changeling* "uncharacteristically intrusive," while skipping over *J. Edgar*'s music entirely. An interview with Eastwood by *Christian Science Monitor* in October 2003 about *Mystic River* compares his directorial approach to his background as a jazz musician, without mentioning that he composed the film's soundtrack.
6 The terms used in quotation marks here were drawn from Dennis Lim, "Pitch Perfect," *Los Angeles Times*, December 5, 2007, and Jack Mathews, "Best Shock: Clint as Actor," *New York Daily News*, January 26, 2005, yet these adjectives and various synonyms are common to reviews of both Eastwood's acting and his soundtrack compositions.
7 William Weir, "Clint Eastwood Is a Great Director. Is He a Good Composer?," *Slate*, November 9, 2011, accessed August 11, 2017, http://www.slate.com/blogs/browbeat/2011/11/09/clint_eastwood_john_carpenter_and_other_director_composers.html.
8 All figures, transcriptions, and reductions in this chapter were created by the author.
9 For an in-depth analysis of Copland's score and its relationship to Hollywood and American musical modernism see Sally Bick, "*Of Mice and Men*: Copland,

Hollywood, and American Musical Modernism," *American Music* 23, no. 4 (2005): 426–472.

10 Eastwood's long-time collaborator/orchestrator Lennie Neihaus conducted the Boston Symphony Orchestra for the film's soundtrack.

11 See Arnie Cox, "Tripartite Subjectivity in Music Listening," *Indiana Theory Review* 30, no. 1 (2013): 1–43. Generally, Cox states, "Corporeally, performers are in the first-person position, while listeners are in the second-person position. The third-person position in this context refers to reflection and the position of observing or picturing wholes: a position from which one compares disparate musical elements, with or without the aid of a score, or from which one reflects on one's experience as it is occurring." Quasi-first-person is an experience whereby the process of mimetic comprehension causes listeners to "vicariously take part in the performance"; intention may be present, but it is not required. Cox notes, "We can mimetically comprehend violin music, for example, not only in terms of the voice or some other instrument other than violin, but also via any other physical modality that matches the pattern, rate, and strength of the violinist's exertions, whether overt swaying or toe-tapping or imagined congruent movements." See also Arnie Cox, "Embodying Music: Principles of the Mimetic Hypothesis," *Music Theory Online* 17, no. 2 (2011).

12 This kind of asymmetry, while not unheard of, may be contrasted with more symmetrical structures commonly found in orchestral scores (e.g., John Williams) and popular songs.

13 This could be placed against numerous counterexamples; one particularly vivid example is the use of Ligeti's music to depict notions of alienation in Stanley Kubrick's 1968 film *2001: A Space Odyssey*. The lack of a predictable, singable melody line, along with the absence of a steady beat and no easily discernable tonal trajectory, attenuates participation, prediction, and, thus, quasi-first-person subjectivity.

14 See David Huron, *Sweet Anticipation: Music and the Psychology of Expectation* (Cambridge, Mass.: MIT Press, 2006). Of particular importance to this cue is Huron's notion of *veridical familiarity*, or the creation of predictable interactions with music through successive repetitions of a particular cue or work itself.

15 Paul Sanden, *Liveness in Modern Music: Musicians, Technology, and the Perception of Performance* (New York: Routledge, 2013), 15, emphasis in original.

16 This also corresponds to Claudia Gorbman's notions of "invisibility" and "inaudibility" in early Hollywood. See Claudia Gorbman, *Unheard Melodies: Narrative Film Music* (London: BFI, 1987).

17 See Robynn Stilwell, "The Fantastical Gap between Diegetic and Non-Diegetic," in *Beyond the Soundtrack: Representing Music in Cinema*, ed. Daniel Goldmark, Lawrence Kramer, and Richard D. Leppert (Berkeley: University of California Press, 2007) for an in-depth explanation of the link between theater practice and listener acculturation toward nondiegetic music.

18 Music by Eastwood, with lyrics by Carole Bayer Sager; performed by Jamie Cullum.

19 William Caplin, *Classical Form: A Theory of Formal Functions for the Instrumental Music of Haydn, Mozart, and Beethoven* (Oxford: Oxford University Press, 1998). See also James Hepokoski and Warren Darcy, *Elements of Sonata Theory: Norms, Types, and Deformations in the Late-Eighteenth-Century Sonata* (Oxford: Oxford University Press, 2006). For detailed analyses of the history of "masculine" and "feminine" sonata themes, see James Hepokoski, "Masculine. Feminine. Are Current Readings of Sonata Form in Terms of a 'Masculine' and 'Feminine' Dichotomy Exaggerated? James Hepokoski Argues for a More Subtle Approach to the Politics

of Musical Form," *Musical Times* 135, no. 1818 (1994): 494–499; and Marcia Citron, *Gender and the Musical Canon* (Cambridge: Cambridge University Press, 1993).

20 Caplin, *Classical Form*, 268n16.

21 The resulting phrase (combining two sentences into a larger weak-strong unit) is referred to as a *parallel period*. See Caplin, 65, for an in-depth discussion of this construction.

22 Variations of sentence structures are examined in Steven Vande Moortele, "Sentences, Sentence Chains, and Sentence Replication: Intra- and Interthematic Formal Functions in Liszt's Weimar Symphonic Poems," *Intégral* 25 (2011): 121–158; Mark Richards, "Viennese Classicism and the Sentential Idea: Broadening the Sentence Paradigm," *Theory and Practice* 36 (2011): 179–224; and Matthew BaileyShea, "Beyond the Beethoven Model: Sentence Types and Limits," *Current Musicology* 77 (2004): 5–33.

Notions of "dissolving" sentences are treated at length in Matthew BaileyShea, "Wagner's Loosely Knit Sentences and the Drama of Musical Form," *Intégral* 16/17 (2002): 1–34. Richards specifically explores phrase design in film music themes. See Mark Richards, "Film Music Themes: Analysis and Corpus Study," *Music Theory Online* 22, no. 1 (2016).

23 Though "Maggie's Theme" most often appears as a period structure, "Frankie's Theme" is regularly truncated and subjected to variation, a practice that evokes an image of Maggie as a stabilizing force in Frankie's life. The Copland-like cues later in the film withhold both a clear tonal/key orientation and a clear phrase structure, evoking a kind of unorganized, loose-knit, unraveled quality that corresponds to the narrative.

24 Weir, "Clint Eastwood, Great Director."

25 Among many excellent accounts, Citron directly engages lyricism and perceptions of compositional femininity in the music of Brahms.

26 Catherine Parsons Smith suggests analogs between the gendering of modernism in music and that in other disciplines, centered around the use of sexual linguistics, the ambivalence of literary women toward previous generations, and the prominence and later suppression of antiwoman statements characterized as "masculinism." See Catherine Parsons Smith, "'A Distinguishing Virility': Feminism and Modernism in American Art Music," in *Cecilia Reclaimed: Feminist Perspectives on Gender and Music*, ed. Susan C. Cook and Judy S. Tsou (Urbana: University of Illinois Press, 1994), 90–106. Ellie Hisama argues that these factors did not necessarily keep women from writing in modernist styles, nor does it mean that the "musical matter itself" is inherently masculine. Hisama agrees that a convincing case has been made for the linking of misogyny and modernist scientific texts. The open misogyny of various fields and the tendency of modernist male composers to speak of their works in exclusively masculine terms and imagery, in addition to female composers' exclusion from education and professional exchanges, certainly support modernism's general characterization as masculinized. Ellie Hisama, *Gendering Musical Modernism: The Music of Ruth Crawford, Marion Bauer, and Miriam Gideon* (Cambridge: Cambridge University Press, 2001).

27 Michael Goldman, *Clint Eastwood: Master Filmmaker at Work* (New York: Abrams, 2012), 17.

28 Elizabeth Widdecombe, "Clint the Composer," *New Yorker*, October 4, 2008, accessed August 18, 2017, http://www.newyorker.com/magazine/2003/03/24/nothing-fancy.

Acknowledgments

Lester Friedman: First, let me thank David Desser, who, as always, has been a great friend and wonderful partner in this endeavor. We have been fortunate to assemble a collection of first-rate scholars to examine Eastwood's movies, and we thank our contributors for their outstanding work, their forbearance as bumps appeared in our path, and their commitment to our book. My wife, Rae-Ellen Kavey, has been a kind and patient advocate as this project progressed over time, and my friend Delia Temes remains the most perceptive and constructive reader of my work. My colleagues and the administrators at Hobart and William Smith Colleges have provided me with both the encouragement and the support necessary to complete this anthology, and I am appreciative of the time I have spent there and the friends I have made during that time. At Rutgers, we have benefitted from the wise and astute counsel of Leslie Mitchner.

David Desser: I would like to thank my good friend Lester Friedman for asking me if I'd like to join this project. Once again, it has been a pleasure. Who knows what will happen now that we are both emeritus professors! To my wife, Frances Gateward, I am grateful for her support all along the route to completion. And to my daughter, Sophie, who put up with Daddy on the computer and whom I hope will continue to grow as a true heroine. Finally, I would like to thank the contributors without whose work this, obviously, could not have come to such fine fruition. It is interesting to work with people whom I have never met, those whom I know only casually, as well as with those who are among my best friends in the field. I thank you all for your professionalism and patience. I should thank Clint Eastwood, whom I have met, though many years ago, for his graciousness at that time and his ongoing career as one of America's most important directors.

Notes on Contributors

LUCY BOLTON is senior lecturer in film studies at Queen Mary University of London. She is the author of *Film and Female Consciousness: Irigaray, Cinema and Thinking Women* and coeditor of *Lasting Stars: Images That Fade and Personas That Endure* (winner of BAFTSS's prize for Best Edited Collection of 2017). She has recently published on Vivien Leigh, Marilyn Monroe, and Melanie Griffith and is beginning a project on the film stardom of Mary Magdalene. She is currently writing a monograph on cinema and the philosophy of Iris Murdoch.

DIANE CARSON, professor emerita at St. Louis Community College, is codirector of *Other People's Footage: Copyright and Fair Use*. She is past president of the University Film and Video Association and served as film specialist for the UFVA American Documentary Showcase. Carson is coauthor of *Appetites and Anxieties: Food, Film, and the Politics of Representation*; has contributed to anthologies on Preston Sturges, John Sayles, and South Korean film; and coedited anthologies on contemporary film performance, feminist film analysis, and multicultural media and pedagogy.

DAVID DESSER is emeritus professor of cinema studies, University of Illinois. He has authored and edited eleven books previously, most recently *Small Cinemas in Global Markets*. His best-known works include *The Samurai Films of Akira Kurosawa*; *Eros plus Massacre: An Introduction to the Japanese New Wave Cinema*; *Reframing Japanese Cinema: Authorship, Genre, History*; *American Jewish Filmmakers*; *The Cinema of Hong Kong: History, Arts, Identity*; and *Ozu's Tokyo Story*. He is a former editor of *Cinema Journal* and founding coeditor of the *Journal of Japanese and Korean Cinema*.

LESTER D. FRIEDMAN is emeritus professor and former chair of the Media and Society Program at Hobart and William Smith Colleges. The author, coauthor, and editor of over twenty books and numerous articles, his areas of scholarly interest include film genres, American cinema of the 1970s, American Jewish cinema, and the health humanities. Additionally, he's written books about Steven Spielberg, Arthur Penn, Peter Pan, and Frankenstein; authored two screenplays that have been the basis of independent films; and is a *Jeopardy!* champion.

ALEXANDRA KELLER is the director of the film and media studies program at Smith College. She specializes in the American Western; cinema and the postmodern, avant-garde and experimental film; and the relationship between cinema and other forms of artistic and cultural production. She is the author of *James Cameron* and *The Endless Frontier: Westerns and American Identity from the Reagan Era to the Digital Age* (forthcoming).

JONATHAN KIRSHNER is the Stephen and Barbara Friedman Professor of International Political Economy in the department of government at Cornell University. He is the author of *Hollywood's Last Golden Age: Politics, Society and the Seventies Film in America* and the author of the novel *Urban Flight*.

CHARITY LOFTHOUSE is associate professor of music theory at Hobart and William Smith Colleges. She has published articles on sonata theory in Dmitri Shostakovich's symphonies and presented papers and lectures on Shostakovich, Russian music, film music, and women monastic composers at Society for Music Theory; Music Theory Midwest; Music Theory Society of New York State; Feminist Theories in Music; University of Massachusetts, Amherst; Eastman School of Music; Louisiana State University; Mannes College of Music; and at international conferences in Austria, Estonia, and Russia.

MURRAY POMERANCE is professor in the department of sociology at Ryerson University and the author of numerous volumes including, most recently, *The Man Who Knew Too Much*, *A King of Infinite Space*, *Moment of Action: Riddles of Cinematic Performance*, and *Alfred Hitchcock's America* and has edited and coedited books including *The Last Laugh: Strange Humors of Cinema* and *Cinema and Modernity*. He is editor of the *Horizons of Cinema* series at SUNY Press and of the *Techniques of the Moving Image* series at Rutgers University Press.

STEPHEN PRINCE is a professor of cinema at Virginia Tech. He is the author of numerous books, which include *Movies and Meaning: An Introduction to Film*, *The Warrior's Camera: The Cinema of Akira Kurosawa*, *A Dream of Resistance:*

The Cinema of Kobayashi Masaki, and *Digital Visual Effects in Cinema: The Seduction of Reality*.

DAVID STERRITT is editor-in-chief of *Quarterly Review of Film and Video*, contributing writer at *Cineaste*, film professor at the Maryland Institute College of Art, professor emeritus at Long Island University, former film critic of the *Christian Science Monitor*, and author or editor of many books, including *Spike Lee's America*; *The Films of Alfred Hitchcock*; *Mad to be Saved: The Beats, the 50's, and Film*; and *The Cinema of Clint Eastwood: Chronicles of America*.

Index

Page numbers in *italics* refer to figures.